Student as Producer

How Do Revolutionary Teachers Teach?

Student as Producer

How Do Revolutionary Teachers Teach?

Mike Neary

Winchester, UK
Washington, USA

JOHN HUNT PUBLISHING

First published by Zero Books, 2020
Zero Books is an imprint of John Hunt Publishing Ltd., No. 3 East St., Alresford,
Hampshire SO24 9EE, UK
office@jhpbooks.com
www.johnhuntpublishing.com
www.zero-books.net

For distributor details and how to order please visit the 'Ordering' section on our website.

Text copyright: Mike Neary 2019

ISBN: 978 1 78904 238 2
978 1 78904 239 9 (ebook)
Library of Congress Control Number: 2019941773

A CIP catalogue record for this book is available from the British Library.

Design: Stuart Davies

UK: Printed and bound by CPI Group (UK) Ltd, Croydon, CR0 4YY
US: Printed and bound by Thomson-Shore, 7300 West Joy Road, Dexter, MI 48130

We operate a distinctive and ethical publishing philosophy in
all areas of our business, from our global network of authors to
production and worldwide distribution.

Contents

For my students and teachers.

Labour seems quite a simple category
(Karl Marx, Grundrisse 1993 103).

Introduction

Student as Producer is a curricula for revolutionary teaching that emerged from inside an English university at the start of the twenty-first century. Grounded in a pedagogy derived from Marxist social theory, *Student as Producer* provides a practical and critical response to the on-going assault on higher education by the social power of Money and the State, with a focus on Police. This account of *Student as Producer* is set within a particular moment in time: between the student protests and urban riots that erupted in England in 2010–2011 and the 2017 General Election in the UK, when students and young people played a significant role in protesting against the politics of austerity and supporting the politics of Corbynism. This book explores the intellectual origins of Student as Producer, with particular reference to Walter Benjamin's *The Author as Producer* (1934), and develops the concept of Student as Producer through an engagement with the work of major writers on revolutionary education: Jacques Ranciére, Paulo Freire and Paula Allman. Student as Producer's revolutionary curriculum is framed around unlearning the law of labour as a critique of capitalist work and the institutions through which the law of labour is enforced, including the capitalist university. The critique proposes a new form of higher education institution, a co-operative university, as a moment of revolutionary transition towards communism: making a clear link between democracy and Marx's law of value. This moment of revolutionary transition is consolidated by drawing on the power of Strike, not to defend labour but to move towards the abolition of capitalist work. And, finally, at the end of the book, a thought experiment about how such a university and its communist sociality would be defended: not by Police, but another form of Authority and, its derivative, Authorship. The theoretical frame for an alternative to Police is taken from the

1

work of the Soviet legal theorist Evgeny Pashukanis (1891–1937) based on common purpose and social defence. Authority comes from a critique of authoritarianism recovered from Roman philosophy. Authorship is after Walter Benjamin's *The Author as Producer* inflected with a dialectical twist.

1. Curricula

This book suggests a *curricula*, or course of action, for revolutionary teachers and students everywhere. Written from inside an English university and with a focus on higher education, the curricula is in solidarity with teachers and students and other workers in education who labour under the oppressive rule of capitalist work, the law of labour, and are seeking to change the world, i.e., abolish capitalism, rather than teach it. The name of the curricula is Student as Producer.

Student as Producer works across a number of dimensions. Student as Producer is concerned with teaching in the classroom but, more than that, it aims to create radical change at the level of the institution and to recover the idea of the university as a revolutionary political project. Student as Producer does not use the term co-producer. Co-production is favoured in public management systems involving service users in the provision of facilities, as well as students in their own education (McCulloch 2009). The concept of co-production does not challenge the social relations of capitalist production, affirming a system it appears to critique. Student as Producer involves students, but its real focus are the social relations of capitalist production and their revolutionary transformation. The overwhelming character of capitalist production turns the modern world into a labour camp, with waged work 'a form of living death' (Dinerstein and Neary 2002 11). This is why labour must be abolished, or unlearned.

Student as Producer emerged in a moment when higher education was being transformed in England and around the world into a financial machine: sometimes referred to as 'academic capitalism' (Slaughter and Rhoades 2009), set out here as the pressure on higher education institutions to succumb to the law of Money enforced by the power of the State and Police. This process is overwhelming the academic project that underpins the core activities of higher education: teaching and research; where critical intellectuality is being replaced by the brutal rationality of the law of Money. This rush to financialisation is not a new phenomenon, having been introduced in the UK during the first Thatcher government in the 1980s, as Monetarism, but has intensified in the recent period, following a right-wing political coup in 2010 under the coalition government, 2010-15 (Amsler and Cannan 2008, Shattock 2012, McGettigan 2013) and, since 2015, by Tory rule. Academic life is now dominated by the law of Money and its associated protocols: regular audits and other forms of performance management, with academics cast as self-entrepreneurs and students as consumers; all part of a process of income generation fuelled by speculation and debt.

Critiques of this on-going process have been written up in a wide range of academic papers, books and conferences, creating a whole new sub-discipline: Critical University Studies (Williams 2006, Newfield 2016, Naidoo 2018, Morrish 2019, Hall 2018). The problem has been well described, but there has been a gap between critical writing and practical action: between academics and activism. The course of action suggested in this book is not simply to connect academics to activists, but to consider ways in which critical theory and practice might be integrated in a manner that avoids 'pseudo-concrete' actions that sustain the capitalist project rather than undermine it (Kurz 2007, Adorno 1998). The intention to develop a critical, practical curricula is what underpins the question 'how do revolutionary teachers teach?'

The project to abolish capitalism is energised by the fact that capitalism is in crisis and might be on the point of collapse. There is nothing new about capitalism in crisis. 'Capital is Crisis' (Endnotes 2011, After the Fall: Communiques from Occupied California 2010). What distinguishes this crisis from earlier crises, e.g., The Wall Street Crash in the 1930s or the 'Oil Crisis' in the 1970s, is that this time capitalism may have reached the limit of its own expansive capacity (Cleaver 2017, Kurz 2014); or, at the very least, its current mode of regulation, neoliberalism, has lost the ability to reproduce itself other than in ways that bring to the fore its powerfully destructive potentialities (Fleming 2019). So, for the moment, the idea of post-capitalism is getting increasing attention as a matter of urgent necessity (Mason 2015, Pitts and Dinerstein 2017a, Pitts and Dinerstein 2017b, Gilbert 2016).

The defining moment of this crisis was the economic crash of 2007–2008, where writers at the time were calling into question the neoliberal ideology on which this market-based model of social and political development is based (Haiven 2014, Hall 2018). The Global Slump (McNally 2014) appears to be far from over in a situation where 'the catastrophic consequences are still unfolding' (Hall et al 2013 8). The response by governments to the 'Great Recession' has been a series of austerity measures, including drastic cuts to public funding, layoffs of public sector workers, economic stimulus programmes, bank bailouts and, somewhat counter-intuitively, the intensification of privatisation policies, described as 'austerity for ever' (Corporate Europe 2011). These measures have been imposed through an increasingly militarised police force and state security systems (Roberts 2011, Neocleous 2014) in what might be characterised as a global civil war (Kurz 2013). This has led the Marxist historian Eric Hobsbawn to argue that we know the era of neoliberalism has come to an end but we do not know what it is to become. The intensification of market-based policies and privatisations has been particularly prevalent in the UK. In the recent period these policies have included higher education policy and practice, resulting in extraordinary levels of trauma and turbulence across the sector (McGettigan 2013, Brown 2013, Shattock 2012).

This crisis and its disastrous consequences have generated massive protests and resistance around the world, often connected to wider movements of struggle for housing, employment, the environment and against war and the Police-

State (Harris 2011), as well as demonstrations in the UK (Bailey and Freedman 2011, Solomon and Palmieri 2011, Haiven 2014). At the heart of these protests have been students erupting in demonstrations and resistance even in places where student and political participation by young people was thought to be moribund.

The student protests of 2010 in England, which form the starting point for this book, may have looked as if they had come out of nowhere, but students have long been recognised as 'unruly subjects' (Edelman-Boren 2001), as 'a continually occurring, vital and global social phenomenon' (2001 3) with student resistance and rebellion having a 'profound impact on the political structures and the histories of many countries' (2001 3). It may only be in the UK where students are not thought of as politically significant actors (Budgen 2011).

If the student protests had happened without warning, the urban riots of 2011, following shortly after, were not so unexpected: urban rioting is not uncommon and, as we shall see, has intensified in the UK since the 1970s. The urban riots in the late summer of 2011 started in Tottenham, following a protest at the police shooting of Mark Duggan, which resulted in his death, and spread across London and to cities throughout the country, between 6–11 of August, including Bristol, Liverpool, Manchester and Birmingham. Each disturbance followed a similar pattern of burning cars and buildings, taking goods from shops without paying, 'looting'/ 'free shopping', with anger and protest directed against the police.

It is important to contextualise this very specific expression of resistance in the moment in which it occurred, and to resist its naturalisation as a political event in ways that undermine its sociological significance: the students are not 'hooligans' (Pearson 1983), nor are they an expression of another 'moral panic' (Cohen 1973, Bloom 2012), and the rioters are not simply 'criminals' (Cameron 2011); rather, both groups are kicking off

against the poverty and boredom of student life in the middle
of maybe the deepest crisis of capitalism, as part of a movement
of resistance on-going around the world, in opposition to the
ways in which the Police-State are responding to the crisis; it
is within this context that their actions must be considered.
The Police-State responds always and everywhere with savage
violence to any threat to the law of Money (Neary 2015). The
focus on Police in the book is through the science of Police; not
Police Studies or Criminology, but the recovery of Police as a
political category and theoretical device derived from political
economy (Neocleous 2000). In this case the main activity of
Police is not capturing criminals or solving crimes, but the
imposition of poverty on populations through enforcing the law
of labour (Neocleous 2000). The focus on Police will interrogate
the police as a philosophy of the political through an exemplary
'police logic' (Ranciére 1999 34). The argument presented in this
book is that a fundamental resistance to the Police-State means
unlearning or undermining the law of labour as an aspect of
class struggle for communism.

Joshua Clover makes the link for us between these two
events: student protests and urban riot, in his book *Riot-Strike-
Riot: the New Era of Uprisings* (2016) where he describes the
student protests of 2010 and the urban riots in England that
came immediately after them in 2011 as 'a double riot':

> The shape of the double riot is clear enough. One riot arises
> from youth discovering that the routes that once promised
> a minimally secure formal integration into the economy are
> now foreclosed. The other arises from a racialised surplus
> population and the violent state management thereof. The
> holders of empty promissory notes, and the holders of
> nothing at all.
> (Clover 2016 180).

For Clover the riot or street protest is based on his notion that the politics of consumption have come to replace the importance of the strike and the politics of production at a time when the world of work is collapsing. The project for Clover is to reveal the underlying processes out of which the double riot occurs, what Clover, after Marx, describes as 'to bring forward the real movement' of struggle and transformation (2016 180), not only as an empirical fact, but as a cogent and compelling theoretical account of riot in which: 'A theory of riot is a theory of crisis' (2016 1) so that a meaningful political response can be made. Cleaver's approach assists unlearning the law of labour by situating political economy in the centre of his theoretical analysis, along with other sociological and philosophical inspirations, including value-form theory, postcolonialism and anarchism, as well as social and economic history. Clover's point is that labour or capitalist work in an era of increasing automatisation is diminished, undermining the power of the strike, and that production has been replaced by the politics of distribution, hence the importance of riots as a form of free shopping. Riot prime is the moment when racialised and other surplus populations confront the Police-State as an emergent form of radical subjectivity. I will develop this analysis later in the book through a critical engagement with Clover's riots and strikes, but for now, the point I want to stress is that labour is not simply a word that describes the activity of work; rather, labour is the concept for the generalised social relation that dominates human life, even when there is high unemployment and not enough waged work to go around.

Student as Producer has emerged at a time when the world of work is collapsing across the UK and around the planet, in a scenario that has been described as 'the end of work' (Rifkin 2004). The situation is particularly acute for young people, who are described as 'the lost generation' (Ainley and Allen 2010), or the 'scarred generation' (Morsy 2012) and 'a generation at risk'

(ILO 2013); and, in relation to higher education, 'students without a future' (Mason 2012). In 2011 the rate of youth unemployment in the UK was 18 per cent, and is now recorded as 12.4 per cent, with the figures for black and ethnic youth between 7 and 11 per cent, roughly the same for male and females (Powell 2018, Statista 2018). With regard to graduate employment at the time of the riot, students in jobs at the top end of the pay range were experiencing some increases in starting salaries, but the Higher Education Careers Service Unit figures showed most salaries for graduates were under £20k, with £15k not uncommon, and with a marked difference between students graduating from the top and new universities. The statistics reveal that one out of three graduates were not in graduate jobs, and six out of ten art and design graduates were struggling to find work for which they were qualified. This extended to science graduates, half of which were in jobs that did not require scientific knowledge (Ainley and Allen 2013), creating a new category of employment: GRINGOS (Graduates in Non-Graduate Occupations) (Blenkinsop and Scurry 2007, 2011). This situation had a knock-on effect for less qualified young workers, pushing them down the job ladder into less well paid more insecure work, so that those without degree qualifications were four times more likely to be without work (Ainley and Allen 2013). Another issue is the rise of unpaid internships where graduates work for no pay in order to secure an entry into the job market. These figures about jobs and salaries now form part of the Key Information Statistics displayed by universities in England on their websites, encouraging students to regard the main purpose of higher education as seeking employment (Unistats – https://unistats.ac.uk/).

One result is that young people were staying in education for longer, with a delayed transition to adulthood. Ainley and Allen argue: 'In the absence of work, education has little economic rationality. It functions instead as the main means of social control over youth by enhancing existing divisions amongst young people and replacing the social control formerly exercised in the workplace by wages' (Ainley and Allen 2013).

Post riots, the situation for young people in England is worsening in terms of job prospects. In 2015 the Chartered Institute for Personal Development reported that 58.8 per cent of graduates were working in jobs that did not need a graduate qualification, with a 'depressing mismatch between the rising graduate population and declining number of graduate jobs, with 31 per cent of students still not in work' (2015 data published in 2016 graduate labour market statistics). In 2017 the figure is that nearly half, 49 per cent of employed graduates, are working in a non-graduate job (Office for National Statistics 2017).

While the lack of 'good jobs' or even 'bullshit jobs' (Graeber 2018) is demoralising and depressing for young people in a world in which work is the defining principle of social life, the problem for revolutionary teachers is not how to create more jobs, but rather to treat the nature of capitalist work itself as problematic (Weeks 2011). The revolutionary project's challenge is to create new forms of human and natural activities not based on the value of capitalist money, but, rather, on forms of life-enhancing life. I will refer to this process as unlearning the law of labour, as the first lesson for revolutionary teachers to teach and to learn, forming the underlying pedagogic principle for Student as Producer.

Student as Producer

The concept of Student as Producer first emerged at the University of Warwick in 2006, where I was working as a sociology lecturer as part of a project I directed: *The Reinvention Centre for Undergraduate Research* (Reinvention Centre 2007, Reinvention Centre 2010). The Reinvention Centre promoted the development of undergraduate research, in a process referred to as research-engaged teaching, as a core principle of curriculum development in higher education with the fundamental objective that undergraduates came to be regarded as actively part of the research mission of their universities where they were studying.

The idea of 'Reinvention' came from the title of a report: *Reinventing Undergraduate Education: a Blueprint for America's Research Universities*, published by the Boyer Commission (1998), that was set up to improve the unsatisfactory student experience at North American research-intensive universities. The commission evolved out of the work of Ernest Boyer (1928–1995), the educationalist and teacher, who in a series of publications argued for a reconfiguration of the relationship between teaching and research, with teaching recognised as an important and fundamental part of academic life. Boyer provided a framework and a baseline on which to consider the relationship between teaching and research in the US and elsewhere. As he put it: 'The most important obligation now confronting colleges and universities is to break out of the tired old teaching versus research debate and define in more creative ways what it means to be a scholar' (Boyer 1998 xii).

Boyer formulated this debate with the creation of four categories of what he referred to as 'scholarship': the scholarship of discovery – *research*; the scholarship of integration – *interdisciplinarity*; the scholarship of engagement – *knowledge applied to a wider community*; and the scholarship of teaching – *research and evaluation of one's own teaching* (Boyer 1990). The Boyer Commission, established in his name, set out to create its own charter for students in the form of an Academic Bill of Rights, which included the commitment for every university to provide 'opportunities to learn through enquiry rather than simple transmission of knowledge', together with a programme for institutional change that made research-based learning the standard experience, started in the first freshman year, developed throughout the programme and culminating in final year/capstone projects, in a context of interdisciplinarity and a strong academic community (1998 14–36).

This dysfunctionality between teacher and research, identified by Boyer, and the gap it creates between student and teacher, has been described as a form of 'apartheid' (Brew 2006 164). The relationship between teaching and research has profound implications not only for teaching and learning, but for the meaning and purpose as well as the structure and organisation of providers of higher education:

> The relationship between teaching and research is intricately embedded within ideas about what universities do and what they are for. It is fundamental to what is understood as higher learning and to ideas about the nature of the academy. Understanding this relationship raises substantial questions about the roles and responsibilities of higher education institutions, about the nature of academic work, about the kinds of disciplinary knowledge that are developed and by whom, about the way teachers and students relate to each other, about how university spaces are arranged and used, indeed, it raises fundamental questions about the purposes of higher education.
> (Brew 2006 3).

This close relationship between research and teaching as the defining issue of higher education was confirmed around the same time as the Boyer Commission was reporting by the Rectors of European Universities gathered in Bologna in 1988. These Rectors agreed the *Magna Charta Universitatum*, in which they set out the framework for an integrated system of European higher education, as part of a wider debate about the role of the university in contemporary society.

As they said in the preamble to the Charta: 'the future of mankind depends largely on cultural, scientific and technical development; and that this is built up in centres of culture, knowledge and research as represented by true universities'.

The Charta set out some fundamental principles about the future of higher education in Europe, as well as outlining the means by which these fundamental principles could be achieved. Key to all of this was the issue of academic freedom for tutors and students and that central to the issue of academic freedom was the relationship between teaching and research.

The fundamental principles set out by the Charta were:

1. To meet the needs of the world around it, research and teaching must be morally and intellectually independent of all political authority and economic power.

2. Teaching and research in universities must be inseparable if their tuition is not to lag behind changing needs, the demands of society, and advances in scientific knowledge.

The Charta set out the means to realise these principles, including:

1. To preserve freedom in research and teaching, the instruments appropriate to realise that freedom must be made available to all members of the university community.

2. Each university must – with due allowance for particular circumstances – ensure that its students' freedoms are safeguarded and that they enjoy conditions in which they can acquire the culture and training which it is their purpose to possess.

Clearly, there is more at stake than teaching students research skills. What is at issue is the recovery or the continuation of the university as a liberal-humanist institution, based on some notion of the 'true university' and the 'public good'.

Germanic Higher Education

This idea of a liberal-humanist university based on a symbiotic relationship between teaching and research was not something that the signatories to the Charta and Boyer had invented, but was based on the model for higher education that had been established in the Germanic states in the eighteenth and nineteenth centuries. The University of Berlin, created in 1810, is regarded as the epitome of this model, but the groundwork for this type of university had been established earlier at the universities of Halle and Gottingen. These universities' teachings were based on a broad curriculum, 'modern studies and a worldly orientation' (Pritchard 1990 14), against 'the narrowly prescribed curriculum of the medieval university' (1990 14). Teaching and learning was to be practical and realistic, based on a reasoned, rational and 'modern intellectual outlook' (1990 15) supporting freedom of thought against dogmatic theology. At Halle this resulted in 'the university pioneering original scientific research and assuming a role of academic leadership based on free enquiry' (1990 15). Gottingen's main contribution to the modern university, as Pritchard tells us, was the prominence given to the Department of Philosophy and Law with a downgrading of theology alongside an emphasis on personal education.

The University of Berlin was set up in an attempt by the Prussian state to recover some cultural and political prestige following the defeat of Napoleon in 1815. The University of Berlin has become the model for what is known as the Humboldtian University, named after Wilhelm von Humboldt (1767-1835), the philosopher and legal constitutionalist who held the post of Director of Education in Prussia during the period of the university's inception. The philosophical basis for the founding of the University of Berlin was further enhanced by contributions made by the idealist philosophers Johann Fichte, Friedrich Schleiermacher, Friedrich Schelling, Henrich Steffens, Friedrich Schiller, Immanuel Kant and Georg Hegel (Pritchard

1990). At the University of Berlin the life of the mind was given prominence before empirical, vocational or utilitarian pursuits (Pritchard 1990). At the core of the curriculum lay the 'unity of knowledge' as a basis for the relationship between teaching and research, and between teachers and students. It was around this idea of 'unity of knowledge' that the infrastructure of the institution was based.

Humboldt (1810) argued:

It is furthermore a peculiarity of the institutions of higher learning that they treat higher learning always in terms of not yet completely solved problems, remaining at all times in a research mode [i.e., being engaged in an unceasing process of inquiry]. Schools, in contrast, treat only closed and settled bodies of knowledge. The relationship between teacher and learner is therefore completely different in higher learning from what it is in schools. At the higher level, the teacher is not there for the sake of the student, both have their justification in the service of scholarship.

(quoted in Elton 2001 44).

In Humboldt's model of what he referred to as 'organic scholarship' the simple transmission of knowledge through lectures would be abandoned, with teaching taking place solely in seminars. Students were to be directly involved in the speculative thinking of their tutors, in a Socratic dialogue and in close contact, without strictly planned courses and curricula. Students should work in research communities with time for thinking and without any practical obligations.

This approach was grounded in the philosophical ideal of absolute knowledge, encompassing both what philosophers like to call the real and ideal, the abstract as well as the concrete. Philosophy was seen as the most integrative subject 'embracing all of knowledge in its organic wholeness' (Pritchard 1990 42).

This approach meant universities were required to teach a broad range of subjects, with the emphasis on philosophy reflected in the provision of Doctorates of Philosophy (PhD) for the most advanced research degrees.

This understanding of philosophy as the most integrative subject survives through the award of a Doctorate of Philosophy (PhD) as the most advanced higher education degree classification, across all academic disciplines.

However, this unity of knowledge was undermined by industrial and commercial science emphasising empirical, amoral, utilitarian and instrumental research. Alongside this was a preoccupation with interdisciplinarity, focusing on complexity and difference, rather than the idea of generic scholarship, and a more collective way of learning and teaching. Nevertheless, as Pritchard puts it: 'A growth in our awareness of the complexity of knowledge does not exclude the possibility of an ultimate synthesis nor the possibility that unity does indeed exist' (Pritchard 1990 44).

This pursuit of the unity of knowledge is more than an academic exercise, but is itself a political project to create a more democratic relationship between teacher and student, although this was not realised at the University of Berlin, nor universities which espouse its model. Pritchard suggests a more prosaic reason for combining research and teaching in one institution was as a money-saving device for the cash-strapped Prussian monarchy. Pritchard is concerned that: 'the ideal cannot be sustained in a mass education system' (Pritchard 1990 48). But is this really the case? Student as Producer claims that a democratic education system is not only possible but necessary and required, based on a more radical model than that established by liberal-humanist philosophers, European administrators or American educationalists.

16

The University and the State

A key issue involved in understanding what a more radical version of higher education could look like includes understanding the nature of the university and its relationship with the state.

The role of the state and its relationship to the university is central in terms of the development of the modern university. This was a matter of great intellectual and practical import for Humboldt as a legal constitutionalist. Then, as now, in the UK at least, it appears that the University is 'constantly on the defensive against possible state demands that the university should demonstrate economic or practical "usefulness"' (Pritchard 1990 53).

Humboldt framed this relationship in terms of academic freedom, not only between the students and their teachers, but in terms of the relationship between the university and the state. Humboldt's point was that in guaranteeing the academic freedom of the university, the state itself is regenerated by the way in which the university promotes and preserves the culture of the nation; and, in so doing, establishes what he described as a 'Culture State', which included a genuinely cultured population who would be trained to act as independent and autonomous citizens. Humboldt's model was overwhelmed by what he feared most: the rise of industrial capitalism and the subsumption of the 'Culture State' by the 'Commercial State' to which the university became increasingly tied through government and private sector research contracts, in a process where teaching became not only detached from research, but also came to be regarded as a subordinate and less profitable activity (Knoll and Siebert, 1967).

Humboldt set out his political philosophy in the book *The Limits of State Action* (1791). In this book Humboldt presents the basis for his commitment to an extreme laissez-faire philosophy (Burrow 1993). For Humboldt, political philosophy was based on 'the proclamation of complete self-sovereignty of the individual' or 'extreme individualism' (Knoll and Siebert 1967 17 and 19). The state was to have no positive role in the area of social welfare, but was a necessary evil whose main purpose is to protect its members from external threats; every effort by the state to interfere in the private affairs of the citizens was to be 'absolutely condemned' (Humboldt 1993 16). For Humboldt the state was not to have any influence on education, which was to be a private rather than a public affair: public education was to lie wholly outside the limits within which the state should exercise its effectiveness (Humboldt 1993). Humboldt had to temper his thoughts on public education while working for the Ministry of Education in Prussia, but he did not wholly abandon his reservations about the state and, with regard to his university reform, devised a model with considerable autonomy (Knoll and Siebert 1967).

The University of Berlin, founded in 1810 by idealist philosophers, exemplified this trend so much so that the university was seen to embody the spirit or life of the Prussian nation (Lyotard 2005), privileging moral and ethical speculation as well as providing 'functionally useful knowledge' (Delanty 2001 34), while remaining autonomous from the rest of society as a sort of 'social utopia' (Delanty 2001 33). Knowledge finds its validity in a model of self-governance or freedom, where knowledge is not the subject but in the service of the subject so that 'it allows morality to become reality' (Lyotard 2005 36). In the Prussian political reality of the time, this culminates in Hegel, one of the university's founding philosophers, producing his theory of the state, providing a justification for the Prussian monarchy and a system of authoritarian governance (Kay and Mott 1982).

Student as Producer is against this liberal idealist model of higher education: the point is to invert Hegel's philosophy by grounding knowledge in a new form of political association based on class struggle: bringing the capitalist state and the ideology on which it is based down to earth (Neary 2016).

To the extent to which these Germanic universities trained state officials and bureaucrats, acting on behalf of the state, this training was described as Police Science, based on an administrative concept of Police: 'Police is concerned with maintaining the total wealth and substance of the state's internal structure and increasing it' (Wellmon 2015 158). These universities had their own form of 'academic police', which extended to scrutinising the content of lectures, academic publications and student behaviour to maintain the reputation of the institution (Wellmon 2015).

The relationship between the state and the university is key to the framing of this book, not in terms of supporting an idea of liberal-humanist state, but acknowledging the modern state as the capitalist state described not in instrumental or functionalist terms (Miliband 1973, Poulantzas 2013) but recognising the state as a form of the capital relation, between labour and capital (Clarke 1991a), that emerges out of a process of class struggle (Holloway and Picciotto 1977). From this analysis the state is not able to provide a solution to the contradictions of capitalist society as it is itself derived from out of those contradictions. Or, to put it another way, 'the state is not simply a tool of capital, it is an arena of class struggle' (Clarke 1991a 195).

A key part of this analysis is the relationship between the state and money, not regarded in this analysis as discrete aspects of the political economy of the capitalist world, but complementary forms of the capital relation, providing the logic and substance for the development of capitalist society (Clarke 1988). If the state is the political form of the capital relation, then money encompasses capital's economic form. Marx explains the domineering and determining role of money in the first chapters of *Capital Volume 1*, where the accumulation of money as the economic form of capital becomes the logic for social development. For Marx, money is not merely a means of exchange, unit of account and store of value, as it is for economists, but Money-Capital is the supreme form of social power (Clarke 1988 13-14) with its own supernatural transformatory powers. The basis for an appreciation of the social power of money lies in understanding the law of labour.

The Law of Labour: Generic and Generative

This book is grounded in the history of student protests and urban riots through a particular understanding of the concept of labour, elaborated by Karl Marx in his labour theory of value, most fully in *Capital* (1990) and *The Grundrisse* (1993). Remember Student as Producer is unlearning the law of labour, but how does the revolutionary teacher consider labour? For a start, according to Marx in *The Grundrisse*, labour is not simply work that people do; but is, rather, a generic word that describes all work in capitalist society in general. The ubiquitous nature of capitalist work and the fact that labour can refer to all kinds of work, paid and unpaid, means that the concept readily naturalises itself. The concept of labour in capitalist society describes not only in general terms all aspects of work, but is also used to describe each specific work activity. Marx refers to these specific types of work activities, e.g., butcher, baker candlestick maker, as concrete labour and the general concept of work as abstract labour. Labour, then, for Marx is a generic concept, or abstraction, but it is also something real: in that sense we can refer to the concept of labour as a real abstraction, not something that exists in the mind as an ideal or thought abstraction, but the determining logic of capitalist social life. It is only in capitalist society where such an idea is possible, where labour becomes the organising principle for the whole of capitalist society (Cleaver 2000). Labour in this sense is unique to capitalist society. As Marx puts it in *The Grundrisse*:

Indifference towards any specific kind of labour presupposes a very developed totality of real kinds of labour, of which no single one is any longer predominant. As a rule, the most general abstractions arise only in the midst of the richest possible concrete development, where one thing appears as common to many, to all. Then it ceases to be thinkable in a particular form alone. On the other side, this abstraction of labour as such is not merely the mental product of a concrete totality of labours. Indifference towards specific labours corresponds to a form of society in which individuals can with ease transfer from one labour to another, and where the specific kind is a matter of chance for them, hence of indifference. Not only the category, labour, but labour in reality has here become the means of creating wealth in general, and has ceased to be organically linked with particular individuals in any specific form. Such a state of affairs is at its most developed in the most modern form of existence of bourgeois society...Here, then, for the first time, the point of departure of modern economics, namely the abstraction of the category 'labour', 'labour as such', labour pure and simple, becomes true in practice. The simplest abstraction, then, which modern economics places at the head of its discussions, and which expresses an immeasurably ancient relation valid in all forms of society, nevertheless achieves practical truth as an abstraction only as a category of the most modern society.

(Marx, Grundrisse 1993 193)

This law of labour, for Marx, is not benign. Labour is the unavoidable organising principle of capitalist society, imposing a particular way of life, or rather absolute law enforced by the social power of the Police-State and money, poverty and wages, in order to create a particular form of wealth, capitalist value, where people and the planet are the resource not the project. The notion of real abstraction and its contradictory consequences will be considered in detail later in the book, specifically in relation to Marx's labour theory of value, and how the law of labour can be unlearned so that people and the planet are the project and not the resource. This unlearning means the creation of new forms of social institutions through which new forms of human activity and social wealth not driven by the law of labour can be learned as a moment of revolutionary transition.

The significance of this approach can be demonstrated by setting the theory and practice of Student as Producer against a book that deals with the student protests of 2010, *Student Revolt: Voices of the Austerity Generation*, written by Matt Myers, based on interview recollections of people involved in the protest. Like many historians Myers takes history for granted, as a movement in time, rather than a particular form of time in a very particular society that includes present time and concrete history (Neary 2017a, Postone 1993). Paul Mason, who writes an introduction to the book, characterises Marxist theory as the remit of 'grey beards and leather jackets' (Mason in Myers 2017 xi). For Mason the working class are no longer the subjects of revolution, but have been replaced by a new generation of protesters, described by Mason as 'part of a wider global social phenomenon, which moved to different rules compared to the old proletariat and the old intelligentsia'. This has been, for Mason, a revolt of the so-called networked individuals, 'the new sociological type called into being by the information society and assumed, until now, to be immune to protest and addicted to selfishness' (Mason 2017 xv). Myers' history is not devoid of all conceptual framing, he uses the notion of 'generation' from Karl Mannheim's *The Problem of Generations* (1952) and, more specifically, 'the austerity generation' and 'the Millbank generation' (Myers 2017 27), linked as an 'emotional community' (2017 27) or a student movement that acts as 'a transitional social community...organised...to assert their rights collectively in a unity greater than the sum of its parts' (2017 28).

Student as Producer makes use of the concept of generation, not as in cohorts of the population, but by using generation as a prefigurative idea: that which is generative or genetic. Student as Producer grounds the process of generation in Marx's theory of labour, as the groundwork on which capitalist civilisation is based, and which must be undermined if a new form of social life is to be established, not based on the law of Money but by unleashing the law of life.

Student as Producer makes its own claims on history, with particular reference to the student protests of 1968, when students, together with workers and trade unionists in Paris and around the world, kicked off, demanding an end to the boredom and poverty of everyday life (Lefebvre 1969, Debord 1984). I have described this historical moment and its legacy as a 'pedagogy of excess' (Neary and Hagyard 2010). What I mean here by excess is, as Ross (2002) describes it, the really transforming aspect of the '68 protest' was that the participants did not perform the roles that had been accorded to them by sociologists, journalists, historians and politicians, i.e., those who defined the events of May 1968 as a 'student protest'. The significant point, argues Ross, is that the students refused to act as students: 'In the so called "student action" students never acted as students but as revealers of a general crisis, of bearers of a power of rupture putting into question the regime, State, society' (Blanchot 1998 quoted in Ross 2002 25). This refusal to act as students was compounded by the students' refusal to speak about student issues, choosing only to speak about 'common affairs' raising the protest to the level of society. As Badiou maintains, the events of 1968 were 'something that arrives in *excess*, beyond all calculation...that proposes an entirely new system of thought' and which 'led infinitely farther than their [the students'] education...would have allowed them to foresee; an event in the sense of real participation...altering the course of their lives' (Badiou 1998 quoted in Ross 2002 26, author's emphasis).

The Author as Producer

The slogan for the revolutionary teaching practice developed in this book is Student as Producer. Student as Producer is ripped off from the title of a paper written by Walter Benjamin called The Author as Producer, to be presented to the Committee for Anti-Fascists in Berlin in 1934. Writing during the aftermath of World War One and the rise of the Nazi party in Germany and in the shadow of another forthcoming European war, Benjamin sought an answer to the basic question of how do radical intellectuals act in a time of crisis. Benjamin's solution was by finding ways in which objects-victims of what is claimed by oppressors as their history become subjects-protagonists of their own history, not simply by participating in creative practices, but by revolutionising the process of production and the meaning and the nature of history itself: refunctioning production and operativism so as to 'contribute constructively' to social life (Gough 2002 73).

Benjamin was a 'Maverick Marxist' (Lowy 2005, Arendt 1999, Leslie 2000), part of a group of intellectuals who sought to extend Marx's critique of political economy out of the factory and the labour movement into all areas of social life (Eiland and Jennings 2014). Benjamin is very much influenced by the work of Bertolt Brecht and the Russian Constructivists: a group of artists after the Russian Revolution for whom the artist is producer (Gough 2002, Gough 2005, Palmier 2006).

In this book I want to bring Benjamin back to life – not as in David Kishik's 2015 book *The Manhattan Project*, where he imagines Benjamin did not commit suicide on the French/Spanish border but escaped to live in New York, but by refunctioning his revolutionary sensibility through a reappraisal of Marx's law of value, with a strong link to Russian Constructivist politics and practice. In *The Author as Producer*, Benjamin was focusing on the creative arts, literature and painting as well as journalism, but in other related work he focused on the life of students with specific ideas about how to connect research and teaching in higher education to develop radical and disruptive modes of knowledge production (Benjamin 1931, Charles 2016) The work of Benjamin will be a recurring theme in the book. Benjamin is not a ghost that haunts this book, but a story board on which to develop a curriculum for unlearning the law of labour.

Benjamin on Higher Education

Walter Benjamin wrote extensively and critically about education, including higher education, recognising the limits of the university curriculum and how the role of universities as progressive institutions might be recovered. Writing *The Life of Students* in 1914-15 (Bullock and Jennings 2004) he suggests how students can contribute to the function of the university as the essence of criticality, i.e., 'to disclose the immanent state of perfection and make it absolute, to make it visible and dominant in the present' (2004 37). This is not possible, he argues, by writing an empirical account of events or about institutions and their practices. It is achievable, he maintains, by grasping the life of the university and its students as a 'metaphysical structure' (2004 37), as an 'idea of the university', understood in its entirety as a 'system as a whole' (2004 38), framed, indeed, as 'the highest metaphysical state of history' (2004 37). Benjamin understands the system as a whole as 'the conscious unity of student life' (2004 38), which he explains as 'the will to submit to a principle, to identify completely with an idea' (2004 38) based, in this case, on a notion of generalised scholarship and 'community of learning' (2004 38), culminating in the more expansive and non-empirical 'unity in the idea of knowledge' (2004 38). For Benjamin this community of learning and unity in the idea of knowledge can be further enhanced by students connecting with radical and progressive aesthetic movements of the period, something they had, up until that time, avoided. Benjamin notes that insofar as the university has become an organ of the state such idealist thinking becomes unacceptable. The German university had become overwhelmed by vocationalism, individuality and service to the state. He writes: 'The perversion of the creative spirit into the vocational spirit, which we see at work everywhere, has taken possession of the universities as a whole and has isolated them from the nonofficial, creative life of the mind' (2004 41-2).

So much so that, for Benjamin, 'The uncritical and spineless acquiescence in this situation is an essential feature of student life' (2004 39). And that, 'The secret tyranny of vocational training...poisons the essence of creative life' (2004 43). This is exemplified for Benjamin in the way that German universities operate against the Humboldtian principles on which they were established:

> The most striking and painful aspect of the university is the mechanical reaction of the students as they listen to a lecture. Only a genuinely academic and sophisticated culture of conversation could compensate for this level of receptivity. And, of course, the seminars are worlds away from such a thing, since they too, mainly rely on the lecture format, and it makes little difference whether the speakers are teachers or students. The organisation of the university has ceased to be grounded in the productivity of its students, as its founders had envisaged. They thought of students as teachers and learners at the same time; as teachers, because productivity implies complete autonomy, with their minds fixed on science instead of on their instructor's personality. But where office and profession are the ideas that govern student life, there can be no true learning. There can no longer be any question of a devotion to a form of knowledge that, it is feared, might lead them astray from the path of bourgeois security.
> (Benjamin 2004 42)

Benjamin's solution is for the student to become 'an active producer, philosopher, and teacher all in one, and all these things should be part of his deepest and most essential nature' (2004 42). This should not operate by reference to any specific scientific principle, but provide the basis for 'the community of the university' (2004 43) which for him is 'a life more deeply conceived' (2004 43). He concludes:

This is what would prevent the degeneration of study into the heaping up of information. The task of students is to rally round the university, which itself would be in a position to impart the systematic state of knowledge, together with the cautious and precise but daring applications of new methodologies. Students who conceived their role in this way would greatly resemble the amorphous waves of the populace that surround the prince's palace, which serves as the space for an unceasing spiritual revolution – a point from which new questions would be incubated, in a more ambitious, less clear, less precise way, but perhaps with greater profundity than the traditional scientific questions. The creativity of students might then enable us to regard them as the great transformers whose task is to seize upon new ideas, which spring up sooner in art and society than in the university, and mould them into scientific shape under the guidance of their philosophical approach.
(2004 43).

Elsewhere in his writings (1932/1999) he makes the point about the significance between research and teaching more explicit, not in terms of developing more scholastic practice but in a way that would 'establish rigorous new forms: not the pernicious spectrum of critical methods...to make way for more enterprising researchers...[and]...less banal, more considered learning'. By which he means 'we should not look to research for *a revival in teaching; instead, it is more important to strive with a certain intransigence for an...improvement in research to emerge from teaching'* (1932/1999 419).

And, for this to be done in such a way that 'a rearrangement of the subject matter would give rise to entirely new forms of knowledge' (1932/1999 420).

As Mathew Charles (2016) puts it:

> Benjamin gives the outlines of a practice of teaching-led research here: it does not ground teaching on the expertise of established research, nor attempt to turn students into producers of research on an imitative model of the 'master' teacher (producing more 'masters' within a system of higher education that has no place for them), but rather opens up the expertise of the academic's own research to the lived experience and interests of the emerging generation. As Benjamin suggests, in the era of mass systems of higher education, there is the possibility that the new strata of students can function as agents in the educational process in a way that posits them not as 'creators' or 'reproducers' of scholarly knowledge but its deformers and destroyers.

And so how to make this work? How can students become deformers and destroyers, and what can be built in place of the system of master teachers?

Student as Producer Conference

The first appearance of the slogan Student as Producer was as the title for a conference organised by the Reinvention Centre in 2007, in what might have been the first UK event that featured academic and student research. The conference included papers from academics and students from the University of Warwick and Oxford Brookes University, on a range of different topics, as well as colleagues and students from other universities across the UK and other international speakers as well as students from a sixth-form college. The conference also saw the launch of an online electronic journal featuring student research that has now developed to become: *Reinvention – An International Journal of Student Research* [https://warwick.ac.uk/fac/cross_fac/iatl/reinvention/].

The two keynote speakers at the conference were Steve Fuller, Professor of Sociology at Warwick, and Eric Newstadt, a graduate student and former Chair of the National Graduate Caucus of the Canadian Federation of Students in Canada 2004-6. The themes for their talks were two core issues for the topic of revolutionary teaching: democracy and the law of value. Both of these terms, democracy and the law of value, and their relationship define the critical intellectual space within which this book is written.

The title of Steve Fuller's presentation was Can Universities Retain their Edge as Knowledge Production is Democratised? In this talk Fuller acknowledged that universities have always been in the business of reproducing the structures of knowledge and power in society. However, as these structures have become more democratised, universities are set to become victims of their own success. In other words, as more people acquire academic training, a competitive advantage increasingly accrues to those who use traditionally non-academic means of producing knowledge that nevertheless manage to reach large numbers of people. Fuller argued that projects like the Reinvention Centre are ideally poised to make the case that these skills are as integral to the curriculum as ordinary literacy and numeracy. However, he cautioned that the ultimate challenge facing universities as they broaden their skills base in this fashion is whether they can retain control over intellectual standards, since most of the knowledge is happening outside academic settings, often in a self-organising fashion. If universities are to do more than merely follow market trends, the question of standards will have to loom large. However, the constituency of universities provides a unique opportunity for academics and students to collaborate in the production of knowledge.

Writing in a book published around the same time, *The Sociology of Intellectual Life* (2009), Fuller discusses how science might be democratised, favouring the institutional process invented by Humboldt at the University of Berlin, where academics through their teaching function 'redistribute the advantage that new knowledge initially accrues to its producers', but this can only take place with a strong commitment to the academic freedom of students and academics 'to inquire freely in each other's' company' (Fuller 2009 164).

The title of Eric Newstadt's keynote was *Devaluing the Value-Form: Pulling on the Roots of Everyday Life to Get Beyond the Neoliberal University*. Newstadt argued that the last few decades have witnessed the emergence of a new kind of university, the neoliberal university. Grounding his argument in Marxist terms, he pointed out that the neoliberal university reflects the myriad ways in which the logic and extension of the value-form works, where knowledge is cast as a collection of measurable and interchangeable variables that can be almost mechanistically produced. Newstadt maintained that the work and rhythms inside the neoliberal university are intimately tied to the emergence and operation of a globalised and finance-based capitalism. Newstadt argued that in order to get beyond the neoliberal university it is important to understand the political economic structures that underpin and support neoliberalism, which, for Newstadt, crystallised around understanding the real nature and character of the value-form: 'the veil behind which Capital becomes ever more extensive and deeply embedded'. Newstadt argued that because 'the logic of value is absurd' there are plenty of opportunities for creating schemes to *parody* this absurdity and for developing strategies that can be effective in creating the opportunities for solidarity and for helping individuals deal with the pain associated with neoliberal policies in universities and elsewhere. In Newstadt's terms, Student as Producer might be seen as a parody, undermining the neoliberal university, based on the absurd logic of its own financialised principles. Newstadt (2013) developed these arguments in his PhD on *The Value of Quality: Capital, Class and Quality Assessment in the Re-Making of Higher Education in the United States, The United Kingdom and Ontario.* The main point of this thesis is that a quality assurance regime 'neither measures nor helps to produce anything that could meaningfully be described as being of "high quality"'. Rather quality assurance is effective in helping to reproduce commercially orientated but hardly ground-breaking research and a more 'flexploitable' labour force. In other words, 'systems of Quality Assurance were developed to evaluate the exchange value of new knowledge and graduates within the context of neoliberal capitalism' (Newstadt 2013 ii).

The Value of Democracy

These keynotes provide a strong conceptual framing for the theoretical debate that sustains this book, between *democracy* and a critique of the *law of value,* out of which could emerge the basis for revolutionary teaching.

There is a strong relationship between the issues of democracy and communism. Marx was a democrat before he was a communist, although his move towards communism is consistent with his democratic ideals (Rubel 1962). The clear distinction between the two categories is that the former is considered as a political revolution in what might be described as 'the dictatorship of the proletariat' premised on the capture of the state, while the latter is a social revolution requiring the abolition of all social classes and political power as the basis for a fully human rather than political society (Rubel 1962).

Democracy, for Rubel, is not an end in itself, but part of the struggle against authoritarian and absolutist societies, a form of 'political self-education' (Rubel 1962 89) that underpins the transformation of the whole society; or 'an association in which the free development of each [individual] is the condition for the free development of all', quoting from *The Communist Manifesto*. How then to recover the basis for this kind of political self-education arranged around a development of the relationship between democracy and a critique of the law of value? In this book, Student as Producer and the co-operative university will be suggested as just such a form of political self-education.

The relationship between democracy and the law of value can be considered with regard to the debate between reform and revolution. This debate is reflected most acutely in the dispute between Rosa Luxemburg (1871-1919) and Eduard Bernstein (1850-1932) in Germany in the early years of the twentieth century. Bernstein favoured the social democratic model where the state would enable capital to reform leading eventually to socialism. Luxemburg was for the revolution, to be led by the working class. This debate is developed by Miliband and Liebman (1985), who argue in favour of a 'revolutionary reformism' as a model for social development. The revolutionary teacher of Student as Producer advocates a version of revolutionary reformism, which recognises the state as a capitalist state derived out of the capital relation, understood as a site of class struggle (Holloway and Picciotto 1977). The conflictual factors in the capital relation are labour and capital, but what distinguishes Student as Producer from orthodox Marxism is not a critique of capitalism from the perspective of labour but rather is based on a negative critique of labour, following the work of Moishe Postone, as part of *Critical Theory and the Critique of Labour* (Neary 2017a). The question of labour in a book about capitalist production is key and will be revisited in places throughout the text. The logic of Student as Producer's critique of labour is that it focuses not on how to capture the state; but, rather, how to dissolve the social relations of capitalist production in real time. This will involve, as Marx argued in the *Critique of the Gotha Programme* (1875/1966), a transitional period made up of revolutionary ideas and practices, e.g., co-operatives, which will be discussed at the end of the book, including a thought experiment for how this new revolutionary society might be defended.

Student as Producer, Lincoln, England

I was appointed the Dean of Teaching and Learning at the University of Lincoln in 2007. I came to Lincoln with the intention of establishing a model of curriculum development based on the concept of research-engaged teaching that had been established by the Reinvention Centre at Warwick and Oxford Brookes universities. The University of Lincoln was already committed to this approach, so there was much on-going work in this area that could be developed. In my position as a senior manager and working closely and collaboratively with academics and students as well as administrators, estates and other professional services staff we developed a model for curriculum development that was accepted by the university in 2010 as the organising principle for teaching and learning across all subjects and all levels, to be rolled out across the university over the next 5 years, and beyond. The project was supported with external funding from the main government institution to support university teaching, the Higher Education Academy, as well as gaining the support of other academics in other institutions in the UK and around the world. The title for this new project was Student as Producer.

From the beginning, it was made very clear that Student as Producer was not simply a new teaching and learning initiative to, in the managerialist language of the time, 'enhance the student experience'; but that Student as Producer sought to recover the university as a radical political project, with its roots in the student movement of May 1968, and with very clear references to its Marxist antecedents. This was set out in the User

Guide Manual for Student as Producer for all university staff and students:

> Research-engaged teaching is not new, but is grounded in the intellectual history and tradition of the modern university. In a period when the meaning and purpose of higher education is far from clear, some academics maintain that higher education is being defined by government policy in ways that undermine the academic project. The research-engaged teaching and learning initiative is an attempt to restate the purpose of higher education by seeking to reconnect the core activities of universities, research and teaching, in a way that consolidates and substantiates the values of academic life.
>
> The core values of academic life are exemplified by the type of students that are produced at Lincoln. Student as Producer refers to the objects and resources and processes that students create and invent, but it also refers to the ways in which students are the creators of their own social world, as subjects rather than objects of history (Benjamin 1934). This capacity for student subjectivity is found in the human attributes of creativity and desire (Lefebvre 1991), so that students can recognise themselves in a world of their own design (Debord 1970).
>
> (User Guide 2012)

Student as Producer was implemented across the university through a number of infrastructural platforms: making use of the quality assurance bureaucratic processes, institutional support for teaching and learning, and the design of teaching and learning spaces and technology (Neary et al 2010). What underpinned all of this was a theoretical framework based on Marxist social theory, running counter to the dominant managerialist discourse that pervades higher education, following Newstadt, as a sort of parody. It was not necessary to be a revolutionary

Marxist to be engaged with Student as Producer, indeed the project encouraged critical debate, but this was the framework within which teaching and learning at Lincoln was now to be conceived against the mainstream managerialist discourses, 'managementese' (Docherty 2015 54), that had overwhelmed university life.

The main instruments through which Student as Producer was implemented were the quality assurance processes: the bureaucratic processes and protocols by which universities ensure the quality of their degree programmes. When academics were designing new courses they were challenged and invited, Student as Producer was not compulsory, to engage with the core principles of Student as Producer that had been agreed across the university. At the heart of the principles was the extent to which undergraduate research forms a key component of the teaching programme at all levels and how much are students involved in the design and delivery of the programme. Academics were encouraged to consider issues of space and spatiality with regard to the teaching rooms in which they were working as well as the wider 'learning landscapes' environment beyond the institution (Neary et al 2015). The principles encouraged academics to consider how they would make use of the emerging digital technologies to facilitate the production of undergraduate research, as well as supporting the more subversive aspects of computer 'hacking' to find ways by which students could build the new technologies rather than just using them (Lockwood and Winn 2013). And, wrapped around all of this, was a support structure for academic teaching. The most radical expression of this was the creation of a Teaching Academy, designed as an informal network of support for teachers, lying outside the mainstream provision, but supported by the university.

It is important to note that none of this was compulsory; academics were invited and encouraged to engage with Student as Producer. The reason for this was to avoid Student as Producer becoming another manager-led initiative, but also to encourage critical debate and an attitude of *dissensus*, so the project would not go stale and so that we could all learn from each other's teaching practice and theory. This desire to generate a critical debate has been supported by the large number of publications that have been produced by colleagues and students involved with Student as Producer at Lincoln, giving the project academic credibility as well as a strong theoretical and conceptual framework through which to develop the work.

Student as Producer has been well received across the institution and was taken up by other universities who adapted the model in their own way, usually without the Marxist inclinations. This whole institutional approach was well received by government external quality reviewers, the Quality Assurance Agency, who awarded Student as Producer their highest commendations. A core purpose of Student as Producer was to radicalise the mainstream (Neary 2013).

Student as Producer did not transform the neoliberal university – it was recuperated within the capitalist university, but the project remains unfinished, and has yet to be established in more radical forms (Neary and Saunders 2016). This book does not include an extensive review of the project, which can be found elsewhere (Neary et al 2015, Neary and Saunders 2015). The purpose of this book is to reveal the conceptual and theoretical approaches that have been developed by Student as Producer, and to understand the historical and political context out of which it emerged, as well as showing the direction in which it is now moving, so that we can develop a set of principles and practices to answer the question 'how do revolutionary teachers teach?' In order to attempt to answer that question the book will be set out as the following series of chapters.

Chapter 2 Protest, Pedagogy and Police
This chapter contextualises Student as Producer as a moment of

resistance to the assault on higher education and the politics of austerity. The chapter makes a link between the protests of 2010 and 2011 as 'a double riot' (Clover 2016), in response to 'a double crisis', by which I mean the economic crisis and the crisis of the university (the Edu-Factory Collective 2009). Written from the standpoint of my own position within this movement of protest, I am responding to the problem identified by Myers (2017), when he argues that 'Much of theorisation of 2010 came from outside the movement – from journalists and writers – rather than being retrospective intellectual production from inside' (Myers 2017 22). Along the way, I raise the question of what it is to be a Marxist working in higher education today. This chapter deals with the role and nature of Police in relation to the riots (Bloom 2012); as the instrument of a repressive state and function of the way in which the repressive state is policed at a time of crisis (Hall et al 2013); as the imposition of labour and poverty and the avoidance of communism (Neocleous 2000), and as the antidote to a type of institutional democracy that seeks to prevent the emergence of revolutionary subjectivity (Ranciére 1999). The debate about Police is extended at the very end of the book, in the afterword, to consider a form of social security that is appropriate to communism: not-Police which I call Authority and Authorship. The not-Police are derived from the writings of the Russian legal theorist Evgeny Pashukanis (1891-1937), as well as a critical engagement with modern interpretations of Roman political philosophy.

Chapter 3 Student as Producer and the Labour Debate

This chapter takes a closer look at the work of Walter Benjamin and, in particular, his paper *The Author as Producer* (1934). It pays particular attention to his engagement with Marx and Marxism and how this has been scrutinised in parts of the Benjamin literature: by TJ Clark (2003), Esther Leslie (2000) and Hannah Arendt (2007). Following these accounts of Benjamin and Marx, I conclude, after Wiggershaus (2007) among others, that Benjamin's approach was not dialectical enough, particularly with regard to his celebration of the proletariat as the revolutionary subject. I set out a dialectical account of labour through the work of Moishe Postone (1993). I will focus in this book on the writings of Moishe Postone as he exemplifies a particular approach to Marx's labour theory of value that has come to be known as the new reading of Marx (2017). This more dialectical account allows me to identity the way in which labour works as a form of social mediation in the development of capitalist social relations, and that this is the matter that needs to be fundamentally addressed in order that the social relations of capitalist production can be dissolved and revolutionised through a form of revolutionary teaching. I will do this with reference to a key voice in the debate about critical theory and the law of labour, Theodor Adorno (1903-69), whose own experiences of teaching university students during the student protests in 1968 in Germany, and his unwillingness to support direct political protests, avoiding protests against capitalism that merely reflect capitalism's instrumental attitude as quasi/pseudo-concrete solutions, has much to teach the revolutionary teacher.

Chapter 4 Learning from Revolutionary Teachers

This chapter engages with three major revolutionary teachers: Jacques Ranciére, born in 1940, Paulo Freire (1921-97) and Paula Allman (1944-2011), setting out key learning points from their theoretical and practical work. These authors have been chosen for their engagement with and capacity to be read through Marx's labour theory of value and, therefore, have much to teach about unlearning the law of labour. Specifically, Ranciére promotes the power of a socially reflexive critical Marxism, not dominated by elite theorists but as a social revolution that emerges from the practical activity (praxis) of workers themselves. Of particular interest to Student as Producer is how practical activity can create new knowledge as a form of collective critical intelligence or the emancipation of the intellect. Ranciére makes a strong argument about the way in which intellectual emancipation works as an antidote to Police through a politics of dissensus. It is the role of the revolutionary teaching to conjure up this collective critical intelligence, not only within the classroom and education institutions, but at the level of political society. This is what Ranciére refers to as communism without the communists. And, above all, where possible do nothing that is instrumental for capitalism. Paula Allman reminds us of the power of reading Marx's primary texts, unfiltered and uninterrupted, as a way of substantiating our revolutionary teaching. Allman makes a claim to have much in common with Moishe Postone and his critical reappraisal of Marx's social theory, emphasising the dialectical struggle between labour and capital as the key to human emancipation. As we shall see, a critical reading of her work needs to avoid the contaminating idealism of liberal humanism and the seductiveness of theory itself, both of which can undermine the importance of what her version of revolutionary pedagogy has to say. Allman's work is significant because she connects the reality of critical theory and practice with her own emotionality, as anxiety and pain of higher education, as part of what Hall (2014) calls 'the anxiety machine'. In the section on Allman, I will look at the work of a group of writers gathered around her as a milieu of Marxist educators, including Glenn Rikowski and Peter McLaren. I will examine Allman's claim to be close to the work of Moishe Postone, showing that he takes a very critical approach to the type of critical pedagogy advocated by Allman. Paulo Freire is identified in the book as a sophisticated social theorist, showing how his conceptual approach to pedagogy is applied in practice as part of a critical dialogue between teacher and student. Freire grounds his theory in a Marxist account of class struggle with the power of labour as a fundamental aspect of social revolution. Freire does not theorise labour as a real abstraction, choosing to deliver a motivating message through more idealist abstractions, e.g, the pedagogy of *hope*. I shall elaborate on the power of the idea of hope when read through a materialist version of the labour theory of value (Dinerstein 2015). The powerful message from Freire is to take the theory and practice of revolutionary teaching outside of the classroom and to use it to formulate educational policy. He shows the importance of operating at the local and national state and internationally, linked always to the classroom in a way that is sensitive to the political, social and cultural context. He is very clear about the dangers of recuperation. His life and work reminds us to remember the violence and brutality of the capitalist state. Freire is working from an understanding of power and the need for new forms of social institutions based on the reinvention of the concept and practice of power that comes close to Holloway's exhortation 'to change the world without taking power' (2002). Holloway argues revolutionary power does not mean taking over the state, but dissolving the capital relation on which the capitalist state is based, as a form of 'anti-power'. Freire understands higher education as being based on a dialectical and dialogical relationship between research and teaching, and like Student as Producer, he argues, the university must be revolutionised.

Chapter 5 The Co-operative University: Democracy and the Law of Value

The final chapter tells the story of the work that I have been doing with others to create a form of co-operative higher education, as the culmination, for the moment, of Student as Producer. The co-operative university is not the revolution, but is a moment on the way to a communist future. This communist future is discussed in relation to key debates set out at the start of this book, between democracy and the law of value, where the democratic principle is embodied in a progressive form of labour organisation, the co-operative university (Winn 2015 a Winn 2015 b), and between reform and revolution (Luxemburg 2006), arguing in the end for a type of revolutionary reformism (Miliband and Liebman 1985). I set this out as a critical engagement with Joshua Clover's notions of riot and strike (Clover 2016). Where Clover argues for Riot prime as the moment when a new radical subjectivity emerges from the confrontation of racialised and surplus populations with Police, I argue for Strike prime, not only to recover the power of the labour movement, but, following Postone, as a way to abolish the social relations of capitalist work. I make a connection here with the #MeToo movement and the Women's Strike. All of these debates, taken together, act as types of political education, or Student as Producer. The discussion in this chapter is contextualised within the rise of Corbynism, seen as the culmination of a process that students kicked off in 2010 where the book began, with a focus on the future of capitalist work as a movement towards its abolition, or unlearning.

Afterword: Authority and Authorship

At the end of the book I provide a version of not-Police, which I call Authority and Authorship, as a new form of social institution, a non-institution, to defend the kind of society needed to sustain communism as a sort of thought experiment. This version of not-Police is grounded in the work of the Bolshevik legal theorist Evgeny Pashukanis, set alongside Hannah Arendt, Alexandre Kojeve and Giorgio Agamben's denial of authoritarianism and Benjamin's take on authorship with a dialectical spin. Authority and Authorship have the pedagogic function of sustaining common purpose and social defence: how to live life and prosper, or life-enhancing-life: a perfect life. This is what I mean by revolutionary teaching.

Methodology and Method

The argument throughout the book is framed using the

methodology of critical political economy, a form of intellectual enquiry denounced by those who represent the interests of capital. Critical political economy seeks to uncover the logic that lies behind the everyday structures of capitalist life, and how those structures can be subverted (Bonefeld 2014). Critical political economy identifies those structures as organised by Marx's labour theory of value, not simply as an economistic theory, but as the organising principle of capitalist civilisation. Value here does not refer to bourgeois morality, ethics or principles, but, rather, what is the real value and nature of things: the measure of their social worth. Marx argued that the value of things in capitalism is social labour, i.e., human energy measured by time. These useful values, commodities, are then sold on the market as exchange values when the surplus value is realised as profit and payment for other expenses. Commodities are expressions or forms of value: hence Marx refers to commodities as the commodity-form. Marx's theory is a theory of social form. The value of labour is itself a commodity, referred to by Marx as labour-power, which has its own value – what workers need to sustain their lives and the lives of their families. The unique quality of social labour is that it can produce more value than it is worth, creating what Marx refers to as surplus value. The way in which labour is put to work by capital to create surplus is what Marx calls exploitation. The revolutionary principle is that capital relies on labour, but labour does not rely on capital. As a social law the labour theory of value can be modified or transformed depending on the circumstance. The current circumstance is the crisis of capital. This crisis sustains the possibility of creating another form of social value or wealth not based on the exploitation of social labour, a form of social wealth that Marx calls communism. The value of things in communism is based, Marx argued, on the reconciliation of the needs and capacities of humanity and the natural world.

My writing method includes an amount of direct quotations.

I do this so the reader can read the words of the writers quoted in this book and come to their own conclusions. I hope the reader will read the texts beyond the extracts I have presented, as Paula Allman suggests, unfiltered. I am anxious to avoid overbearing explanations of other writers' work. Jacques Ranciére argues explanations by teachers to students are a form of stultifying oppression. He suggests, in place of teacherly explanations, the creation of what he calls 'the thing in common': an 'egalitarian and intellectual link' between teacher and student (Ranciére 1991 13). The thing in common is for those with the will to learn so they can liberate their collective critical intelligence, as a form of intellectual emancipation. Bearing Ranciére's position on explanation in mind, I present this book as such a common thing.

2. Protest, Pedagogy and Police

Student as Producer was launched at the end of 2010 at the University of Lincoln, during a time of turbulence and trauma for higher education in England as the Tory-led coalition government sought to intensify the concept of student as consumer (Boden and Epstein 2006) and the pedagogy of debt (Williams 2006). In 2010-11 student organisations arranged a series of actions to protest against the governing coalition's higher education policy, in the form of marches in London and elsewhere, as well as more spontaneous occupations of university premises by groups of students. In other sites across the country students, academics and activists set up free universities and held 'teach-ins' to protest the Tory-led coalition policy for higher education. These protests were not just against higher education policy, but included students and pupils and their teachers and lecturers from other parts of the education sector, all of whom felt under attack by the Tory-led coalition funding cuts and privatisation policies, specifically in relation to the Education Maintenance Allowance and the Adult Learning Grant. This movement of resistance achieved a high rate of intensity in the last months of 2010, before dissipating in what looked like defeat after the fees and related policy were voted into law, and the students were subjected to excessive police force at the demonstrations, together with a punitive use of the criminal law to process the protesters through the courts (Power 2012). However, what appeared to be the end of the matter exploded back to life in the 'summer riots' of 2011, with students playing a significant part in the disorders, citing government education policy and police brutality as reasons for their involvement (The Guardian 2011). In the period following the protests student acts of resistance tended to be local and sporadic, with some success, e.g., forcing the University of Warwick in 2015 to abandon the setting up of an employment agency for part-time teachers who would not be employed by the university, and setbacks, e.g., increasing repression on campus by police and security (Bandhar 2013). There was a noticeable maturation of demands by students beyond the question of fees and cuts to more democratic forms of university governance (Neary and Winn 2019) and signs of more strategic developments beyond occupations that include the organisation of student strikes (Berlyne 2016), the establishment of student housing co-operatives and a boycott of the National Student Survey. And then, quite unexpectedly, the engagement of young people in politics burst dramatically back to life in the 2017 General Election in the UK, when large numbers of young people, against all expectations, voted for Labour and Jeremy Corbyn, the left-wing leader of the party.

In what follows I want to review the movement of student protest and summer riots during 2010-11 and their significance. Far from regarding the movement of protest as having been defeated, I want to emphasise its impact as part of a historical movement of political protest and to consider its future possibilities. The protest should not be regarded as a one-off event, but as part of a history of protest that had emerged in England since the eighteenth century (Thompson 1971, Pearson 1983), and with increasing regularity since the early 1970s. In that context the 2010 student protests need to be seen together with the 'summer riots' that kicked off in cities across the UK less than 12 months after the last student had clashed with police in Parliament Square in London. The police will feature centrally in my analysis, not only to report on their violent behaviour towards the students, as a functional instrument of the state, but as a fundamental actor in the whole drama, through a science of police (Neocleous 2000, Endnotes 2011), to reveal their real nature (Ranciére 1999, Hall et al 2013) as a significant actor in student protests, framed in terms of a theory of Police. I will develop this theory of Police with reference to the work of Clive

Bloom (2012), Joshua Clover (2016), Stuart Hall et al (2013), Mark Neocleous (2000) and Jacques Ranciére (1999). A science of Police reveals the true story of *what is at stake* not simply as a critique of political economy but, more practically, as the violence of theory in action and, most importantly, to point out how this violence can be undermined. If the police, as I will argue following Neocleous, are essentially about the imposition of the law of value, poverty and (un)employment, then the lesson to be learned is the necessity for dissolving the law of value. This is the essence of Student as Producer and the answer to the question 'how do revolutionary teachers teach?'

To understand the full significance of the student protests they need to be seen in a wider European and global movement of protest at that time against various forms of government repressions, including the 'Arab Spring', but also the Occupy Movement and its variations around the world, including the Spanish Indignados, the German student mass campaign against fees and as student protests in Latin America for an extended period (Dinerstein 2014, Simbuerger and Neary 2015, Simbuerger and Neary 2016). It is important to note the energy and the impetus the student protests gave to the more general opposition to the politics of austerity in the UK, particularly the trade union movement. Most significant is the effect the protest had on the 'behind the scenes' manner in which the government attempted to make higher education policy, through statutory instruments rather than legislation, and the shambolic way higher education policy has unfolded in England (McGettigan 2013). Finally, I want to argue this movement of protest is not over; it is possible to see the student movement in the UK springing back to life, with the new Tory government in 2017 giving the student movement of protest and resistance an extra dynamism. What gives these protests a renewed intensity is that these student protesters are now paying the massively increased fee, and living the new poverty of student life in the reconstituted, marketised higher education environment. And, most significantly, the student movement in England can be seen as the opening moment of the expression of an anti-austerity campaign that culminated in the surprise election of Jeremy Corbyn to the leadership of the Labour Party in 2015 (Chessum 2015, Myers 2017, Kumar 2011), as well as having a significant impact on the 2017 General Election. And, in the aftermath of that election, the way in which student fees became a central question of national political debate (Mason 2018).

Phrase and Content

The period 2010-11 was an extraordinary time for Student as Producer, providing it with a dynamic energy and vibrancy. Student as Producer had lived off its historical reference points: the formation of the University of Berlin in 1811 with its emphasis on linking research and teaching, and, of course, May 1968 (Neary and Hagyard 2010); but now Student as Producer was in the middle of what felt like history being made with students at the heart of the process. The student protests of 2010-11 were not a repeat of May '68; they shared many similarities and strongly identified with that moment of student revolt, but had their own critical sensibility pumped out to the boom box dubstep rhythms and musical intonations of the student protests (Mason 2012). Student as Producer is predicated on the critical power of students and academics and here for all to see were students being powerful, making it up as they went along, learning from previous generations as well as providing their own radical twist, sometimes theorised sometimes not, writing their own poetry of the future when 'the phrase cannot get ahead of the content: here the content gets ahead of the phrase' with radical action now running ahead of theory and enriching it (Karl Marx 2003). The protest was substantiated with various types of 'disobedient objects' (Victoria and Albert Museum 2014)
So where did it all begin?

University Paris – 8

University Paris – 8 is situated in the *banlieue* (suburb) of St Denis, at the end of Metro line 13 on the north-eastern edge of the city of Paris. The street names that enclose the campus, Lenin Avenue, Liberty Street and Stalingrad Avenue, reflect the area's history as a stronghold of the French Communist Party (PCF). Following years of decline in its industrial manufacturing base, and with an inevitable rise in unemployment, St Denis now appears as a 'dormitory of the dispossessed', a ghetto with low income families, high crime statistics and a diverse population, including many of African and Arab descent. It is notorious as the place where on 27 October 2005 two youths died escaping from the police, setting off weeks of rioting across France, leading the government of Nicolas Sarkozy (the President of France 2007-12) to declare a nationwide 'state of emergency'.

Yet, there is another way of interpreting the psycho-geography of St Denis: the conflagration of 2005 was not the result of 'extreme dispossession' but, rather, the outcome of sharing 'a common language and a common enemy' with more life and energy among the *banlieusards* than is found on the fashionable Left Bank, for all its radical chic (Invisible Committee 2009: 56). The common enemy was the necro-social living death that typifies life in a capitalist city, the common language was the language of revolt sprayed graffiti-style on public buildings and campus walls: *Vive le Commune (Long live the Commune); Occupe Tout, N'exige rien (Occupy everything, demand nothing)*.

The first site of University Paris-8 was on the Bois de Vincennes in the centre of Paris, originally known as the Experimental University Centre Vincennes (*Centre Experimental Universitaire de Vincennes*). University Paris-8 was established as one of a number of innovative universities in 1969, designed to modernise the French higher education system, while, at the same time preventing a repeat of the student uprising that had started in Paris the previous year. University Paris-8 was, from the beginning, determinedly avant-garde: staffed by academics committed to interdisciplinarity and interactive teaching, in seminar rooms filled with students from a wide range of backgrounds and the very latest teaching technologies. Aware of the tendency of academic introspection, Paris-8 found ways to connect with matters outside of the campus through a series of teach-ins designed to engage with workers in factories and farmers in the countryside (Cohen 2010).

The academics working at University Paris-8 at that time read like a list of contributors to an anthology of modern European social and political thought. Faculty included Michel Foucault, Helene Cixous, Gilles Deleuze, Felix Guattari, Jacques Ranciére and Jean-Francois Lyotard. The curriculum was stuffed with radical new disciplines, including courses on Cinema, Computer Studies, Psychoanalysis, Linguistics as well as Women and Gender Studies. The radical content of the taught programme was mirrored by the university's democratic governance structures, with students and staff employed at all levels working to create a new model of higher education.

For the students Paris-8 was 'a victory for their movement and a new revolutionary battleground' (Cohen 2010 209). No sooner had it opened than it went into occupation, strained by intellectual disputes arranged into different factions of Marxist-Leninism, communists, Gauchistes, Maoists and Trotskyites, fighting for control of the institution and with the Ministry of Education. The extent of the antagonism between Paris-8 and the Ministry of Education is evident by a remark made by the French Minister of Education, Alice Saunier-Seite, who had a low opinion of the quality of their degrees: 'Is it true that at Vincennes they gave a degree to a horse?' (Dosse 2011 350).

Jacques Ranciére describes his experience teaching at Paris-8:

The university, created from scratch in the summer of 1968, was supposed to give rebelling students the novelty they were hoping for. It was a nursery of young academics marked by their Marxist convictions and by the theoretical novelties of the time: structural linguists and anthropologists, Althusserian philosophers, Lacanian psychoanalysts, sociologists trained by Bourdieu and literature professors instructed by Roland Barthes' semiology and by the 'literary theory' of the Tel Quel group. The whole thing had the look of what we called at the time a 'recuperation' of the May movement, and it seemed bound to dissolve that movement's political potential into academic and cultural novelties. The Marxist professors who had congregated there soon split into violently opposed camps. One rejected the 'recuperation' and tried to use this out-of-the-box university as a base to continue the fight against the institution of the university as such. The other embraced the thesis of the PCF, which said that Vincennes was a 'victory' of the May movement and had to be consolidated and defended against leftist 'provocateurs' intent on sabotaging it. Althusserianism became, as a matter of course, the theoretical weapon of this second camp, and drew to its side new recruits who were no longer attracted by subversion but by the desire to put an end to it.

(Ranciére 2011a 127)

Whatever Ranciére's view, in a short period of time, Paris-8 became 'the most exciting intellectual centre in France in the 1970s...and the most famous French University in the world... and the only spaces in France's fossilised university landscape where innovative and critical thought was possible' (Cohen 2010 214). But the success of this 'absurdist utopia' (2010 214), which turned 'institutional dysfunction to an art form' (2010 214) meant that Paris-8 had enemies within the Ministry of Education. The fact that it was attracting many more students than it was built to cope with (designed for 8000, by the mid-1970s it had enrolled more than 30,000) gave these enemies the justification to have the Vincennes campus bulldozed and ordered to move out to St Denis. In spite of the move it retained its leftist credentials, with ground-breaking courses in Dance and Photography established in the 1980s. It still managed to attract leading leftist intellectuals, including Toni Negri, and the students and academics maintained their radical connection with the world through a series of campaigns on immigration, anti-globalisation and against imperialist wars. The campus remained open to the public, retaining 'a loose anything goes atmosphere...convivial and combative' (2010 216). So much so that even in 2010 'a barely tamed chaos still reigns in an institution which has never fully made its peace with authority, and its faculty are still connected by a strong sense of solidarity and readiness to oppose the powers-that-be' (2010 217). In other words, Paris-8 remained as a vision for an alternative version of higher education.

At the time of writing its 40-year history, Cohen (2010) records that the ghost of '68 is fading fast. The new generation of students appear less politicised; although still drawn from poor working-class families they are more instrumental about their reasons for wanting a degree. In this context the institutional memory is disappearing as the radical cohort of teaching staff who established Paris-8 are now retired or retiring. Paris-8's radical teaching methods have been recuperated and mainstreamed in other French universities and around the world. The building is showing signs of dilapidation and under-investment. The whole radical enterprise was placed further at risk from Nicolas Sarkozy's attempt in 2008-9 to privatise and commercialise the French higher education sector. The prevailing condition appears to have become a mixture of *plus ca change* and *deja vu?*

But now something is stirring again – the radical history of University Paris-8 is being recovered. No one can be sure when it started – when the apathy turned to activism, but when it exploded it was like it had never gone away.

Edu-factory – the University is a Factory

On a damp grey February weekend, before winter turned to spring, hundreds of student activists and some academics from all over Europe and other parts of the world congregated in Paris, France to consider the future of the European university. The main meeting place for the event was Paris-8 in the *banlieue* (suburb) of Paris, St Denis.

The meeting was the latest in a series of events that had begun with 'Bologna Burns' in Vienna, London, Paris and Bologna the previous year, as well the Commonversity meeting in Barcelona in 2010. The title for the event was *For a New Europe: University Struggles Against Austerity*. This meeting was organised by the Edu-Factory Collective and the Autonomous Education Network with the purpose of resisting the Bologna Process, and to counter cuts in social welfare expenditure. The Bologna Process is a European wide programme to create a business and employer friendly standardised higher education curriculum across Europe, named after the place in which it was first agreed by government ministers (Corbett 2005). The overall aim of the Paris event was to develop a collective political capacity for a new university, a new Europe and a new future for everyone.

Those who came had been attracted by the call: 'The time is now upon us to rise up, together, collectively and singularly, to reclaim our lives and build a New Europe based on rights and access. The time has come for us to reclaim what is ours: the common.'

The groups who attended the event included the University of Utopia, All Nepal National Free Student Union, the Carrott Workers Collective, Critical Legal Thinking, Direct Action from Ukraine, the Slow University of Warsaw, Fakultat Null from Berlin, Pan Africa Student Council (Gambia), Street University (Russia), Öğrenci Kolektifler (Turkey), the Association of the Blacklisted Students of Tokyo, Upping the Anti (Canada) and many unaffiliated individuals. Some groups coming to the event from North Africa and the Gambia had not been allowed to enter France to take part. The meetings took place in the context and an awareness of struggles on-going elsewhere, in the Maghreb and the Gambia in particular.

The lecture theatre for the opening plenary was packed with people sitting on the floor and in the aisles, mostly students and young activists and some academics. The overwhelming number of participants was reflected in the chaotic workings of the timetable. Nothing started on time, but no one minded. Groups who had only read about each other were now meeting face to face, revelling in the situation and the impact they were having. Even the English students, not known for their radicalism, had taken on the status of vanguard activists, with the other participants interested to know about what had been going on in London and elsewhere in the UK with regard to the marches and occupations.

The event was organised like a formal academic conference with a series of presentations, workshops and panels where key issues were discussed in the traditional setting of classrooms and lecture halls. The issues under discussion included autonomous knowledge production, self-education, networking, transnational organisations and the concepts of 'the common' and 'precarity'. Indeed, the terms 'commons' and 'precarity', as was increasingly the case in academic and activist circles, were the defining principles of the event.

This was not a fractious gathering. There was a general consensus about the nature of the problem in higher education and what was to be done. The conference was able, without much difficulty, to come up with an agreed statement, known as the Joint Declaration, which said:

We, the student and precarious workers of Europe, Tunisia, Japan, the US, Canada, Mexico, Chile, Peru and Argentina, met in Paris over the weekend of the 11th-13th of February,

2011 to discuss and organize a common network based on our common struggles.

Students from Maghreb and Gambia tried to come but France refused them entry. We claim the free circulation of peoples as well as the free circulation of struggles.

In fact, over the last few years our movement has assumed Europe as the space of conflicts against the corporatisation of the university and precariousness. This meeting in Paris and the revolutionary movements across the Mediterranean allow us to take an important step towards a new Europe against austerity, starting from the revolts in Maghreb.

We are a generation who lives precariousness as a permanent condition: the university is no longer an elevator of upward social mobility, but, rather, a factory of precariousness. Nor is the university a closed community: our struggles for a new welfare, against precarity and for the free circulation of knowledge and people don't stop at its gates.

Our need for a common network is based on our struggles against the Bologna Process and against the education cuts Europe is using as a response to the crisis.

Since the state and private interests collaborate in the corporatisation process of the university, our struggles don't have the aim of defending the status quo. Governments bail out banks and cut education. We want to make our own university. A university that lives in our experiences of autonomous education, alternative research and free schools. It is a free university, run by students, precarious workers and migrants, a university without borders.

Lina Dokuzovic (2016), who attended the event, writes:

The Paris meeting thus initiated a large-scale shift among European knowledge-based activists and their organisation of transnational meetings to a transcontinental struggle that focused on the relationships between the university and structures of inclusion, primarily those within border and migration regimes. Furthermore, they expanded beyond examining the relationships between knowledge and capital to approaching the links between the state and corporations and education and migration today. This gave rise to new perspectives on cross border solidarity.

(2016 151-2)

Student Protests in the UK

The British students and academics at the Paris event enjoyed their new-found celebrity status as vanguardist revolutionaries. The power and effectiveness of the English students' protests against fees and cuts was certainly unexpected, overcoming the stereotypical characterisation of students and young people as apathetic and apolitical, even among those who might be expected to support radical action. 'Students were simply not supposed to care about their own education' (Solomon 2011 12). Mark Fisher's *Capitalist Realism* (2009) had already provided an account of his own students' inaction before the kids kicked off.

In the world of *Capitalist Realism* Fisher diagnosed his students like psychiatric patients. They are said to be suffering from *'reflexive impotence'*, *'depressive hedonia'* (made miserable by the pursuit of pleasure) and addicted to the Control Society (2009 21): 'They know things are bad, but more than that, they know that they can't do anything about it' (2009 21).

The book describes the scene in a Capitalist Realist classroom in a further education institution in England:

During lessons at our college...students will be found slumped on desk (sic), talking almost constantly, snacking incessantly (or even, on occasions, eating full meals)...The carceral regime of discipline (Foucault) is being eroded by the technologies of control, with their symptoms of perpetual consumption and continuous development...The lack of an effective disciplinary system has not, to say the least, been compensated for by an increase in student motivation. Students are aware that if they don't attend for weeks on end, and/or if they don't produce any work, they will not face any meaningful sanction. They typically respond to this freedom not by pursuing projects but by falling into hedonic (or antihedonic) lassitude: the soft narcosis, the comfort food oblivion of Playstation, all night TV and marijuana... Ask students to read for more than a couple of sentences and many – and these are A-level students mind you – will protest that they can't do it. The most frequent complaint teachers hear is that it's boring...it is the act of reading itself that is deemed to be boring. (2009 23)

Students in the world of *Capitalist Realism* are defined as experiencing 'Oedipod consumer bliss' (2009 24) living life as an 'ahistorical anti-mnemonic blip culture – a generation...for whom time has always come ready cut into digital micro-slices' (2009 25). Fisher says that, while many appear to be dyslexic, what they are suffering from is *'post-lexia'*: 'Teenagers process capital's image-dense data without the need to read – slogan-recognition is sufficient to navigate the net-mobile-magazine informational plane' (2009 25). In this 'hypermediated consumer culture' (2009 25) teachers are caught between being 'facilitator-entertainers and disciplinarian-authoritarians' (2009 26).

It would be hard to imagine a more damning critical judgement against a section of working-class youth. The most significant response comes from the students themselves: within a year of the book's publication the students were out on the streets protesting against cuts in education. As the students shouted out in *The Coming Insurrection* (2009): 'We are not depressed; we're on strike' (2009 34).

Later Fisher, following the emergence of the student protest movement, was to describe the new critical attitude among students in terms of young people 'emerging from a deep depression': 'There's the rush that you get from simply not being depressed anymore – the occasional lurching anxieties, a sense of how precarious it all seems...and yet not only is it maintaining itself, its proliferating, intensifying, feeding on itself – it's impossible, but it's happening – the reality programme reasserting itself' (Fisher 2018 476).

Millbank: 10 November

The first main event in this period of protest was a march in London on 10 November, organised by the National Union of Students (NUS), under the presidency of Aaron Porter, and the University and College Union. The march was against the proposed huge increase in student fees in England from £3000 to £9000 and the intensification of neoliberal policies for education. After the NUS were initially praised for the organisation of the march, the events of the day were to split the student movement, with the NUS marginalised in the face of increasingly militant groups of students among the most prominent of whom was Clare Solomon, the President of London Students' Union; as well as emerging new groups: Students Against Fees and Cuts, the London Students Assembly and Education Action Network, a group made up of students and academics.

The route of the march, comprised of about 50,000 people, passed through Central London to the Houses of Parliament, along the north side of the River Thames embankment, to end at the Tate Britain Art Gallery for speeches and a rally. Near the end of the march the students would pass Millbank Tower: the headquarters of the Conservative Party, a building that featured heavily in the events of the day and how they were reported. The police had failed to secure the building which was entered by students, who gained forced access to the offices and roof, smashing windows and with one student throwing a fire extinguisher to the ground below. The fact that the students surrounding Millbank on the ground had chanted to the students on the roof to 'stop throwing shit' was not widely reported. The throwing of the fire extinguisher and window smashing enabled the press to label the students as irresponsible, and for Aaron Porter, the President of the NUS, to describe it as a 'despicable' action of 'rogue protesters' and an attempt 'to hijack a peaceful protest' (NUS 2010).

History (Change) in the Making

I stood on the small roundabout on the north side of Lambeth Bridge. I felt the march stream past me on either side of the road. There were some banners identifying institutions, but this was not a day for making distinctions. This was the university as one voice, against the cuts. The idea of the university in action: noisy, vibrant, funny, intelligent, angry, passionate, daft, serious, worried, critical, exhilarating, musical, articulate, smart, powerful, thoughtful, calm, considered, beautiful, ugly, civilised, urbane, irritating, pushy, cultured, anarchic, compelling, conflicted, logical and rational. A long stream of academics and students, mostly students, as far as the eye could see and beyond, spread across the road stretching one way to Trafalgar Square, and the other way to Millbank and the Vauxhall Bridge Road.

The police looked overwhelmed. They were wearing their 'Police as Service' gear, high-visibility yellow jackets and flat caps, a long way from the Robocop 'Police as Force' uniforms of the G20 demonstration. The police blog sites discussing the event complain about the failure of leadership and poor planning by their superior officers. Ironically, they point out that the lack of police presence was a result of their own 25 per cent cuts in funding.

Our coach had taken a wrong turn and dropped us off at the end of the route of the march at Tate Britain. I walked the march from back to front with a group from the University of Lincoln. We set off towards the front of the protest and met it coming towards us. We carried on against the flow, bumping into friends and colleagues and ex-students from other institutions along the way. It took us more than an hour to get to the back of the long queue, which by this time was not so much marching as shuffling along. The route of the march was not long enough for the crowd to stretch its legs. We were bottlenecked from the beginning. After about 10 minutes of shuffling forward down Whitehall and across Parliament Square, stewards with loud-hailers told us the event was over, that we should disperse and go home. It felt like it was over before it got started. We didn't want to leave. Eventually we met colleagues from Lincoln coming the other way. We left, reluctantly, to find the coaches to take us back to Lincoln. I never got to hear the speeches. I wasn't too bothered, I'd heard all I wanted to hear from the chants of the crowd: 'No ifs, No buts, No education cuts'.

On the way back on the coach I talked to students about the event. This was their first experience of direct political action. They were exhilarated. One student talked about how she read about this kind of thing on her course but this was the real deal, and she was in the middle of it. Some had been at Millbank when the protest kicked off. They were not sure how to think about it. They did not condone flying fire extinguishers but they could sense the power of defiance in what for them was a just cause. They were worried that the media would focus on events at Tory HQ and miss the point of the day, which for them had been a deeply significant event. These are not privileged middle-class kids, but a group for whom the lack of money is a constant grinding relentless reality. These are not even the students who will be charged the proposed new fees, but still they felt the need to defend free public higher education.

Some of the students worried that the day had not achieved very much. I told them that what they had done was important and admirable. They had been the main actors of an important public event, which was attracting national and global attention, and that this is how history is made. All of the students I talked to said they were glad they had been there.

The numbers of Lincoln students attending was impressive. As for academic colleagues, it was great to spend time together on a common cause that extended beyond the interests of our own institution, but it felt like we could have done with more of us being there.

When I got back home the late-night TV news focused on the events at Tory HQ. Elsewhere students and academics have set up a free university on Parliament Square, all are welcome to attend. As the headline in The Guardian put it the following morning: 'This is just the Beginning'.

The Real Dynamic

It is important to contextualise this very specific expression of resistance in the moment in which it occurred, and to resist its naturalisation as a political event in ways that undermine its sociological significance: the students are not hooligans (Pearson 1983), nor are they an expression of another 'moral panic' (Bloom 2012), but they are kicking off against the poverty of student life in the middle of what is maybe the deepest crisis of capitalism ever seen, as part of a movement of resistance on-going around the world, in opposition to the ways in which governments are responding to the crisis; it is within that context that the actions of students must be considered.

The context for the protest was the crisis of capitalism. This crisis is not the result of some malfunctioning technical economistic system of regulation, or the misrepresentation of a new ideology emerging out of a government sponsored think tank which has yet to assume a hegemonic position; but is, rather, the logic of the process of capitalist valorisation in which the endemic dynamic contradiction between labour and capital is the driving energy for the whole process, and in which the organisation of work is the central preoccupation, characterised by intensification, casualisation and shedding workers from the production process (Cleaver 2000). This is the dynamic of the real movement: the way that labour moves (Neary 2002). This is not a rational and functional state managing the crisis (Jessop 1990) or founded on a smart new intellectual proposition like 'shock doctrine' (Klein 2008) nor a Foucauldian model of governance based on some disciplinarian imperative (Amsler and Canaan 2008), but a panic paranoid reaction by the capitalist state, which is itself a form of the crisis (Clarke 1988) as the logic of class struggle intensifies. This paranoid response has had various manifestations around the world: in the UK as 'Thatcherism'; in Chile as the brutal Pinochet Dictatorship, Pinochetism; in France as Mitterand's 'liberalisation without liberals'; in the US as Reaganomics; in Australia and New Zealand as 'New Right' economic policies. In the more recent period this activity has come to be referred to as neoliberalism (Harvey 2007, Clarke 2005), providing a sense of rationality to what is a chaotic panic and a sense of powerlessness as to how such repression can be undermined (Postone 1993). Some writers have argued that, following the Great Recession, neoliberalism is dead, and we are in a period of 'necro-neo-liberalism' (Haiven 2011) as part of a very uncertain future in which the law of value will be imposed by militarised capitalist states against their own populations (Kurz 2013). In other words, Capitalism *is* the crisis, or to put the same thing another way, Students *are* the Crisis! (Communiques from Occupied California 2010, Holloway 2019).

Student protests against fees and cuts in England are not a new phenomenon. In 1988 in response to the Thatcher government's attempt to abolish student loans, ratified by the Higher Education Act in 1990, there was a student confrontation with the police known as 'The Battle of Westminster', after which plans to introduce fees were shelved. There were student walkouts and protests in 1998 when student fees were first introduced by New Labour, and more student protests in 2004 in opposition to a rise in student fees that was put into place without an electoral mandate (Alley and Smith 2004). As well as these historical precedents there was a general sense of student unrest during this period, specifically as a protest against government foreign policy in relation to the Israel-Palestine conflict and the Israeli occupation of Gaza in 2009, leading to the occupation of more than 50 universities. The cuts to higher education finances sparked off occupations, protests and strikes by academics and students and other academic workers at Middlesex University against the proposed closure of the Philosophy department, and at Sussex University as well as Leeds, Kings, Cumbria and Wolverhampton (Endnotes 2011). It was during this period that the largest peaceful demonstration in the UK in 2003 took place against the second Gulf War (Sinclair 2013). And in Ireland the students' protest in 2010 against a proposed increase in registration fees was met with police violence. The outcome of the protest against the Poll Tax still haunts Tory administrations and is a factor in their strategic decisions about policy making. At an event, in December 2015 in London, a civil servant close to ministers said: 'They fear higher education legislation will turn into their poll tax moment.'

The main issue for the students in England in 2010 were proposals that came out of the government's response to the Browne Report (2010) *Securing A Sustainable Future for Higher Education: an Independent Review of Higher Education Funding and Student Finance*. The Browne Report set out a series of recommendations for the future funding of higher education in England. There were other arrangements being made for the other devolved regions of the UK, all of which involved fee support for undergraduate students. The government was proposing a massive increase in student fees in England from £3,000 up to £9,000 for undergraduate fees per year, as a capped amount, not removing the cap as Browne had suggested. And, in an extension of the policy to students in other parts of the educational sector, the withdrawal of the Education Maintenance Allowance worth £30 a week to students in further education with families earning less than £30,000 a year (Amsler and Canaan 2008), as well as abolishing the Adult Learning Grant. The student anger against these cuts and the raise in fees was intensified by the fact that the Liberal Democrats, the junior partner in the new Tory-led coalition government, had broken their promise to abolish student fees made during the General Election campaign of 2010, which had garnered many university student votes on that basis. This was all in addition to cuts introduced as part of the Public Spending review, which included an 80 per cent reduction of public funding for teaching the arts, social science and humanities in higher education. From now on funding would follow the students whose new consumerist and proto-employee attitudes and choices would be driven, as policy makers assumed, by market knowledge gained from Key Information Statistics, including the results of National Student Satisfaction surveys and average starting salaries of students 6 months after leaving university (https://unistats.ac.uk/

Occupations 24 November: Leeds – Reimagining the University

Along with the marches, this period of protest included many university occupations, about 50, some of which were reported on in great detail as collaborative projects between academics and students (Myers 2018). These occupations were part of a global movement of occupations that were transforming the way in which political protest was being imagined, as a new pedagogy of space and time (Neary and Amsler 2012).

I was closest to occupations at the universities of Leeds and Lincoln. The occupation at Leeds was a spontaneous event that came out of the march against government higher education policy on 24 November. These marches had been organised as regional protests following the national protest march in London at Millbank earlier in the month.

Andre Pusey, a postgraduate student at Leeds University, takes up the story, describing the crowd of student protesters walking back to the university on the march against fees and cuts with a mobile sound system banging out the beats 'with no real plan of where to go [or what to do] if and when we got there' (Pusey 2014 297). The marchers gravitated towards the Michael Sadler Lecture Theatre at the university as it had easy access near the front of the main university building. At the beginning of the occupation there were several hundred people crammed into the lecture theatre.

An interesting aspect of the Leeds Occupation is that it happened at the same time as another event, organised as an act of resistance to higher education policy by the Really Open University (ROU), of which Andre Pusey was a founding member.

The ROU described themselves as:

an on-going process of transformation by those with a desire to challenge the higher education system and its role in society. Instigated by students and staff of higher education institutions in the city of Leeds (UK), the ROU is non-hierarchical and open to anyone who wishes to see an end to the commodification of knowledge and the creation of a free and empowering education system where creative and critical thought is fostered. (http://reallyopenuniversity.wordpress.com/what-is-the-rou/) and see (Pusey 2017 http://eprints.leedsbeckett.ac.uk/3888/1/90-1244-1-PB.pdf

The event was called 'Reimagining the University'. Originally planned for earlier in the month, it was rescheduled to coincide with the national day of protest. From the 24-26 November, the ROU was to host a series of events aimed at 'Reimagining the University'. All the events had been organised by students and staff from across higher education institutions in Leeds. The publicity proclaimed that the event looked to challenge the state of the universities, their role in society, and the capitalist crisis, while acting on the desire of students and academics to create a different world. Starting with the national walkout on 24 November, a series of workshops, lectures, events and 'interventions' were going to be happening across Leeds – at the Music and Art Colleges, Leeds Metropolitan University and the University of Leeds (http://reallyopenuniversity.wordpress. com/2010/11/12/join-us-and-reimagine-the-university/).

I was in Leeds for the Reimagining the University event and to take part in the march. I had been an undergraduate at Leeds in the 1970s and so felt an affiliation with this particular student community. My contribution to the Reimagining the University event was to run sessions on Student as Producer, the Social Science Centre, Lincoln and the University of Utopia, with my friend and colleague from Lincoln, Joss Winn. Other events planned to take place between 24-26 of November included sessions on academic freedom, anti-neoliberal experiments in education taking place in Latin America, talks about counter-projects going on elsewhere in UK universities as well as other strategies of resistance, including counter-mapping.

The Reimagining the University event was to be based in the Leeds Students Union with activities taking place across campus and in other sites of higher education in the city. However, as a result of the occupation, it was decided that some of the workshops planned over the 2 days could be moved to the occupation site, giving the ROU event a real sense of 'resistance and political antagonism' (Pusey 2014 298) as well as providing the opportunity for those in occupation to critically reflect on the occupation itself. However, while most of the sessions were well attended, with between 15 and 20 students, academics and activists at each event, there was a separation between those who were part of the occupation and those who were talking about it, as most of the occupiers did not attend the Reimagining the University event.

At the beginning of the Leeds occupation there was a diverse mix of university and further education students, school pupils and activists, giving the space a sense of energy and dynamism, as if it might be the basis for the start of a real social movement. There was a sound system and films projected on the lecture screen, as well as the rolling BBC news programmes that were showing the student protests taking place around the country. However, despite the energy and dynamism at the beginning of the occupation, the opportunity for a real movement was quickly lost:

> The atmosphere was edgy, almost out of control but utterly electric. The music amplified the sense of unity while cheering the protest footage politicised that unity. Unfortunately this remarkable scene lasted only two and a half songs before some veteran student activists switched the music off. A small argument ensued, the sixth-formers wanted the music back on, while others shouted them down. The undergraduate activists, who had control of the microphone, argued that 'this has to be a serious occupation', and that a list of demands should be drawn up to put to the university. After an ill-defined vote it was announced that those who wanted to continue dancing could go outside, although the sound system was never turned back on. Within an hour people were proposing the election of an occupation steering committee. This sparked an interminable and bad-tempered debate, but by this time the excitement and energy had gone—along with 80% of the people.

(Free Association, 2011 quoted in Pusey 2014 308).

The young people were told to turn the music off 'because occupation is a serious matter' (Pusey 2014 308).

This occupation was torn between different groups, the Socialist Workers Party and Anarchists: the former wanted to organise as a Trotskyite Central Committee, while the latter wanted to create task-based working groups that had been the hallmark of less structured protests, e.g., Climate Camp. As it turned out the decision-making structures were arranged as General Assemblies, but even then some people said they felt excluded, with little room for a new generation of activists to constitute itself and the movement (Pusey 2014 309). Increasingly the organisation and leadership of the occupation was taken over by a group from orthodox left-wing groups in what felt like an 'occupation within the occupation' (Pusey 2014 309) with increasing tensions over extending the occupation into other parts of the university as 'flash occupations' (2014 311). Many of those involved in the occupation were concerned that it was a replication of power structures in the university and elsewhere. If this is what democracy looks like it had been a real experience of how hard it is to make democracy work. The conclusions of ROU and the Freedom Association were that the occupation, which was to last until the start of the Christmas vacation, had not disrupted the administration of the university, nor had it made any real challenge to the university management, who had tolerated the occupation, waiting for it to finish when the occupiers went home for Christmas at the end of term.

At the University of Lincoln, where I was working, the students occupied rooms in the Main Administration Building following a march in the city on 24 November 2010. The occupied building is, as its name suggests, the main building on campus with offices and classrooms and lecture theatres, catering facilities and the Vice Chancellor's Office. The actual space they occupied had been used to launch Student as Producer as a university-wide teaching and learning initiative in 2010. The space had been designed by myself with colleagues in the estates department at Lincoln, using some of the interactive and democratic principles taken from the Reinvention Classroom at the University of Warwick (Lambert 2011). The occupying students saw a clear connection between their movement of protest and Student as Producer. As one of them said to me after the occupation was over:

> For the students who took part in the occupation at the University of Lincoln in November to December 2010, Student as Producer provided a theoretical framework *that influenced our actions and strategies, as well as a* rhetoric not only in terms of the occupation, but for what we wanted students to become in Higher Education, and politically at the national level. For me, Student as Producer underpinned the political motivations of the student occupiers at Lincoln. The problem was we didn't get enough people to join us, and the external political situation worked against us in the sense that the student movement was brutally suppressed by an increasingly militarised police force and legal system. The Right are very effective at eradicating oppositional and subversive forces. But we have to fight back and keep on fighting, we can't be deterministic.

9 December: The Vote

The vote on raising student fees was set for 9 December 2010, in the Chamber of the House of Commons. The National Union of Students, together with the newly-formed National Campaign Against Fees and Cuts, organised a day of protest and action. The NUS leadership called for a candle-lit vigil on the eve of the protest in Parliament Square, but the more militant students, energised by the success of their militancy at Millbank, were in a very different mood.

The Power of the Powerless

This time they were ready. An army of occupation with battle vectors drawn, diagonally and in parallel, across Parliament Square. With clear lines of sight, the trap was set around the House of Commons, waiting for the enemy to arrive.

The police knew they were coming. They could follow the progress of the movement of resistance as it made its way through the West End of London. Their advance was given away by TV and police helicopters, circling above in the clear blue winter sky. I caught up with the march at Trafalgar Square. It looked as beautiful as it always does, but this time younger and more urban. Black and Asian working-class youth with their own beat and boom and beat and boom and beat and boom soundtrack. Alongside school children and college kids were university students and their teachers, and many others besides. This is a group that cannot be easily classified or contained. The route down Whitehall was blocked. The march was funnelled through Admiralty Arch, around the back of the Treasury and up Birdcage Walk. The movement of resistance knew they were walking into a trap, but still they kept walking, knowing at some point they would be taken prisoner: kettled, but still they kept walking, with no weapons to defend themselves other than their sense of righteous indignation, they still kept walking, with lessons learned from the history of progressive struggle behind them, still they kept walking. On all sides surrounded by police officers in full riot gear, and dogs and horses, while with every step the trap was tightened. I retreated as I felt the police pincer closing. I lied to get through the police lines. 'Where are you going?' the police officer asked. 'Victoria station,' I said, 'To catch a train.' He let me through, deciding I was no threat to public safety. In the relative tranquillity of St James Park, I felt depressed and despondent. I had bottled it. Other people withdrew to avoid the trap, and stood around as bystanders, no longer participants in the movement of resistance, which kept on walking and walking. Wandering about I found a group of black youths, boys and girls, at the top of Whitehall, confronting the defensive police lines. For these marching youths the battle with 'Babylon' is an everyday event, not a one-off political protest. Most protesters eventually did what they were told to do and took another route. The youths had no fear of police, they've been fighting them for the last 50 years, in Notting Hill and Brixton and St Paul's and other places besides. They wanted to know why they couldn't walk down WHITEhall. 'Why won't you let them through, officer?' I asked. 'To prevent a breach of the peace', the officer replied, unconvinced by his own explanation. Behind his reply was a phalanx of robo-cops with full body-armour, riot helmets and faces hidden by black balaclavas, intensifying their menacing stares. I made my way back to Westminster Bridge via a roundabout route, avoiding police barricades that were set up all around. Reports were coming out that the students in Parliament Square were taking a beating, and had been charged by police on horses. The group of protesters on Westminster Bridge was angry and defiant. They unfurled a flag, 'How Dare You', across the road. The university coach that had brought us to the demonstration was parked next to Vauxhall Bridge. I wanted to collect my thoughts before the journey home. I sat in the Duveen Galleries in the nearby Tate Britain. The gallery was hosting an exhibition, Harrier and Jaguar, by Fiona Banner. The show had decommissioned jet fighters in unusual settings. The Harrier, known for its ability to perform vertical take-offs, was hung upside down, pointing vertically to the floor from a hook in the ceiling, like a carcass. The Jaguar lay upside down on the ground, devoid of its aeronautic capacities, with its fighting power drained away. These were no longer killing machines, but defenceless bits of metal whose powerful invincibility had been made powerless. I arrived home that evening in time to watch the coverage of the protest on the late-night TV news. The police, to my surprise, were having to defend themselves. Not for beating up the students, but for allowing protesters from the day's march to surround the Royal Rolls Royce Phantom V1 carrying Prince Charles and Camilla, the Duchess of Cornwall. The pictures on TV showed the Duchess of Cornwall, with a frightened look on her face. For one brief moment we had a glimpse of excessive reality, stripped bare for all to see. This is what revolution looks like. What a victory this has been.

Significance of the Protest

This day of action appeared to mark the high point for this period of protest. In spite of the incident with the royal couple in the royal car the day had been dispiriting, with students kettled for hours on Westminster Bridge (Indymedia 2010).

This march and the Millbank protest had been very important: they shattered the illusion of lazy, apathetic, apolitical students (Hallwood in Solomon 2011 69), revealing a radical student sensibility beyond the formalised NUS who had organised the march but condemned the attack on Millbank (Hallwood 2011): 'Its energy and idealism had become an inspiration for all those confronting austerity' (Meadway 2011 17). The students had 'transformed the political atmosphere' around Tory-led coalition cuts (Rees in Freedman and Bailey 118), pointing beyond the issue of student fees and university funding against the politics of austerity in general. 'The birth of the new student movement had allowed millions to enter a debate about the legitimacy and ideological purpose of the ConDem spending cuts' (Freedman 2011 6), and served as a call for action to the union movement whose formal opposition had, until this point, been understated:

Britain's students have certainly put the trade union movement on the spot. Their mass protests against the tuition fees increase have refreshed the political parts a hundred

debates, conferences and resolutions could not reach.
(Len McCluskey, The Guardian, 19 December 2010, quoted in
Freedman and Bailey 2011 84).

Millbank had been a 'dramatically symbolic event [which]
had induced a shift in the horizon of possibilities: gone was
the inevitable boredom and futility of the conventional central
London A-B demonstration, and in its place the possibility at
least for some destructive and powerfully symbolic fun for a
generation of kids born after the Poll Tax riots' (Endnotes 2011).

And, out of this emerged various forms of organisations to
continue the struggle, including the London Student Assembly,
UK Uncut, Campaign Against Fees and Cuts, the student
occupations, as well as alternative forms of higher education,
for example, the ROU, People's Political Economy and the Social
Science Centre, Lincoln joined up with transnational networks,
e.g., Edu-factory, as well as other organisations, e.g., Education
Activist Network.

The full significance of the event, with the benefit of a
historical perspective, is that it can be seen as the first stirrings
of an anti-austerity politics that culminated in the election of
Jeremy Corbyn to the leadership of the Labour Party:

Corbyn's victory is actually a product of the social movements
of 2010 and thereafter. The student movement of 2010 may
have been anti-political – and it would be absurd to claim
that it made the weather on its own – but it did crystalise the
mood of anger and injustice in the wake of the 2008 financial
crash, and it kickstarted the anti-austerity movement. It is that
mood that made Corbyn possible, and, more than that, it is
the same generation of young radicals who have constituted
much of the Corbyn surge.
(Chessum 2015)

Paul Mason makes the same point: 'Tuition fees were enacted in 1998 as a symbolic act of financialisation: the replacement of mutual social obligation with credit obligations. The fight for free university education is the issue that woke a generation of individualists and conformists out of their slumbers' (Mason 2017 xviii).

One of the most dramatic images of the protest is the students using mocked up book covers as shields to protect themselves from police truncheons, an idea ripped off from Italian student protests of the 1970s. As Sarah Amsler put it:

The photograph of students marching down the streets of London behind body-sized book shields entitled 'One-Dimensional Man', 'Negative Dialectics', 'Catch-22' and 'Deschooling Society' is worth more than a thousand words; the image of a police officer pushing back an oversized edition of Aldous Huxley's 'Brave New World' is simply too ironic to be called so. The accomplishments of the performance are breathtaking. Wrenched from the abstractions of formalised education, with all but the barest of text abolished from view, social theory is materialised not only in practice, but as practice. By visualising immaterial value, students restore to the figure of the book a gravitas that years of digitisation and commodification have depleted. They do not shield themselves behind knowledge, but hold before them the symbolic promise of all the radical traditions of oppositional knowledge and politics signified through these works. The resulting spectacle of oppression is profound: students communicate symbolically the intellectual and cultural violence of the state's abdication of education, and the authorities, ridiculously, actually interpellate themselves. (Amsler 2010)

Political Reportage

The student protests provided a spectacular story for the mainstream media, (Cammaerts et al 2013). One reporter who got closest to the movement was Paul Mason, a journalist for the BBC and Channel 4 with a background as an academic lecturing in the social sciences, who kept a running commentary on the protest. He published two books around this time: *Why it's Kicking Off Everywhere* (2012) and *Why it's Still Kicking Off Everywhere* (2013), that sought to understand not only the student protests in the UK, but why political protest is 'kicking off' everywhere around the world, building on early writings about working-class struggle: *Live Working or Die Fighting: How the Working Class Went Global* (2009). Mason figured that the students and young activists protesting around the world were responding to their new sociological condition, which he identified as 'the graduate with no future' (Mason 2013 263), i.e., a future based on unemployment and the dole queue. He argues this grievance was substantiated by a sophisticated understanding among students and young people of the nature of power in capitalist society and how it was reproduced, which they had learned from lecture theatres and teach-ins. Out of this came ideas to avoid a life of wage slavery in the form of 'alternative economic practice', i.e., bartering and sharing as the basis for non-capitalist economics, as a place where 'the radicalised youth meet the dispossessed poor' (Mason 2013 291). He stressed that the students and protesters were now armed with a new weapon, social media like Facebook, Twitter, blogging and Tumblr, to facilitate the spread of real time information, as a sort of instant knowledge, facilitating the organisation of protest and one-off events, as well as a host of other activities, e.g., writing publications, setting up protest camps, marching and fighting the police. Mason argued that what characterised these activists was that none of them were full-time. Another feature was the strength of personal relationships made online and at demonstrations, where they got to meet and to know each other in a form of networkism. These associations were characterised by a lack of hierarchies and leadership or dogmatic ideologies and hence an absence of the factionalism that limited old style labour movement politics; and in this new movement women played a key role.

Mason chose to characterise the rapid expansion of all of this resistant activity in socio-biological terms; like a virus or genes or germs, through the idea of memes infecting and spreading, by writing, speech rituals, street art, graffiti and other 'imitable phenomena' (2013 278), citing V for Vendetta as a pertinent example. And so, out of all of this, the students and protesters were creating a new social life, 'something that did not exist before', like it was their own poetry of the future (Mason 2013 281).

For Mason this is all highly significant: expanding the space and power of the individual, representing 'a shift in human consciousness and behaviour' (2013 292) as a form of 'counter-power' as powerful as 'electrification, and it will condition all politics going forward' (2013 293). The protests, he argued, are in response to the 'one militating factor against a return to stability and order: the economy' (2013 262) generating a state of emergency that is likely to see the rise of fascism. He reported that due to the nature of economic crisis the next form of resistance is yet to be developed, but it is likely to be beyond 1-day strikes and occupations and goading mainstream parties beyond their comfort zones.

This is perceptive work, neither romanticising nor rubbishing the movement, but taking it seriously on its own terms, although not all those students who took part in the protests agree with him. Alessio Lunghi and Seth Wheeler edited a critical response: *Occupy Everything: Reflections on Why It's Kicking Off Everywhere* (2012). In their contribution to this book, Thomas Gillespie and Victoria Habermehl (2012) focus on new forms of experiments in higher education of which Mason makes no mention. They see a network that is attempting to break with the neoliberal university: groups:

> who are actively trying to create a 'new' university that breaks with both the post-war-public and neoliberal-private paradigms of higher education. While these groups were involved in the protests that swept the last months of 2010 and into 2011, they are also looking to move beyond the logic of protest to an affirmative politics of transformation within and against the university.
> (2012 15).

Gillespie and Habermehl stress the problem of precarity that 'is emerging as the basis for political organisation and class struggle on a global scale' (2012 16) and view the student protests as 'a collective rejection of debt and precarity and in discovering new reasons to learn that cannot be subjected to an economic calculus of cost versus benefit' (2012 17). They include in this group the ROU, the Social Science Centre, Lincoln, as well as Student as Producer and the University of Utopia as examples of this new form of protest. The Free Association in the same publication are critical of Mason's concept of memes, and want to emphasise the concept of 'resonance' rather than 'contamination' (2012 26), which they characterise as a politics of excess of capitalist determinations: 'For a movement to move, it must exceed the emergence of its own conditions' (2012 31). Following on with the biologistic theme, Camille Barbagallo and Nicholas Beuret see death not life as the organising principle of political life; or 'necropolitics – where death and not life is the function of governance' (2012 52). There is disagreement about Mason's underplaying of the importance of the labour movement as a site of resistance, as well as Mason's associated notion of part-time protest. Antonis Vradis contests Mason's account: 'As it is the capitalist onslaught that takes their days away, taking a day off their struggle becomes a non-option. All facets of social resistance have swiftly merged into one, and their days seem to blend into one. These are extended moments of struggle to take back all of their days – to take back their entire lives' (2012 67). Andre Pusey and Bertie Russell argue that these new lives will not be written up as traditional class models, but, using Mason's focus on electrification, will become 'the electrified worker' (2012 77) who is able to build our own common as 'fields of sense' (2012 79), even though 'we don't yet know how to be organised in a way that will precisely allow us to move in, against and beyond capitalism' (2012 80).

Academic Tomes

Throughout the protest the voice of academics was muted. The University and College Union (UCU) had organised the first demonstration together with the NUS on 10 November 2010, but UCU staff tended to be focused on terms and conditions of employment during this period with some notable exceptions, e.g., Goldsmiths College, London, who did support the occupations (Mute 2010). Some academics put their heads above the parapet, but generally this period of student protests was marked by a culture of conformity and silence by academics (Neary 2016). Some protest groups emerged which involved academics, including the Campaign for the Defence of Higher Education in Britain, and the Campaign for the Public University as well as the Academic Activist Network, but these groups failed to make a really significant impact on the events.

Around this time a number of books appeared, written by academics, as part of the debate about the meaning and purpose of higher education, getting beyond the preoccupation with fees and funding. The books were sole-authored by professors of English for whom education policy was not their main academic interest, including Stefan Collini's *What are Universities For?* (2012), Thomas's *For the University: Democracy and the Future of the Institution* (2011), as well as an edited collection by the sociology professor John Holmwood (2011), whose work is more associated with sociological theory than the sociology of education, titled *A Manifesto For the Public University*. Each author, in their own way, sought to recover and recapture the notion of the liberal-humanist university.

For Collini 'intellectual enquiry is in itself ungovernable' (2012 55). He argued universities:

... are bound, by their nature, to be constantly going beyond whatever particular menu of tasks society may set for them. The very open-endedness of their principal activities threatens to legitimate forms of enquiry that may run counter to the aims of those who founded or supported them. One begins to wonder whether societies do not make a kind of Faustian pact when they set up universities: they ask them to serve various purposes, but if they are to be given the intellectual freedom necessary to serve those purposes properly, they will always tend to exceed or subvert those purposes.
(2012 7).

Holmwood's manifesto for the public university is grounded in what he refers to as well-established public values – 'the crisis of the public university is also a crisis of public life' (2011 5), exemplified by the emergence of neoliberalism and the rise in inequality: 'The public university matters to everyone...because it is a condition of citizenship and full participation in economic, cultural and political life. Whatever diminishes it, diminishes our life in common' (2012 11).

Holmwood situates his argument in John Dewey's notion of 'collective intelligence' from his book *The Public and Its Problem* (1927), where it is through the university as 'an instrument for "collective intelligence" that we can begin to understand its fundamental role for culture and public life' (2012 19). Holmwood, after Dewey, seeks to re-conceptualise the concept of the public not based as 'a theory of the state…[but]…as a theory of the public' (2012 21).

Holmwood argues that 'the individual is necessarily a social being in "associative life"' which is democratic and participative' (2012 22). The state is understood in functionalist terms as a set of public authorities, and the organisational form of associate life. The state can be authoritarian and act for its own or specific interests, but 'it takes its meaning from the idea of the public and its interests' (2012 22). The problem is when the state is set against the public and when corporate capitalism seeks to undermine the power of the state, the individual is not protected and is vulnerable to the market, undermining what Holmwood refers to, after Dewey, as the 'Great Community' (2012 24). For Holmwood, the university has a role to play in facilitating the great community through the promotion and improvement of debates and discussion. So the university is part of the solution for a socially just and democratic society, which has 'social justice at its heart' (2012 25).

Thomas Docherty pursues a similar theme. As he puts it:

It is no longer appropriate for us to have 'the idea of the University'; but it is extremely important to replace that with what we can call the search to make the University of the Idea, as it were: the possibility is where we can figure out the future in terms of imagining possibilities through the making of an idea. Thus, the university becomes the institution in which the first principle is actually the search for first principles. (Docherty 2011 3-4)

In this sense he describes the university as an 'event' (2011 17), and rather than the idea of the university, the 'university of an idea' where the university exists to critically reinvent itself, so far as this goes.

Despite the importance and power of this work, it is marked by a very real distance between anything that was taking place within the student movement. The appeal to liberal values, in what amounts to a liberal critique of liberalism, through philosophical speculations and functionalist theory of the state are a long way from the radical theory of the state on which Student as Producer relies (Clarke 1991a, Holloway and Picciotto 1977).

The dynamic energy of the student protest movement subsided as it came up against the realities of its own limitations: factionalism within the student movement, a punitive legal process, overwhelming militarised police power, minimal support from academics, lack of public support from university senior managers, few resources, exhaustion, demoralisation arising from losing the vote on student fees, limited media outlets to be able to articulate its demands and no coherent theoretical critique or strategy. The outcome was that the Christmas vacations emptied the university occupations as students went home for their winter holiday and, very significantly, no other exogenous/external shocks occurred to further destabilise the UK's political economy which was attempting to recover from the Great Recession of 2008-9 (Endnotes 2011). And yet, within a year it was kicking off again: public disorder on the streets, not specifically about higher education, but students were at the heart of it.

Summer Riots

The 'trigger' event for the riot was the shooting of Mark Duggan by the police in Tottenham on 4 August 2011. It was later decided by the courts that Duggan had been lawfully killed by the police

(Taylor 2017, Institute of Race Relations 2014 -http://www. irr.org.uk/news/framing-the-death-of-mark-duggan/). That part of North London was very volatile in terms of police and community relations, with a history that included the killing of a police officer on Broadwater Farm as well as deaths of black men and women in police custody. The police killing of Mark Duggan was compounded by the way in which the police dealt with the aftermath of this event. A key factor was the police's failure to provide information to the family, which initiated a protest march by the family and supporters to the Tottenham police station, leading to a demonstration outside the station in the afternoon and evening. During the evening demonstration a young woman was beaten up by police officers, sparking off the riot that ensued. Initially the riot involved smashing police cars and attacking the police station with bricks and stones. This riotous activity escalated with the burning of cars dragged across the road as barricades, setting fire to shops and public buildings, as well as looting: 'proletarian shopping' (Endnotes 2011): what had begun as a riot against the police had become a 'commodity riot' (Aufheben 2011). News about the riots was spread by use of mobile phones and across social media. The result was rioting around the UK that lasted for 4 days in what were the most extensive riots ever seen in the country.

Neither of these riotous assemblies, the student protests and the urban riot, should be seen as isolated events, but rather as part of a 'riot-wave' (Endnotes 2011) that had struck the UK since the 1970s, after the last great financial crash. A feature of the UK scene is the frequency with which these protests/riots took place and the similarity in their modes of operation, although each having their own specificity. These riots included the Notting Hill Riots *in West London the 1960s and 1970s*; the *summer of riots across the UK in 1981*; the *Miners' Strike in the 1980s; the attempt by bosses to break the newspaper unions in Wapping in* 1986, *and the disturbances on Meadow Well Estate in Newcastle* and *Blackburn,*

Lancashire in 2001.

These events, the student protests and the summer riots, had very similar motivations: anti-police, against racism, unemployment and poverty. By including the student protests and the summer riots as part of the same discussion I am not bringing two separate events together; but, rather, looking at two events which cannot be considered apart: as a 'double riot' (Clover 2016). Less than a year since the student protests, and while the courts were still working through the backlog of criminal cases against the students, things kicked off again and in such a way that made the student protest look like a dress rehearsal for the main event: 'this was a real protest' (Endnotes 2011).

The reaction of academics was mixed: ranging from the patronising to offering significant critical insights. Slavoj Zizek makes the distinction that while the students were able to articulate their grievances, the rioters in the summer of 2011 were like a rabble with 'no message to deliver' (Zizek 2011). Bateman (2012) disagrees, making use of Le Rude's analysis of riotous behaviours, he argues that while the mob are 'generally reactionary or without political meaning' (Bateman 2012 94), the riots of 2011 were able to articulate their grievances as is evident from the reports and reviews of the events, (e.g., see The Guardian report Reading the Riots: Investigating England's Summer of Disorder). Bateman argues the extent to which the rioters are not able to articulate their grievances is in part due to 'a manifestation of a decline of the organised left and the erosion of a politically aware black solidarity movement unable to give effective political expression to underlying grievances which are, nonetheless, of a political nature' (Bateman 2012 105).

What was quickly established was the relationship between those who took part in the student protests and the riots, as well as their motivations. The 2011 riots began as an anti-police riot, but the causes extended beyond police repression to other forms of capitalist violence: poverty, employment, unemployment, the removal of funding for youth and social services, and education. These issues affected all aspects of society, including students. More than half of the rioters in a Guardian/LSE survey on the riots were students who mentioned that 'the increase in student tuition fees and the scrapping of the education maintenance allowance' was a significant factor. The students and those who took part in the 2011 riots engaged in various forms of insecure employment, so that it would be wrong to see the students as privileged middle-class kids, rather the student population had been significantly proletarianised into a more 'negative, rebellious composition, as it felt the emptiness of its own demands' (Endnotes 2011). Student protests began as being against education cuts and fees, but, due to the behaviour of the police at the student protests, became anti-police, particularly for those who had no experience of the police (Indymedia 2010). The battle against the police was intensified on the 9 December marches by those young men and women for whom the low intensity war with Babylon was an everyday preoccupation. An important feature is the extent to which 'hate for the police' (Briggs 2012 32) was a major issue.

The riots of summer 2011 were anti-police from the get-go. In order for the revolutionary teacher to consider the nature of their own revolutionary capacity it is important to consider the police not only in terms of the way in which they policed the protests, but, more significantly, in terms of the real nature of policing. The real nature of policing is an important issue in unlearning the law of labour. The argument of this book is that Police are not simply maintaining order but imposing a particular form of order: the law of labour. This can be uncovered through a science of police.

Science of Police

A key feature of this book is the relationship of higher education to the State. This relationship was brutally expressed during the student protest and the student involvement with other young people in the urban riots of 2011 in terms of their encounter with the police as the enforcer of state law, or Police-State (Neary 2015). The police are a presence in the literature on the protests but they remain under-theorised; or are considered in a way that stresses the police as domination, rather than as theory of emancipation or resistance. A theory of emancipation is necessary and required for the revolutionary teacher if the Police-State is to be undermined. This is a key aspect of unlearning the law of labour.

The police are a highly significant presence at student demonstrations, often the reason for disorder kicking off, although their nature and purpose tends not to be fully elaborated beyond crude functionalist descriptions of the role of the police as agents of the capitalist state, a position from which the police have sought to distance themselves through claims about the origins of policing being based on consent rather than force (Reiner 2010). The literature on student demonstrations and riots tends to follow the functionalist account of the police, where they are mentioned it tends to be with little analysis of the real nature of Police. In this section I want to interrogate the real nature of Police not through criminology or the sociology of crime and deviance or Police Studies, but in terms of a science of police.

I will argue that Police are not simply about the maintenance of public order, but rather the imposition of a particular form of public order, based on the law of poverty and labour, elaborated with reference to Marx's critique of political economy. This is not a functionalist argument, rather I will suggest that Police are a particular form of pedagogical power that emerges out of the logic of the protest. Walter Benjamin has written on Police. He argues that Police can never be anything other than the violence that is implicit in capitalist social relations, existing above the criminal law, as a first principle of capitalist order (Benjamin, 1921, Neary 2015, Neocleous 2000). Functionalism is when institutions are described by the social roles and functions that they fulfil. The limit of this approach is that it does not ask the more fundamental question as to what is the nature of the social relations out of which those functions are derived. Nor does it provide any idea of how the Police-State can be undermined. As the first principle of revolutionary teaching is unlearning the law of labour this cannot be anything other than an important issue for the revolutionary teacher.

Police and Riots

Clive Bloom provides an important account of police practice with regard to the student protests and urban riots in 2010-11 entitled *Riot City: Protest and Rebellion in the City* (2012).

Bloom's publication is a history book, looking at public protest in London since 2000, contextualised in a much longer time frame drawing parallels between urban riots in London in the 1960s and 1970s as well as The Gordon Riots in 1781. Bloom's purpose is to provide an historically based context for the more recent disturbances.

Bloom explores the extent to which the police were themselves a major factor in both of these events, the student protest and the summer riots, in terms of their preparedness, as well as actions and behaviour during the protests. A part of his account of police behaviour at this time includes a review of the morale of the force when they are having to deal with their own cuts to funding. Bloom is interested in the aftermath of these urban upheavals, including the way in which the criminal law was used to punish and prosecute the protesters through the courts.

Bloom's reflections on police practice capture what he regards as the conflicted nature of their role 'as the active agents of state repression' (2012 1) and 'instruments of the rulers' (2012 2) while still carrying out their duties as 'the servants of the general public'

(2012 2). Bloom's Police are the 'armed wing of the state' (2012 14), as part of a political society in which 'live protest remains at the heart of our democracy and at the heart of what it means to live in a free society' (2012 16), even though political society is becoming increasingly authoritarian and undemocratic. He presents the police as the filler in a sandwich between protesters and the general public, a position that is ultimately 'untenable' (2012 36). The issue for Bloom is how much longer the police can continue to serve both the general public and an increasingly authoritarian government.

Policing the student protests and urban unrest in 2010-11 was taking place during a period when the police were themselves coming under increasing scrutiny. The police had been criticised over their policing of the G20 demonstrations, the death of Ian Tomlinson, in what was eventually judged as the use of reasonable force, and riot police clashes with protesters in demonstrations against the Israeli occupation of Gaza in 2009. And there continued to be the on-going controversy over the police use of 'kettling': corralling groups of protesters in an enclosed space for long periods of time denying them access to food and lavatory facilities. A full-scale review of how the police policed the protest, *Adapting to Protest: Nurturing the British Model of Policing (2009)*, concluded that policing protests 'must be lawful and consensual rather than aggressive and provocative' (Bloom 2012 3).

The main focus of Bloom's book are the 2010 student protests and 2011 riots. He is interested in how the two events are related, as well as the police response and strategy. He admits there has been 'a growing criminalisation of space and movement' as authority seeks to retain control (2012 7) against a new form of 'leaderless protest' (2012 11). This leaderless protest is manifest as Black Block, UK Uncut, Anonymous, Pirate Parties in what amounts to horizontal, networked, utopian, non-hierarchical types of political activity that appear to be very different from the Marxist-Leninist organisational structures of the past. There is no attempt by Bloom to theorise Police, nor indeed to find the basis for this new form of political activity. Indeed, he demonstrates a disregard for what he refers to as avant-garde theory of protest in a section at the end of the book of what he calls 'The Revolutionary Model Redefined'. This review of revolutionary theory does not get beyond the 1970s with no discussion of more contemporary theoretical work.

Bloom is interested in what a new type of police force might look like operating in *'the current structures of ghettoised life'* (2012 125 – author's italics) and in an economic and political context in which disturbances are likely to be repeated. Part of this new Police would be based on more effective police intelligence and tactics. His solution for rebellious youth is a mixture of punishment and rehabilitation in the form of militarised prisons to build character, self-discipline and team working so as to give 'a sense of purpose and moral compass' (2012 124).

Bloom is very clear about the link between the two major disturbances and their significance not only for policing but UK society. He argues: 'The destruction at Millbank on 10 November 2010 changed the shape of extra-parliamentary politics, where young people had taken their fight to the centre of power, with no apparent fear of authority, and had wrong footed the police, so that for a short moment, [they] had rekindled the energy of political struggle' (2012 18). The student action 'heralded a new politics and a new space for political action' (2012 53). The students were against being consumers, '"calculating investors", in their own overpriced future' (2012 19) and did not want their professors becoming 'vocational managers' (2012 19). At the core of student protests and the summer riots, for Bloom, was a class struggle about 'who owns the future' (2012 19) where the future appeared to have disappeared, as well as looking for a new kind of hope in a period of disastrous economic downturn. The substantive reasons for the two events were based on similar circumstances: both the student protests and the summer riots are expressions of the 'bleak landscape of austerity' and the 'age of scarcity' (2012 19) against neoliberal aspirations, which is a feature of 'disturbed times' (2012 20). However, despite the similarities, Bloom felt the two protests had different motivations: 'The students rioted to restore equilibrium; the summer rioters to permanently disturb it' (Bloom 2012 123). Both groups of young people had shown no fear of the police, even if the anti-police nature of the protests was arrived at through different experiences: the summer riots were anti-police from the 'get-go' in response to a lifetime of racist policing, whereas students were not so anti-police initially, until confronted by police violence in kettles and on the protest marches.

The relationship between the two events, the student protests and the urban riots, is further explored by Joshua Clover in *Riot-Strike-Riot: the New Era of Uprisings* (2016) through what he describes as a 'double riot' (2016 180).

Clover sets out to provide an account for the development of strikes and riots through a version of historical materialism that explains strikes as protests to defend wages, where the focus is on production (work), and riots as a protest against the price of food and other commodities, where the focus in on the market (prices). Clover's aim is not simply to theorise riots but to theorise crisis: 'A theory of riots is a theory of crisis' (2016 1). Like Bloom he provides a historical analysis of political unrest, starting in the eighteenth century from 'the golden age of riots through the age of strikes and back again' (2016 8) up to the collapse of mass industrialisation in the 1970s, leading to what he refers to as 'the Long Crisis'. He argues the collapse of productivity leads capital to look for the accumulation of profits in the processes of circulation rather than the factory floor. In this account Police are an ever-present reality as the personification of state power.

Clover's historical materialism extends to an understanding of the contradictory social relations that underpin capitalist accumulation, where value acts as 'the self-undermining dynamic' (2016 84), as 'the invisible essence of capital' (2016 22), where the source of surplus value, human labour, is removed and replaced by technology, leading to a decline in profitability and the creation of surplus populations, that has a heavily racialised character, mostly affecting people of colour. He argues that in the pre-Long Crisis period capitalist accumulation was dominated by productivity growth, strikes were the major form of political protest; but, in an era when global productivity is in decline, and as capital moves to focus its commercial activity in the realm of consumption, then the riot not the strike assumes major significance.

He considers the student protests of 2010 and the urban riots in the UK of 2011 in this context, referring to them as a 'double riot' (2016 180): 'One riot arises from when youth discovering that the routes that once promised a minimally secure formal integration into the economy are now foreclosed. The other arises from racialised surplus populations and the violent state management thereof' (2016 180).

The key aspect of the current process is that the crisis has produced surplus populations for whom even the market is now out of reach, especially for black and racialised groups, in a situation where the market has been replaced by the state, so that 'the police now stand *in the place of* the economy' (2016 125), where the police are 'the occupying army' (2016 164) in a 'civil war' (2016 173). This is a dialectical drama, drawing out the relationship between Police and riot, 'where police and riot thus come to presuppose each other' 2016 47): and where 'the police appear as necessity and limit' (2016 47).

Clover draws on the work of *Endnotes*, a writers' collective persuaded by the same version of value-form theory that informs Student as Producer, to express this dialectic relation:

The police...are not an external force of order applied by the

state to an already rioting mass, but an integral part of the riot: not only its standard component spark-plug, acting via the usual death, at police hands, of some young black man, but also the necessary on-going partner of the rioting crowd from whom the space must be liberated if this liberation is to mean anything at all; who must be attacked as an enemy if the crowd is to be unified in anything; who must be forced to recognize the agency of a habitually subjected group.
(Endnotes 2011 in Clover 171)

The dialectic contradiction through the value-form is compelling but is not explored by Clover in relation to Police. His analysis is reduced to a focus on Police function, standing in the place of the economy and as the servant of the commodity (2012 126). He defines this confrontation as Riot prime: a new situation has emerged due to the collapse of the world of work, where protesters are confronted by the police as the main agency of capitalist repression.

I will come back to Clover at the end of the book, when I will make a claim for the efficacy of strike, rather than riots, as Strike prime: not Riot-Strike-Riot but Strike-Riot-Strike, where Strike prime is not the defence of capitalist work but a key strategy in unlearning the law of labour.

Policing the Crisis

Clover draws on the work of Stuart Hall et al (2013) to argue that not only is the riot a modality through which class is lived, but that 'race is the modality in which class is lived' (Clover 2016 168), and, in a situation where he argues race forms part of the surplus population, then *riot is the modality through which surplus is lived* (Clover 2016 170, author's emphasis).

Hall et al (2013) had famously produced their own analysis of policing: *Policing the Crisis: Mugging, the State and Law and Order* where they traced the emergence of a particular form of crime coming out of the streets of South London in the 1970s, dubbed as mugging in the tabloid press, more accurately defined as robbery under the criminal code, where young black men appeared to be the main perpetrators. The strength of the book is the way in which it connects crime, the law and the state to produce not only a theory of domination, and the way it is enforced by policing, but a theory of resistance, based on the way in which young black men respond to the imposition of capitalist order and how the matter is theorised in terms of the nature of capitalist work. The result, Hall et al argue, is not simply a crisis of authority, but a crisis of the state in a period when political power is being increasingly contested.

This is a book about policing rather than a theory of Police, describing the transformation of police on the street – 'Bobbies on the beat' – to professional crime fighters and as increasingly militarised defenders of public order. This is going on alongside the development of an antagonistic relationship with black youth as a factor of society in which race is becoming an increasingly politicised issue.

The police themselves are not problematised, rather their role as agents of the state in creating a controlling discursive practice is described: 'The police are seen as society's first line of defence in protecting the liberty of the individual and the rights of private property, and as a bulwark against social anarchy. They are authorised to produce official measures of overall crime levels – the crime statistics – and to provide a rolling commentary on the relation between crime and wider social trends' (Hall et al 2013 xii-xiii). This is expressed by Hall et al as a form of hegemonic domination together with the control of state apparatuses. Ironically, and key to their analysis, is their view that the police are not simply reacting to the problem of crime and disorder but, by providing a rolling commentary on crime, they actually 'amplify the deviance they seem so absolutely committed to controlling' (2013 55, authors' emphasis). There is a recognition that the police adopt the role of educators about a particular form of private property law that acts as the organising principle for capitalist society.

The highly significant aspect of the book from the perspective of Student as Producer is the connections that are made between crime, work, the law, poverty and resistance. The book sets out the relationship between the black proletariat and the colonial labour market as it applies to the UK so as to understand what 'worklessness' means: very high rates of unemployment among young black men alongside high rates of exploitation – as a structural feature of contemporary capitalism. The result is that young working-class black men develop a new form of 'negative consciousness' against the category of work and being unemployable, as 'a temporary negation of the system' (2013 349) in which a culture of worklessness becomes not only 'a survival strategy' (2013 346) but 'a quasi-political act' (2013 383). This culture of worklessness is nourished by the Rasta attitudes of refusal to work: not for them the boredom of the factory, but, rather the more 'free-wheeling' life of the street, 'dossing' and 'drifting' (2013 351) 'hustling' (2013 366), feeding off the buzz that comes from criminal intent. As Marcus Howe puts it, in relation to the Trinidadian perspective, this culture of worklessness means that 'somehow your whole social personality develops skills by which you get portions of the wage' (2013 366) and, through all of this, 'sections of the working class, although not disciplined, organised, unified by the very mechanisms of capitalist production itself, were necessarily concentrated and socialised through hustling' (2013 367) in ways which allowed them to affect a form of political power and intervention. Referring to black revolutionary leaders, Frantz Fanon and Amilcar Cabral, Hall et al show that it is precisely this group, 'the wretched of the earth' in a colonised context, who make up 'one of the most spontaneous and the most radically revolutionised forces of a colonised people' (2013 371). To be clear, none of this is based on choice or some natural propensity to criminal behaviour, but is the outcome of the position in which these young men find themselves.

However, the question remains for the authors of the book: to what extent does crime provide liberation or an accommodation to the exploitation and brutalisation of capitalist work that these young men are attempting to avoid in yet another violent form; in what amounts to an expression of powerlessness as well as a quasi-political activity; and how can this resistance inform a strategy of struggle?

This is a brave exposition of the condition of young black men and their predicament, making strong links between crime, the law, work and poverty, and the state, but its limits are that it focuses on the condition of worklessness rather than the nature of work itself. This is the first lesson for revolutionary teachers for whom the real nature of work must always be in full view.

Hall and his co-writers' account is an attempt to theorise resistance in relation to cultural aspects of black resistance, but what is the nature of real resistance if it gets lost in a discursive account of crime and criminality? What is the essence of black power as a form of political agency, if the activity of work itself is naturalised, so that worklessness rather than the nature of work itself is the problem? It is the nature of work itself which is the problematic for Student as Producer. That is the real issue and the lesson that revolutionary teachers must teach. For a theory that considers the real nature of Police and a more fundamental relation to the law of labour we need to look elsewhere.

Police Theory

A more fundamental exposition about the nature of work and policing has been set out by Mark Neocleous (2000) in *The Fabrication of Social Order: A Critical Theory of Police Power*, providing a scholarly account of the emergence of the modern police. The focus is not on riots but more generally on the historical role of the police as enforcers of the law of labour and poverty.

Neocleous is writing through a Marxist theory of Police, undermining the sociological and culturalist assumptions of Police Studies. He aims 'to re-situate...[the science of Police]... into the mainstream of social and political theory' (2000 x) and, not only police, but also as part of a theory of the state, arguing that in criminology as in liberal political science, the theory of the state remains under-theorised.

For Neocleous, police is one of 'the supreme concepts of bourgeois society' (2000 xii). He aims to prioritise police in a way that avoids 'a rather crude functionalism, tending to settle for the argument that the police institution acts as a repressive agency, crushing working-class struggles and guarding private property' (2000 xii). Although he does not altogether avoid functionalism, making a clear connection between 'the centrality of the historically massive police operation on the part of the state to the consolidation of the social power of capital and the wage form: as order became increasingly based on the bourgeois mode of production, so the police mandate was to fabricate an order of wage labour and administer the class of poverty'. (2000 xii)

This extends Police function from crime control and detection to the question of the imposition of poverty administered through a range of welfare state institutions and policy, expanding his concept of Police to social policy and the social police, framed around the wider problematic of social security – 'the highest moment of order' (2000 42). Neocleous argues labour is the source of capitalist wealth, and so indigence and idleness must be denied 'through a wide range of measures to teach the working class the morality of work' (2000 55), or moralising the demoralised to make the working-class work. And so the science of Police: becomes 'the commodification of labour' (2000 58) at the point where the discipline of the market fails. This role is carried out not just by uniformed police officers, but social workers, probation officers, as a form of *'social police'* (2000 58).

The key point here is that Police are concerned with a range of activities that go beyond an interest in crime to include that which is potentially damaging to the communal order: 'In other words, preventing crime was not integral to the definition of police; crime prevention has never been the raison d'être of police' (2000 4). The main function of Police is 'abolishing disorder' and the fabrication of order: 'at the heart of this fabrication is work and the nature of poverty' (2000 5) or the science of governing which is as much about administration as it is about law: 'a bourgeois order, achieved through *the exercise of state power*' (2000 5).

Or, to put this another way: *'The policing of prosperity began the process of the making of the working class, a process which would only be completed once a new form of master had properly emerged on the historical stage'* (2000 20).

The liberal theory of capitalist society insists on the idea of a 'hidden hand': a mode of self-regulation based on a system of the rule of law, founded on rights, limited government and the autonomy of civil society. But, Neocleous argues, capitalist society cannot exist without being fabricated by the state. So the police are the solution to *'the delusion that civil society and the commercial order can exist without being fabricated by the state'* (2000 34).

Police then is the response to a new form of order based not on an absolutist monarchy, but on capital: '...the masterless men brought into being by the breakdown of feudalism were now faced with a new form of master: capital. Capital had by this point been simultaneously enthroned and consecrated; the Divine Right of Kings had become the Divine Right of Property. Capital had become King' (2000 40).

However, while the state's police power is the mechanism for overseeing poverty, crucially 'the police is equally no solution. Since it cannot abolish poverty, because to do so would abolish civil society, all the police can do is to prevent the poverty-stricken class from becoming a criminalised and pauperised rabble' (2000 48-9).

Capital and its masters are not confident of their omnipotence but are 'shot through with their fundamental insight – and fear – that as a system private property is fundamentally insecure' (2000 59). Moreover, 'private property requires and generates insecurity', in order to obtain work, economic actors must be kept in a state of insecurity, and by *'generating political enemies'* (2000 59). This is why the system of private property requires state power as 'a mechanism for *securing the insecure'* (2000 59). And, insofar as the security of civil society is concerned:

> In class terms this means that police is necessary because capital, as the modern master, is forever at risk of losing control of the class of which it is master. The economic inactivity of the class of poverty is the heart of the insecurity of the system, the resistance of this class to the social domination of private property is its next step, and the political mobilization of the class its highest form. Thus security involves not just the prevention and detection of crime but, more importantly, the imposition of a form of social police. The history of police as a security project is a history of private property's fear of its most radical 'other' (communism).
> (2000 61)

And so, one of the police's main roles becomes crushing disturbances, keeping the peace and maintaining security rather than preventing crime, adapting its responses to the rise in working-class sedition in ways that are beyond the capacity of the military in order to maintain an equilibrium that is suited to the newly-emerging marketised society. This means taking on powers that allow the police to operate outside of the law so that capitalist order be maintained, covered by a set of administrative guidance, *Judges Rules*. All of this is exemplified by the concept of *discretion* through which police carry out their work. Police discretions allow for selective law enforcement and order maintenance which discriminates against the poor and working class. In these cases police act 'less as a form of judicial power and more as a form of political administration' (2000 101). As a kind of 'low intensity war against the working class' (2000 82).

'Order' then should be understood not just as the absence of riots or generalised peace and quiet on the streets, but as the imposition of the capital-labour relation, the domination of capital over the working class. However, the nature of the capitalist social relation means that 'this is a war which the state cannot win, for to win it would mean abolishing the condition of private property that gives rise to it, and thus abolishing itself as a state' (2000 82).

The result is a Police-State, which means 'The ultimate truth of the police is that it deals in and dispenses violence in protection of the interests of the state. In class society, this means no more than the police dispense violence on behalf of the bourgeois class' (2000 118). Police really is class war.

The scholarly nature of this account is impressive, but Neocleous does not escape the functional and instrumental account of Police. The result is that he is not able to conceptualise a form of maintaining social order beyond the law of capital and so his theory of Police is an account of social domination rather than social emancipation. Student as Producer, or unlearning the law of labour, will suggest another form of Police: not-Police, based on the principles of Authority and Authorship as a form of social defence, premised on a society of abundance, rather than poverty, in a communist world, not organised around labour but a recalibration of the capacities and needs for people and the planet (Kay and Mott 1982).

The Real Nature of Police

A non-functionalist account of police power and violence is found in Jacques Ranciére's, *Disagreement: Politics and Philosophy* (1999). Like Neocleous, he is looking beyond Police Studies and their preoccupation with cop culture or aspects of police behaviour: neither good cop bad cop but the real 'nature of the police' (1999 31). Ranciére works at a high level of theoretical abstraction, yet manages to ground his thinking within a framework that comes close to a critique of political economy and value-form theory (Neary 2019). Ranciére's early theoretical work is important in formulating the value theory of labour on which much of the argument of Student as Producer rests (O'Kane n.d, Nesbitt, 2017, Neary 2019), although value-form theory is not referenced in Ranciére's later texts, where he works through the concepts of politics and equality as a form of the politics of philosophy in which Police play an important role (Neary 2019). Ranciére recognises that policing is more than upholding the criminal and property law but, rather, has a key role in carrying out all of society's 'despised functions' (Ranciére 1999 29). The police are not simply the enforcer of the state apparatus, rather, he describes an altogether more contingent and spontaneous process that arises out of social relations and through which people are recognised as part of political society: what he refers to as 'a perceptible part of the sensible' as opposed to being condemned by police as 'the part of those who have no part'. As he puts it:

> The police is first an order of bodies that defines the allocation of ways of doing, ways of being and ways of saying, and sees that those bodies are assigned by name to a particular place and task; it is an order of the visible and the sayable that sees that a particular activity is visible and another is not, that this speech is understood as discourse and another as noise. (1999 29)

For Ranciére politics becomes that which is antagonistic to policing, demonstrating 'the sheer contingency of any order' (1999 17) in which those who are defined as having no part, 'the no part' are, in fact, made visible. In this case, 'Politics runs up against the police everywhere' (1999 32); politics is 'a meeting of police logic and egalitarian logic that is never set up in advance' (1999 32). Ranciére uses the example of the strike, after Walter Benjamin's account of the strike as a form of revolutionary action in *Critique of Violence*, where Benjamin argues that a strike is political only when it reconfigures the social relations of work: 'A strike is not political when it calls for reforms rather than a better deal or when it attacks the relationships of authority rather than the inadequacy of wages. It is political when it reconfigures the relationships that determine the workplace in its relation to the community' (1999 32). I will return to the importance of the political strike when I discuss my version of Strike prime at the end of the book.

For Ranciére the police are antithetical to democracy, not the formal democratic conventions of parliamentary politics, but a democracy through which people are able to emerge as forms of radical subjectivity without being constrained by the Police-State. Radical subjectivity depends on Ranciére's exposition of equality which he wants to claim as a core political principle, lending politics its reality: 'it has not objects or issues of its own' (1999 31). 'What makes an action political is not its object or the place where it is carried out, but solely the form in which the confirmation of equality is inscribed' (1999 32). As we shall see Ranciére's principle of equality was established in his work as a pedagogical practice in the classroom. In his book *The Ignorant Schoolmaster* (1991), Ranciére describes equality in education not as a principle to be enforced but 'a mere assumption that needs to be discerned within the practices implementing it' (1999 33). And so the logic of Police, as we shall see, is not only street fighting but within the classroom itself

There is much more to be said about Ranciére later in chapter 4, and, in particular, when his theory of equality is linked to his version of critical pedagogy. What makes Ranciére so significant for Student as Producer and unlearning the law of labour is the way in which his conceptualisations of equality have been derived out of pedagogical practice in the classroom.

Police Review

What this review of Police tells us is that the Police Science puts Police as the imposition of poverty and the law of labour, through the imposition of a type of political society in which democratic politics is denied: or Police-State. If labour then is the key issue in terms of unlearning the law of labour we need to look at labour more fundamentally. I will do this in terms of the way in which Benjamin considers labour, through his reading of Marx and the way in which this has been critiqued not through an affirmation of labour but as a critique of labour in capitalism (Postone 1993), as an exemplary aspect of a Marxism based on critical theory and the critique of labour (Neary 2017a). I will then consider this in relation to the question of how revolutionary teachers teach, by considering how this question affected the work of critical theory's most critical theorist, Theodor Adorno, as a revolutionary teacher in the classroom.

In the next section I will look at labour and the law of value through an exposition of the work of Walter Benjamin and his relationship to Marxism. My main point will be that Benjamin's version of Marxism is not dialectical, i.e., revolutionary, enough.

3. Student as Producer and the Labour Debate

The slogan Student as Producer is an adaptation of *The Author as Producer*, the title of a talk Walter Benjamin was due to give to the Society of Anti-Fascists in Paris in 1934. The main theme of the talk was how do radical intellectuals support the proletarian revolution at a time when fascism was engulfing parts of Europe, and the Soviet Empire had degraded workers' self-organisations to a centralised political party machine. *The Author as Producer* is regarded as one of the most important attempts to theorise 'the role and efficacy of the artist...and, more broadly...the intelligentsia in revolution' (Gough 2002 53). At the core of Benjamin's paper is a very strong pedagogical instruction for intellectuals to put themselves alongside workers in the production of intellectual objects, books, newspapers and art, in ways that transform the process of production itself, based on a desire for communism. It is this ambition to revolutionise the social relations of capitalist production that is the main feature of *The Author as Producer*, not merely the quality of the intellectual objects that are produced, although they have an important role in overcoming capitalism.

Benjamin was part of a mass exodus of German intellectual emigres trying to make their voices heard in Europe and America in the 1930s (Palmier 2006). Benjamin is not just writing about the life of the worker-writer, he is living the life of an intellectual who had been proletarianised and impoverished in a moment when the proletarian revolution had been defeated across Central Europe, 1918-23, in a context where the Soviet model has replaced proletarian self-organisation with a central political party platform (Lunn 1984). The Committee for Anti-Fascism, where Benjamin was due to give his talk, was a front organisation for the Comintern in France (Gough 2002, Palmier 2006). The Soviet dominance of revolutionary thinking extended to an insistence on Socialist Realism as the official channel of revolutionary art, against the experimental forms of Dada and Surrealism that Benjamin championed (Benjamin 1929/1978). Anxieties about the rise of Nazism were compounded by fascist riots reported as the bloodiest on the streets of Paris since the Commune in 1871 (Gough 2002).

The Author as Producer paper is heavily influenced by Benjamin's reading of Georg Lukacs' *History and Class Consciousness*, his friendship with Bertolt Brecht, Russian Constructivism and his love affair with the Latvian communist Asja Lacis. Benjamin's relationship with Marx's writings is, as we shall see, controversial (Clark 2003), but his love affair with a Marxist woman and Marxism as a way of life was undisputed (Leslie 2009).

Benjamin took from the Russian constructivists the central idea that production was not simply about the making of finished works, but that the process of production should contain its own revolutionary organising principle (Roberts and Penzin 2017). For Benjamin, it is not enough that a progressive intellectual declares their commitment to progressive social transformation, but that their work reflects the ways in which the social relations of capitalist society might be transformed. This transformation is expressed by the manner in which progressive political practice is embedded within the nature of the work itself and, most particularly, the way in which the product is produced. Benjamin is important for Student as Producer because of the way in which he presents a revolutionary pedagogy on the basis of the reorganisation of intellectual labour. Benjamin is recasting the productive process, after Lukacs, so that the previously unremarkable object of production for bourgeoisie theory, i.e., the worker, becomes the emancipated subject of their own social world. Benjamin's work suggests that intellectual labour can be radicalised by including the student as the subject rather than the object of the teaching and learning process, i.e., the student as producer not consumer.

At the heart of *The Author as Producer* (1934/1998) paper is the question how does a radical intellectual act in a moment of crisis, or, as Benjamin puts it, 'what is the writer's right to exist'? (1998 85). Benjamin argues that a progressive writer will show a commitment or tendency towards the proletariat, but that on its own this is not sufficient to ensure the quality of intellectual work. Rather: 'the tendency of a work of literature can be politically correct only if it is also correct in the literary sense...this and nothing else makes up the quality of a work' (1998 86). However, in order to avoid reifying the product the commitment to proletarian revolution means more than just the product itself, but the extent to which the intellectual article 'is inserted into the context of living social relations' (1998 87), which are themselves determined by production relations. And so the main issue becomes what is the position of a work of writing *within* the social relations of capitalist production? It is this position within the productive process that Benjamin refers to as technique (1998 87). Technique for Benjamin, as it was for Lukacs, is the 'dialectical starting point from which the sterile dichotomy of form and content can be surmounted' (1998 88). This avoidance of reification extends to Benjamin's understanding of the mind, after Marx, which is that it is not the product of intellectual thought but, rather, material conditions that determine consciousness.

Benjamin describes how this radical intellectual thinking can be brought to life, or operationalised, through the practice and principle of 'operativism', not simply in terms of intellectuals writing about events, reportage, but as a practical intervention, directly as part of class struggle. He cites the activities of a literary figure, Sergei Tretyakov, and his work on a Russian collective farm where tasks are shared among workers, not like bourgeois specialisms or competences (Roberts and Penzin 2017). Benjamin argues it is important for the radical intellectual to be directly involved in practical activities: as the 'operative writer' intellectual (Benjamin 1998 88): 'not to report but to fight: not to assume the spectator's role but to intervene actively' (1998 88). Tretyakov's operativism involved 'organising mass meetings, collecting funds...inspecting reading rooms, launching wall newspapers..., introducing radio, travelling films etc...[and]... the organising of collective farms' (1998 88). Benjamin uses this example to show: 'how wide the horizon has to be from which, in the light of the technical realities of our situation today, we must rethink the notion of literary forms appropriate to the literary energy of our time' (1998 89). Benjamin recognises the historical specificity and relevance of different types of intellectual activity, as in a cauldron 'we are in the midst of a vast process in which literary forms are being melted down...' (1998 89), and out of which new forms of intellectual artefacts will emerge.

An important form of operativism is the production of newspapers with content written by their readers, so that readers become authors. This form of action gets beyond the activity of individuals, allowing Benjamin to use again one of his favourite metaphors to describe the transformation of productive relations as 'a vast melting-down process...[which]... destroys the conventional separation between genres, between writer and poet, scholar and populariser...author and reader' (1998 90).

Even so, this process is limited in so far as production belongs to capital and, therefore, Benjamin focuses on developing a revolutionary means of production, or the 'refunctioning'/'functional transformation' of the process of production, in the direction of socialism. This means literary work that is not just about altering individual experiences, but creating new forms of social institutions. He cites Dada and photomontage as examples from the world of art, capable of producing 'revolutionary use-values' (Benjamin 1998 95), acting in concert with others, leading to, again: 'the melting-down of literary forms...[into an]...incandescent liquid mass from which the new forms will be cast...the temperature at which the melting-down process takes place...is determined by the state of class struggle' (1998 96). He stresses the point about the process of production being the key issue for the radical intellectual: 'He will never be concerned with the products alone, but always at the same time, with the means of production. In other words his products must possess an organising function besides and before their character as finished works' (1998 98).

Although Benjamin refers to literary intellectual production, this can apply to other forms of intellectual activity, including teaching. In fact, he mentions teaching as a key issue in this process of recalibrating the organising function: pointing to the importance of having a 'teacher's attitude' (1998 98), by which he means to: 'instruct others in their production and...it must be able to place an improved apparatus at their disposal. This apparatus will be the better the more consumers it brings into contact with the production process...the more readers or spectators it turns into collaborators' (1998 98).

In *The Author as Producer* Benjamin identifies two techniques that can be adopted by the revolutionary intellectual: interruption and astonishment. The former means re-engineering the relationship between student and teacher as a way not of 'developing actions but representing conditions' (1998 99). The later, not as a 'stimulant' but that which 'compels the spectator to take up a position towards the action' so as 'to expose the present' (1998 100). And all of this must be full of good humour, with laughter being a good place to start.

By the end of the article he is reaffirming the class nature of his project: the author is 'an engineer who sees his task in adapting the apparatus to the ends of the proletarian revolution', as a material and historical process rather than one that believes in the 'magical strength of the mind' (1998 103). As he puts it, finally: 'For the revolutionary struggle is not fought between capitalism and mind. It is fought between capitalism and the proletariat' (1998 103). In what follows I shall point out that this orthodox reading of Marxism as a clash between capitalism and the proletariat is a restricted and underwhelming reading of Marx that has proved vulnerable to the contrary and contradictory historical circumstance. This will become most apparent when I deal with Pashukanis's theory of Marxist law later. Benjamin's reading of Marx is not dialectical enough.

Reading Benjamin

One of the most profound engagements with Benjamin's version of Marxism is by Esther Leslie (2000) who wants to rescue Benjamin from the conformity within which he is trapped by the 'defeatist melancholy' (2000 vii) of reform minded scholars. For her production is a key issue; she captures the ambition of Benjamin as described in *The Author as Producer* through a detailed discussion of the notion of 'technique', which she recognises as involving a fundamental transformation in the nature of production itself, beyond any rearrangement of relations of distribution. For Leslie, after Benjamin, technique is not only a technical process but a social process made possible through political art: 'artistic experimentation as a previewed transformation of the real, or probationary transmutation of subjectivity in relation to the real' (2000 97). This is the basis of what she argues Benjamin means by 'refunctioning' (2000 98): as a liberation of the means of production, or new forms of production in the transition to communism. As she puts it, 'The revolutionising of techniques coincides with the revolutionising of reality and liberation into self-consciously organised production. This experimentation plays a role in emancipating the means of production, acting as a training ground in new modes of interaction between technology and humans' (Leslie 2000 100).

However, it is at that point that Leslie's exposition stalls, the revolutionary subject is, as it was for Benjamin, the 'self-organised moment of proletarian revolution' (Leslie 2000 vii), so much so that while she goes some way to rescuing Benjamin as 'a resource and research tool for overpowering political and cultural conformism' (2000 ix) the full power of Marx's exposition of labour goes unrecognised, and any debate about the real nature of labour is curtailed (Dinerstein and Neary 2002). In order to expose the full extent of Marx's theory of value, as a basis for unlearning the law of labour, we need to engage critically with Benjamin's reading of Marx's social theory.

Benjamin and Marx

Benjamin's Marxism was much influenced by the work of Georg Lukacs (1885-1971), the Hungarian Marxist philosopher and communist apparatchik, widely regarded as one of the founders of Western Marxism (Anderson 1979) through his *magnum opus*: *History and Class Consciousness* (HCC) (1923/1971). Benjamin was introduced to Lukacs' work by his lover, Asja Lacis, and he read the book while on holiday in Capri (Lunn 1983, Eiland and Jennings 2014, Burns 1977). Benjamin regarded HCC as 'the most consistent philosophical work of Marxist literature' (Benjamin in Burns 1977 17). Burns argues that Lukacs gave Benjamin 'a dialectic rather than an economic evolutionist framework, as well as an appreciation of the primacy of the systematic supremacy of philosophy over all other branches of science' (1977 17). Lukacs provided Benjamin with a sense of the dynamic development of history, and the relationship between past and present so as to be able 'to reconstruct history from a single, thoroughly understood moment and transform it' (1977 17). Benjamin took from Lukacs that this dynamic is grounded in the concept of totality, as 'located within the context of a concrete and total historical process' (1977 17); and 'the identical subject-object within that historical process as the class conscious proletariat' (1977 17). This enabled Benjamin to conceptualise the concept of technique as something fully embedded within the social relations of capitalist production; as well as the importance for revolutionary intellectual life, not just the objects and artefacts through which it is produced, but to revolutionise the process of production out of which those objects and artefacts are made (Burns 1977).

Did Benjamin Read Marx?

While Benjamin read Lukacs it is not certain how much Benjamin read Marx and studied his labour theory of value. T J Clark in *Should Benjamin Read Marx?* (2003 31 31-49) considers the extent to which Marx's *Capital* and, in particular, the real nature of the commodity-form was 'a generative force in Benjamin's inquiry rather than a set of surface tropes or citations' (2003 42). Clark's purpose is to recover a Marxist Benjamin from the Benjamin of Cultural Studies.

Clark notes the montage of Marxist quotations in Benjamin's *The Arcades Project* (2002), with their focus on value, labour and the process of capitalist exchange: 'More than once in the notes from this time one comes across him copying out a hoary passage from Marxist scripture—the "theological niceties" paragraph, the sentences from the 1844 manuscripts on the "sense of having"—and then a few pages...later copying it out again, like a slow learner kept after school' (2003 41).

Clark is interested in the extent to which *The Arcades Project* is underpinned by the dream of a collective life brought to bear through Benjamin's commitment to the proletariat, based on the transformatory capacity of bourgeois social relations of production: 'Bourgeois society, Benjamin thought, was slowly, over the generations, waking up – waking to the reality of its own productive powers, and maybe, if helped along by its wild child, the proletariat, to the use of those powers to foster a new collective life.' (2003 33)

Clark wants to rescue Benjamin from Marxicologists, like Theodor Adorno (and maybe myself):

> And given the surrounding circumstances of Marxism in the 1930s, there is a way that the very flimsiness of Benjamin's materialism was an asset. It meant that he never seems to have felt the appeal of high Stalinism, nor even of that of its Dance-of-Death partner, the Frankfurt School. 'Marxist method' never got under his skin. Not for him a lifetime spent, like Adorno's, building ever more elaborate conceptual trenches to outflank the Third International. One has the impression that Benjamin hardly knew where the enemy, within dialectical materialism, had dug itself in.
> (2003 41)

Clark concludes that Benjamin's work remains more at the level of a dream rather than understanding the spectacle of capitalism. Benjamin's reading of Marx is 'pervasive, vital and superficial' (2003 41).

A standard critique of Benjamin's reading of Marx is that Benjamin was not dialectical enough. Rolf Wiggershaus (2007) says Adorno objected to Benjamin's insistence that the revolution depended on the state of consciousness of the proletariat as, for Adorno, 'the proletariat was crippled by class domination' (2007 192). Adorno put this down to the influence of Brecht on Benjamin, that 'wild man', as Adorno called him (2007 192). Wiggershaus tells us Adorno stresses his own commitment to the theory of commodity fetishism as the 'decisive mediation' for capitalist society as 'a negative image of the true world' (2007 195). For Adorno, Benjamin was 'not thoroughly dialectical enough' (2007 211), closer to a psychologisation rather than a materialisation of 'the objective power of commodity fetishism' (2007 211), specifically in relation to Marx's chapter 1 in *Capital Volume 1* where he sets out his exposition of the commodity-form as the basis for his labour theory of value.

Feldman (2011) makes a similar point in 'Not dialectical enough: On Benjamin and Adorno and the Autonomous Critique', which directly deals with the issue. She argues that Adorno objects to Benjamin giving too much credit in the artwork essay to the proletariat and not nearly enough to the theorists: '[You] credit the proletariat...directly with an achievement which, according to Lenin, it can only accomplish through the theory introduced by intellectuals as dialectical subjects' (2011 339). Here Benjamin is said to discount the revolution's need for the dialectically minded intellectual. This failure is attributed to a lack of dialectical theorising on Benjamin's part, insofar as Benjamin places his 'blind trust in the spontaneous powers of the proletariat within the historical process', when, in fact, the proletariat 'is itself a product of bourgeois society' (2011 339).

Esther Leslie wants to get beyond Clark's scholastic reading of Benjamin's Marxism, which needs to be 'understood like a field of possibility, and not something to be pursued academically' (2009 558). Leslie notes if Benjamin was not a fully signed up Marxist he loved the Marxist Asja Lacis for her 'radical communism' (2009 559) and, if he did not fully grasp Marx's social theory, he understood the nature of 'communist things' (2009 560). Leslie argues Benjamin was wedded to the notion that 'the subject of historical knowledge is the struggling oppressed class itself' in the *Theses on the Philosophy of History* (2009 563). It is important to note the significance Benjamin gives to the subject of historical knowledge, which points in the direction of considering revolutionary subjectivity as a form of radical epistemology: a key issue for revolutionary teaching and Student as Producer. Leslie notes that Benjamin is very important 'to current disputes in Marxism and beyond still on-going' (2009 566).

Hannah Arendt has identified Benjamin as an unusual Marxist. Benjamin was 'probably the most peculiar Marxist ever produced by this movement, which God knows had its full share of oddities' (Arendt 2007 11); and not a very dialectical one at that. This non-dialectical approach, she argues, is exemplified by Benjamin's attachment to the figure of the *flaneur*, wandering about the city: 'aimlessly strolling' as 'The true picture of the past flits by' (2007 12). This lack of dialectics was put down, Arendt argues, to Bertolt Brecht's influence and, in particular, his notion of 'crude thinking'; although Benjamin did equate crude thinking with dialectical thinking, as he put it, 'Crude thoughts...are nothing but the referral of theory to practice...a thought must be crude to come into its own in action' (2007 15).

A critique of this Lukacsian version of Marx is made by Moishe Postone, showing in clear theoretical terms the way in which Lukacs is not dialectical enough. Postone is important for Student as Producer as he carries out his reappraisal of Marx's social theory by understanding labour not as the subject of history, as Benjamin and the orthodox and mainstream readings of Marx would have it, but from the perspective of 'a critique of labour in capital' (1993 5), providing the basis of a curricula for unlearning the law of labour. Postone is part of a movement of Marxist theory grounded in *critical theory as a critique of labour*. I have elaborated on this tendency within Marxism elsewhere (Neary 2017a), but for now I want to focus on Postone, in terms of my understanding of Benjamin's dialectical understanding of the labour theory of value, before making a link between Postone and critical pedagogy through an analysis of Paula Allman's work in the next chapter.

Moishe Postone has set out an ambitious project based on 'a fundamental reappraisal of Marx's mature critical theory in order to re-conceptualise the nature of capitalist society' (1993/2003 3). He does this through a critical rethinking of the central categories of critical political economy: the commodity, labour, value, money and capital. He carries this out not by considering capitalism in terms of the private ownership of the means of production or the market, what he calls a politics of distribution and the main focus of mainstream Marxism, but by exploring the centrality of labour for social life in capitalism, with a critical focus on what he calls the 'productivist paradigm' (2003 17). What makes Postone's analysis distinctive is not his affirmation of labour (proletariat) as the revolutionary subject, in the way of Benjamin and mainstream Marxism, but rather through 'a critique *of* labour in capitalism' (1993 5). He does this by a reconstruction of capitalist core categories, including value, abstract labour and capital itself, to reveal them as the outcome of a very determinate set of social relations, grounded in what Marx refers to as the commodity-form.

Marx well understood the importance of his discovery of the substantive nature of the commodity-form and, in particular, the constitutive character of labour-power as a central capitalist commodity. In a letter from Marx to Engels on 24 August 1867, the year that the first volume of *Capital* was published, he wrote:

> The best points in my book are: 1. (this is fundamental to all understanding of the FACTS) the two-fold character of labour according to whether it is expressed in use value or exchange value, which is brought out in the very First Chapter; 2. the treatment of surplus value regardless of its particular forms as profit, interest, ground rent, etc. This will be made clear in the second volume especially.
> (Marx 1987, 402)

Joss Winn (2015b) puts it this way, drawing out how Marx's theory is a theory of social form, set out here as exposition of the commodity-form: 'Marx first elucidated the "two-fold character of labour" in *A Contribution to the Critique of Political Economy* (1859) and then seven years later reworked it into the first chapter of *Capital Vol.1*. There, Marx unfolds his new scientific discovery, one that he regarded as "the pivot on which a clear comprehension of political economy turns".' (Marx 1996, 51).

Winn (2015b) reminds us that: 'Marx's discovery shows how the role, character and measure of labour is central to political economy and therefore to the total "logic" of capitalism's social world. Marx's discovery was not simply that labour is useful and can be exchanged like any other commodity, but that its character is "expressed" or "contained" in the form of other commodities. What is expressed is that labour in capitalism takes on the form of being *both* concrete, physiological labour [use value] and at the same time abstract, social, homogenous labour. It is the abstract character of labour that is the source of social wealth (i.e., value) and points to a commensurable way of measuring the value of commodities and therefore the wealth of capitalist societies.'

Postone has elaborated further on the way in which the 'dialectical tension between use value and value commodity form' (Postone 2002) of capitalist labour is manifest not only in the form the commodity, but also through the apparently independent structures through which capitalist modernity is regulated, including the capitalist state. Postone's conclusion is that post-capitalist or communist society is not the realisation of labour, but its historical abolition/negation (Postone 1993/2003).

In *Lukacs and the Dialectical Critique of Capitalism* (2003) Postone presents his reappraisal of Marx's social theory through a critique of the way Lukacs formulates Marx's categorical analysis of the commodity-form. Postone argues that Lukacs' presentation of the commodity-form is dualistic: as a relation between two aspects of social life: use value (quality – proletariat) and exchange value (quantity – measure), neither of which are intrinsically connected; rather, each has their own ontological status. With this twin track formulation in mind Lukacs argues that the essential aspect of capitalism is that use value, the proletariat, is overwhelmed by exchange value: measurement and quantification. The overwhelming logic of exchange value provides the basis for the logic of bureaucracy and the instrumental rationalisation which underpins the regulatory and administrative forms of capitalist institutions: the law and the state. For Lukacs this logic extends beyond the law, politics and economics to all forms of cultural and social life. However, what prevents this bureaucracy from becoming an 'iron cage' is that workers are not only exploited by capitalist social relations, but are constitutive of them: labour is both the product and the producer of capitalist modernity. For Lukacs, this productive capacity extends to the proletariat's ability to create a form of society beyond capitalism. This can occur at moments of crisis when the working class is able to understand its exploited position as wage labour within the commodity system, and so develop its own revolutionary class consciousness to reconstitute society in its own likeness by 'coming into its own historically' (2003 17).

Postone suggests a number of problems with Lukacs' formulations. Firstly, while Lukacs recognises the rational and institutional form of capitalist institutions, the state and the economy, as the product of rationality and quantification, the institutional form of human life, the proletariat, are presented by Lukacs as if they are transhistorical, pre-formed and ready-made. Ironically, for Marxist theory which is celebrated for its critique of commodity fetishism, the proletariat is reified and fetishised.

The result is that despite what Postone acknowledges is a brilliant essay, it still manages to create a backward looking view of the future, in a formulation of time and space that characterises aspects of Benjamin's work epitomised, as Postone suggests, by Benjamin's famous reference to Paul Klee's painting *Angel Novus* (1920): 'Lukacs's critical theory of capitalism... backs into a future it does not grasp. It is reminiscent of Walter Benjamin's image of the angel of history, propelled into a future to which its back is turned' (2003 21).

Postone looks for an explanation for this backward-lookingness in the way in which Lukacs interprets Marx's categorial analysis of the commodity-form, linked with a particular interpretation of capitalist modernity through the perspectives of major sociological figures, most notably Max Weber (1864-1920) and his thesis on the origins of modernist rationality and bureaucratisation.

Postone defines this approach as mainstream Marxism, which sees revolution 'in terms of class relations structured by the market economy and private ownership of the means of production' (1993 6) in which workers are dominated and exploited by the capitalist class. The structural tensions which characterise the relationship between the type of society based on market and private property relations and the constantly developing technical means of production implies the possibility of the proletariat rearranging the technical means of production based on collective ownership organised around the principles of equality and social justice.

Postone argues that Lukacs provides no sense of how an emancipated proletariat would overcome rationalisation and bureaucracy of the labour process and the division of labour out of which it has been produced. As such, Lukacs offers no alternative way of thinking about the real issues that have troubled socialist planners, so the probable outcome is reinventing another form of society based on the imposition of labour in less mediated forms: more immediate, violent and terroristic. Secondly, there is no real explanation for the historical dynamic of capital, other than as a 'ghostly movement' (2003 16) providing no account of the processes: the friction needed to melt what Lukacs refers to as a 'frozen reality' (2003 16). To use Benjamin's melting metaphor, Postone argues there is no conceptual logic to generate the necessary heat required for revolutionary social transformation.

So, the question becomes how labour gets beyond its own constitutive form – how does the proletariat *generate* hot class struggle: how does the proletariat and all that is solid melt? This is something that neither Benjamin nor Lukacs resolve. The answer to this question lies in a much deeper understanding of the question of labour in capitalism.

We have seen how Postone describes Lukacs's account of the understanding of the role of the commodity as the structuring principle of capitalist society. Postone, after Marx, maintains the focus on the commodity, but in a more dialectical way than Lukacs, enabling a very different understanding of labour. The commodity-form of labour for Postone, following Marx, is not dualistic, rather it is constituted in a way that is both immanently abstract and concrete. The abstract form, abstract labour, relates to the commodity-form's socially structuring dimension: people work (produce) to get money (wages) to consume what is produced by others. In capitalism the way in which waged work is organised operates as a general social principle (exchange value), as well as the organisation of particular productive activities (use value). In capitalism this organisation of labour is not contingent, nor is it based on custom or tradition, as in pre-capitalist societies, but is, rather, dependent totally on the production of expansive social wealth (surplus value), which Marx refers to as valorisation. Abstract labour then has a social function as a process of social mediation through the generalised social activity of commodity exchange. The imperative to generative expansive social wealth (surplus value) means that capitalism is historically dynamic, made real at all times through the competitive reorganisation of the labour process, as industrial technology and science along with associated forms of everyday social life, e.g., education at all levels, including higher education. Given the ubiquity of organised waged work in capitalist society labour appears as an entirely natural process: 'a simple category' (Grundrisse 1993 192).

This means that capital, the expansive dynamic for social wealth, rather than labour forms the basis for revolutionary transformation. Postone offers a very different interpretation of the revolutionary subject in capitalism to that presented by Benjamin and orthodox Marxism. For Postone, the revolutionary subject is capital, understood now in terms of its capacity for historical dynamic expansive social transformation. Capital operates as an impersonal form of social domination (Neary 2017a). Postone finds the justification for this position in Marx's account of Capital as Subject through the process of valorisation:

> It [value] is constantly changing from one form into another without becoming lost in its movement; it thus transforms itself into an automatic subject...For the movement in the course of which it adds surplus value is its own movement, its valorisation is therefore self-valorisation...[V]alue suddenly presents itself as a self-moving substance which through a process of its own, and for which the commodity and money are both mere forms.
> (2003 9) (*Capital* 255-6).

The basis of the self-movement is the process of exploitation by which labour is itself produced as labour-power, or human energy measured by social labour time:

> Capital is a self-moving contradiction [in] that it presses to reduce labour time to a minimum, while it posits labour time, on the other side, as sole measure and source of wealth. Hence it diminishes labour time in the necessary form so as to increase it in the superfluous form; hence posit the surplus in growing measure as a condition – question of life or death – for the necessary.
> (Postone 1993 34, *Grundrisse* 706)

Postone describes Capital as Subject in these terms:

As the Subject, capital is a remarkable 'subject'...it is historically determinate and blind. Capital, as a structure constituted by determinate forms of practice, may in turn be constitutive of form and social practice and subjectivity, yet as the Subject it has no ego. It is self-reflexive and may induce self-consciousness, but...it does not possess self-consciousness.

(Postone 1993 77)

What this highlights is that the revolutionary teacher should focus on labour as the point of critique, in a way that is not instrumental for capital, but rather, serves to undermine or dissolve the social relation of capitalist production, or unlearning the law of labour.

The logic for this abolition of capitalism lies not in a life and death struggle 'between capitalists and the proletariat' as Benjamin argues in *The Author as Producer*, but, rather, in determinate forms of practice established by the contradiction within the commodity-form of labour, i.e., through the unfolding history of the dialectic relation between its concrete and abstract nature in an on-going expansive process of valorisation. In capitalism human labour is essential for the valorisation process: the production of surplus value through the exploitation of workers. However, in the process to increase productivity and avoid labour conflict, workers are expelled from work with their knowledge and capacity increasingly automated, and as a form of surplus population; this gives rise to technological development and the intensification of work, alongside increasing unemployment and poverty. The forced evacuation of labour leads to a tendency for the rate of profit to fall, even while, at the same time, increasing automation leads to the overproduction of commodities. Crucially, the creation of surplus populations, alongside poverty and unemployment, generates forms of resistance, including the real possibility of overproduction providing the basis for a society of abundance, rather than the logic of scarcity on which capitalism is based. Abundance here means not over consumption, but that the productive process is able to satisfy social demands based on the needs and capacities of people and the planet (Kay and Mott 1982).

The key point, contra Lukacs, is not that exchange value overwhelms workers, providing the substance for rationality and a counterpoint for worker struggles, but rather that all social life has been subsumed by the social relations of capitalist work. Human emancipation is not possible by the realisation of the proletariat, but by the abolition of capitalist society as a whole.

The need to appropriate human labour-power is complex and deeply conflictual, generating crisis as the process struggles to maintain expansion. It is out of crisis and contradiction that radical subject emerges: not as some intrinsic capacity that is inherent within the proletariat, as Benjamin has it, but as a dynamic negative aspect of the capital relation. The progressive productive characteristics point in the direction of how human emancipation might be achieved: through the appropriation of accumulated general social knowledge for the benefit of humanity and nature in a non-alienated form (Postone 1993 364); so that 'people control what they create rather than being controlled by it' (1993 373). In a society where people have been controlled by the logic of production, it is likely that a new human emancipation will be a world that is not dominated by production, but a new form of human sociability with a new logic of social wealth. Humanity can recover itself through different forms of social wealth based on a different concept of usefulness not defined within the capital relation (362). Postone refers to this as the 'latent potential' (1993 364) of the use value dimension, no longer constrained and shaped by the value dimension...not as a utopia of labour, but 'disposable time': non-working time not dominated by the logic of work but through a communist concept of wealth and sociability.

And, to further develop Postone's argument, in a passage that is particularly relevant for those of us who work in universities, Marx recognises in *The Grundrisse* the extent to which this new social wealth is based on re-appropriating the general power of science, knowledge and technology, which he defines as 'general social knowledge' (1993 706), 'the social brain' (694) and 'the general intellect' (1993 706) or 'knowledge in an alien form: the power of knowledge objectified' (1993 706). Marx argues that science and knowledge which had previously been used to increase capitalist productivity can now be reclaimed as knowledge at the level of society as a new type of 'social intellect' (1993 709) 'for society generally and each of its members...the development of the individual's full productive forces, hence those of society also' (1993 708). Marx refers to this notion of radical individuality/subjectivity as 'the social individual' (1993 749).

Marx had previously argued in the *Economic and Philosophical Manuscripts* (1844) that 'natural science has transformed human life all the more practically through industry and has prepared the conditions for human emancipation, however much its immediate effect was to complete the process of dehumanisation' (1844 355). Through the on-going crisis ridden development of the capitalist mode of production the stage is set for natural science to 'become the basis of a *human* science...The idea of *one* basis for life and another for *science* is from the very outset a lie...Natural science will in time subsume the science of man, just as the science of man will subsume natural science: there will be *one* science' (1844 355). This is much more than a call for interdisciplinarity, but is a powerful critique of the subject discipline obsessed capitalist university, providing the basis for a new revolutionary science and the foundation for a communist higher and higher education. All of this has very important consequences for the way in which revolutionary teachers teach as the foundation for the revolutionary subject understood as a form of radical epistemology, and is of central significance to Student as Producer and unlearning the law of labour.

The labour theory of value was abandoned in the nineteenth century in the face of the rising power of the working class, and replaced with a theory that focused more on use value, rather than the more social determination of exchange as a form of labour time (Clarke 1982). This act of intellectual avoidance has been referred to as the 'great evasion' (Perlman 1968). For Marx, the substance of capitalist value is calculated as amounts of labour time. This temporal frame of reference is not quantified as the tick tock of absolute clock time: but a measure of socially relative time i.e. the time taken to produce a commodity based on the standard rate of productivity in any given jurisdiction at the moment in time when the commodity is exchanged. Marx refers to this notion of relative time as 'socially necessary labour time' (Marx 1990 129). The new science of economics has it that the value of a commodity now becomes its usefulness to the buyer alongside a market-based formula dependent on supply and demand. The entrepreneur is characterised as the person with the ability to satisfy consumers' needs, whose risk and innovation demands the major share of the profits. The importance of labour is recognised in terms of human capital with ways invented to increase its productivity and as only one factor in the process of production (Cleaver 2017 31-7). Trade unions and other labour associations are tolerated to the extent that demands are contained within the social relations of capital. Workers have sought to self-manage the labour process as worker-co-operatives and have been encouraged to do so as long as these associations do not break the bounds of the logic of capitalist work. This is the understanding of labour that has come to dominate the discourse of labour relations and labour struggles (Dinerstein and Neary 2002). But Postone, after Marx, points to a much more fundamental and critical reading of labour in capitalism. Not then the affirmation of labour, but the negation of labour. This is consolidated by Marx's *Critique of the Gotha Programme* which will be examined in chapter 6 where Marx is arguing not for the freedom of labour but rather freedom from labour. And, as we shall see, Marx does favour worker co-operatives, but only if they are not controlled by the state, and as moments of transition to a communist society.

How Do Revolutionary Teachers Teach?

The question remains how does this work in practice and, with regard to the focus of this book, how do revolutionary teachers teach? Given that social relations in capitalism are mediated by abstract labour, activity needs to deal with this process of mediation in a way that avoids 'pseudo-activity' (Kurz 2007, Adorno 1998), as well as any form of praxism or activism. Adorno saw elements of pseudo-activity in Marx's famous maxim 'philosophers only interpret the world, the point is to change it'. Adorno argued interpretation was required to avoid pseudo-activity: action that affirmed the instrumentality of Capital rather than negated it. For Adorno, praxis was based on the avoidance of labour, and, therefore, praxis must be underpinned by 'reasoned analysis' (1998 264). In the case of Student as Producer this means critical theory as a critique of labour (Neary 2017a), or unlearning the law of labour.

This was a very real issue for Theodor Adorno during the student protests in West Germany in 1968-9. Adorno was a key figure in the reappraisal of Marx's labour theory of value, restoring its revolutionary potential, although his attachment to class struggle was somewhat underwhelming (Neary 2017a). The question for Adorno was how to teach revolution in a way that does not ape the instrumentality of capitalist society, as 'a symptom of alienation rather than the solution to it' (Wilding 2009 25), or as a form of crude Marxism which claims to be overcoming the limits of philosophy 'by its negative relation to everything bourgeois' (Wilding 2009 32), or the praxis of charismatic teachers; all of these might be described as a sort of critical pedagogy. Adorno's students were very critical of his unwillingness to commit to class struggle and the student movement; for them 'Adorno as an institution is dead' (2009 36). He had, after all, called the police to evict students from his lecture theatre who were protesting at his lack of activism at a time, in 1968, when student protest in Germany was at its height. Wilding tells us Adorno's work was not actually detached from the student protests, but that his negative dialectic minds us to bear witness to the contradictoriness of the world. Adorno took a hard-line approach to the theory and practice of negation: 'To negate a negation does not bring about its reversal; it proves, rather, that the negation was not negative enough' (Adorno 1990 159–60). This does not mean do nothing, the dialectic insists that mediation requires immediacy: 'there is no mediation without a moment of immediacy' (Wilding 2009 27, from Adorno 1993 91); but there is no 'illicit shortcut to practical action' (Wilding 25, Adorno 2001 3).

So how do revolutionary teachers teach? Not simply astonish and interrupt, or carry out operativism, as if revolution was about adopting appropriate pedagogical techniques, but in a way that acknowledges the nature of social mediation of capitalist work and its brutal institutional forms: Money and the State.

In addition, and fundamentally, the topics that are taught must be of theoretical-practical significance so as to recognise the world in its totality, and in a way that reflects the social world as being contrary to itself. And, secondly, not only the content of the curriculum, but teaching in a way that challenges the institutional form from which knowledge and science are derived, as a type of 'non-institution', which is how Wilding describes Adorno (2011 37); not, merely at the level of the personal or the political, but at the general and social. Given the nature of what we are dealing with we might start with the creation of new forms of social institutions, based on the way in which Student as Producer considers the process of teaching and learning as the construction of a radical epistemology. Student as Producer suggests work on this problematic can be done by setting up a co-operative university, as a moment of revolutionary transformation. And, given the centrality of Police, a form of social defence based not on commodification and the capitalist law of value, but a society grounded in Authority and Authorship, generating abundance, as well as a new unity of purpose based on the reconciliation/mediation of human needs and capacities as part of the natural world.

But before drawing up a revolutionary curriculum, I want to connect with the ways in which Marx has been used to develop a theory of critical pedagogy. In the next chapter I will explore the work of three revolutionary teachers, Jacques Ranciére, Paulo Freire and Paula Allman, whose work is characterised by a very distinctive engagement with the work of Karl Marx, to see what a revolutionary teacher can learn from other revolutionary teachers.

4. Learning from Revolutionary Teachers

In this chapter I review the work of three major revolutionary teachers: Jacques Ranciére, Paulo Freire and Paula Allman, pointing out the significance of their work for how revolutionary teachers teach. These theorists have been chosen because of the ways in which their work is informed by a Marxist theory of labour, giving substance to the historical materialist theory of pedagogy and knowledge that I have elaborated in this book. I will consider what we can learn from them about making a curriculum for Student as Producer.

Jacques Ranciére: The Ignorant Professor

Jacques Ranciére *might* be the epitome of a revolutionary teacher. Born in Algiers in 1940, he was a student of Louis Althusser, one of the major Marxist intellectuals of the post-World War Two period, at the Sorbonne in Paris during the student protests in the 1960s. Ranciére went on to teach in Paris-8 (St Denis), a prototype institution for radical teaching in higher education. Ranciére is now Professor of Philosophy at the European Graduate School in Switzerland, another pioneering institution that seeks to encourage productive co-operation between academics and students. Ranciére is known as the 'philosopher of equality' (Davis 2010 vii), because of his promotion of the concept of 'intellectual equivalence' although his range of writings defies simple categorisation, in what amounts to more like 'an extraordinary philosophical meditation on equality' (Ross 1991 ix). Ranciére's work deals with the relationship between domination and oppression not simply as a pedagogical issue, but also in terms of art and aesthetics, and more generally as 'matters of ignorance and knowledge' (Power 2010 78). His approach to teaching is elaborated in *The Ignorant Schoolmaster: Five Lessons in Intellectual Emancipation*, published in France in

1987 and in English in 1991, along with a series of other books and publications that develop the politics of education to a wider social context, some of which I will review in this chapter: *Proletarian Nights: The Workers' Dream in Nineteenth Century France* (2012); *The Philosopher and his Poor* (2004) and *Disagreement: Politics and Philosophy* (1999).

An interest in labour and work is an enduring feature of Ranciére's writing (Deranty 2012), encouraging us as academics to consider our own situations as worker-intellectuals and the ways in which our hopes and dreams are supported and/ or shattered by the world of capitalist work (Larson 2013); as well as 'what does it mean to speak *as a Marxist* today' inside an English university (Ranciére 2011a, author's emphasis xxi).

Reading Capital

Ranciére came to prominence as a student of Louis Althusser (1919-90), the French Marxist philosopher and member of a group of students, 'Union des Estudiantes Communistes', who formed part of the Student Communist Party (PSC) in France in the 1960s. Ranciére was expelled from the PSC along with other student followers of Althusser for their unorthodox Marxism. Ranciére contributed a chapter to a volume Althusser published, entitled *Reading Capital* (Althusser et al 1965), where he set out an exposition of the capitalist law of value that deals with Marx's social theory of the value-form. This chapter has been acknowledged as a core text in the development of 'a new reading of Marx', setting out, among other things, the difference between the concept of alienation and abstraction in Marx's work (O'Kane n.d., Neary 2019, Nesbitt 2017). In this way Ranciére was endorsing Althusser's position about there being two Marx's, early and late, distinguished by an epistemological break that marked Marx's transition from idealist humanist to revolutionary materialist philosopher; although Ranciére's chapter on the value-form contradicted Althusser's position of 'the economy being determinate in the last instance'. This paper was published in Althusser et al's *Reading Capital* (1965) but was removed from subsequent editions, including the first English translation, until it was restored in a German and later in English language editions (O'Kane n.d.).

Althusser was renowned for a version of structural Marxism where the impact of human agency was severely constrained within the economic sphere and other determinations in which workers found themselves. Althusser took the elitist position that due to the scientific expertise needed to read Marx's social theory it required intellectuals who were knowledgeable about philosophy to guide human revolutionary actions (Clarke 1980). It was during this period that Ranciére severed his connection with Althusser as a result of Althusser's anti-student response to the student protests throughout the 1960s. The student protest culminated in the student-worker uprising in Paris in May 1968. Althusser set out the reasons for this opposition to the student protests in *Student Problems* (Louis Althusser 1964/2011 11-15).

The article *Student Problems* reflected the on-going dispute between the French Communist Party (PCF) and the National Union of French Students (UNEF) about the future of French universities. The PCF argued for a quantitative increase in universities and staff, whereas the students looked for qualitative improvements in teaching, which they saw in terms of alienation and anomie, demanding a more equal and democratic relationship with their teachers. Althusser conceptualised the issue not as the relationship between students and teachers, but in terms of the content of knowledge itself and the relationship between science and ideology.

In *Student Problems*, Althusser wants to highlight an issue that had come to prominence in this period: the nature of intellectual work itself and its relationship to knowledge. He argues against the way in which knowledge, or 'half-knowledge' as he called it, is used by the dominant class as the basis for their ruling ideology, in what he refers to as the 'thingification of science' (2011 14). He argues in favour of teaching the epistemology of science and disciplines as a way to counteract this effect. At the core of this issue is what Althusser refers to as 'the pedagogic function':

The pedagogic function has as its object the transmission of a determinate knowledge to subjects who do not possess it. Therefore the pedagogic situation is based on the absolute condition of *an inequality between knowledge and a lack of knowledge*. Those to whom society transmits, through its pedagogical institutions, the knowledge that it has decided they should assimilate, represent the side of non-knowledge, or, if you prefer (since a non-knowledge is also a certain knowledge), the side of *unequal* – inferior knowledge. Those whom society puts in charge of transmitting to the non-knowers the knowledge that they possess represent the side of knowledge, or those who have *unequal* – superior knowledge. The famous pupil–teacher, lecturer–student relationship is *the technical expression of this fundamental pedagogic relationship.* (1964/2011 14).

And, more succinctly: 'No pedagogic questions, which all presuppose unequal knowledge between teachers and students, can be settled on the basis of *pedagogic equality* between teachers and students' (2011 14, author's emphasis).

For that reason he is against any form of participatory research activities between student and teacher, which he refers to as an 'anarcho – democratic conception of pedagogy that can only lead to students' disappointment' (2011 15), and to them being stuck in a world of 'half-knowledge' (2011 15). Althusser argued that by protesting for a more egalitarian and democratic form of teaching the students risk alienating their professors against the political causes that the students defend. Students already have inadequate scientific training, which can only be compounded by the type of participatory teaching that the students are demanding, making the students easier to manipulate by bourgeois technocratic governments.

Ranciére recognised that what is clearly at stake is knowledge and its relationship to power and the way in which power is produced. As he put it: 'politics in a new form – in the question of knowledge, its power and its relationship to political power. This would become the ground for a "civil war" among the intellectuals in which the question of whether one *should* be committed could no longer be posed' (Ranciére 2011a 39, author's emphasis). The similarity between the politics of intellectual production that Ranciére is espousing with those of Walter Benjamin in *The Author as Producer* could hardly be more pronounced. Remember, Benjamin argued what mattered is not commitment by intellectuals to the proletariat, but rather the fundamental transformation of the politics of capitalist production.

For Ranciére, there was a clear connection between Althusser's elitist philosophical approach to Marxism and his approach to teaching in higher education: 'Fundamentally, Althusserianism is a theory of education, and every theory of education is committed to preserving the power it seeks to bring to light' (Ranciére 2011a 52), as a kind of 'enlightened despotism' (2011a 54), or 'theory's police force' (2011a 41) set out to protect the slogan 'science belongs to intellectuals' (2011a 47).

Ranciére refers to Althusser's position as being nothing more than 'class struggle in theory' (2011a 111). The problem with this version of Marxist theory, Ranciére argued, is that its proponents 'never entail any disruptive practices' (2011a 112). This is a new kind of academic freedom to 'say anything and everything at the university...provided they perpetuate its functioning' (2011a 112). Ranciére is not against Marxist theory, rather that Marxist academics need to acknowledge the real power relations out of which revolutionary discourse is produced and how those social relations might be transformed, in which the intellectual has a role to play; rather than finding the rationality of class struggle outside of class struggle. Althusser had made the role of professor 'the power of science' (2011a 114), which, at its worst, represents a 'discourse of order in the vocabulary of subversion' (2011a 116), casting judgements about what is revolutionary politics, in what amounts to 'a philosophy of recuperation' (2011a 118) proposed by 'armchair Marxists' (2011a 118).

Ranciére wants to reclaim science from scientists and intellectuals, finding a foundational source in the activities of workers:

> The *capitalist* relation of science to labour cannot be reduced to the use of science to oppress the worker, or to the idea that the privilege of science goes to those who live from the redistribution of surplus value. The appropriation of the knowledge and inventions of the worker is also an important aspect of this relation. Capitalism does not impose from above a scientific work method that replaces the 'artisanal' methods of workers: it forms this scientific method by constantly appropriating the inventions born from workers' practices. (2011a footnote 37 162)

Ranciére's point is that the oppressed do not need to be assisted by the science of philosophers to disabuse them of their illusions, but that from out of workers' struggle emerges 'the space of a new intelligence – the intelligence formed in the struggle, the knowledge reclaimed from the hands of the exploiters' (2011a 15).

The point for Ranciére is, not *contra* Althusser, 'to validate a rectified Marxism' (Ranciére 2011a xv), rather to study: 'the multiple ways thought assumes form and produces effects on the social body' (2011a xv). Ranciére wants to speak against the left's attempt at unifying discourses, that become 'blatant generalities' (2011a 119), rather, he sees Marx as part of 'a multiplication of the discourses of struggle' (2011a 119); otherwise Marxism becomes a 'discourse of order' (2011a 120), speaking on behalf of others from lessons learned from Marxist teachers in university classrooms and other institutional forms of working-class organisation. Marxism will continue to have an ambiguous role, as a: 'system of multiple identifications, of the place where discourses of revolt meet and where the discourse of subversion is perennially being transformed into the discourse of order' (2011a 122-3). So that, 'There is no pure Marxism... Marxist discourse has always been inflected by social practices, inflected by discourses and practices of revolt...and inflected by the disciplines and discourses of power. Still today only mass struggles can shake up the theoretical and political apparatus of representation that blocks the autonomous expression of revolt' (2011a 123). And in another clear example of his ambivalent attitude to Marx:

Maybe there isn't a Marxist conceptuality which must be saved from ideological doom and bourgeois invasion. There is not one logic in Capital, but many logics; it contains different discursive strategies, each of which corresponds to different problems and each of which echoes, in many different ways, the discourses through which classes think themselves or confront an opposing discourse, be it the science of classical economics or the protests of workers, the discourse of philosophers, or the reports of factory inspectors, and so on. The plurality of these conceptualities is also a manifestation, not of 'class struggle in theory' but of the effects that class struggle and its discursive forms have had on the discourse of theoreticians.
(2011a 81)

And so, Ranciére '...declared war on the theory of the inequality of intelligences at the heart of supposed critique of domination' (Ranciére 2011a xvi). He does this by asking the questions: who educates the educators, what is it to be a Marxist today and what is 'the space of a new intelligence – the intelligence formed in the struggle, the knowledge reclaimed from the hands of the exploiters' (2011a 15).

The Ignorant Schoolmaster

Ranciére expands on this position through a theory and activity of revolutionary teaching. The book that confirmed his credentials as a revolutionary teacher is 'The Ignorant Schoolmaster: Five Lessons in Intellectual Emancipation' (1987 [1991]) where he argues education should be predicated on the assumption of an equality of intellects between students and teachers, as part of the process that leads to the emancipation of the intellect and of knowledge.

The Ignorant Schoolmaster is an extraordinary text, part satire, part adventure story, history book, policy analysis, 'how to do' teaching guide (Ross 1991), and 'a skillfully crafted material object, a textured work of art and artifice, as well as a book of ideas' (Davis 2010 29). The book is written in such a way that the stories and the voices of the main protagonists are conjoined/ intertwined, making it difficult to know who is speaking (Ross 1991). On the face of it the book is the story of Joseph Jacotot (1770-1840), a lecturer in French Literature at the University of Louvain during the period of the Restoration of the Bourbon Monarchy in Europe (1814-30), who discovers by chance an effective way of educating his students. This method is based on the presumption of an equality of intelligence/intellect between the teacher and those being taught.

Jacotot's problem was how to teach French to a group of Flemish students as a non-Flemish speaker. The solution was to establish a *thing in common* between him and his students, in this case a bilingual edition of *Telemaque*, a French novel written by

Fenelon in 1699, recounting the epic adventures of Ulysses' son, Telemaque, and his tutor, Mentor, later revealed as Minerva, the Greek Goddess of Wisdom. *Telemaque* is a treatise on good government, defined in *Telemaque* as an aristocratic republic based on a constitutional monarchy, where the monarch is constrained by a caste of patricians. Although set in ancient times, the book was seen as a rebuke to the principle of an absolute monarch and the divine right of kings, personified in the form of the newly restored sovereign, Louis XIV of France (The Sun King), and was influential on emerging political science, e.g., the writings of the philosopher Jean-Jacques Rousseau. Like *Telemaque, The Ignorant Schoolmaster*, although referring to the Restoration, is seen by many as a critique of its own contemporary situation with regard to education processes and policy in France in the 1980s (Ross 1991).

Jacotot asked his students, through an interpreter, to learn French using the translation of *Telemaque* by repeated readings and rote-learning. The results of this approach were spectacularly positive. Key features of this way of learning were that students who had the will to learn required no explanations from their teachers. The idea that learning requires an explanation by the teacher for the student is *the* taken for granted aspect of teaching and learning, yet, Jacotot's method was contrary to this defining pedagogical principle, revealed in the book as 'the myth of pedagogy' (1991 6). And, not only that, the myth of pedagogy implied a fundamental presupposition, that there are two forms of intelligence in the world: inferior – student, and superior – teacher, as if helping students to understand was the first principle of an enlightened progressive teacher. *En contraire*, Jacotot's experiment revealed the so-called explanatory mode of progressive teaching as a process of making the student stupid or *'enforced stultification'* (1991 7). The student was being taught through the method of explication that in order to understand she must submit 'to a hierarchical world of intelligence' (1991

8): what the teacher already knows. Against this common pedagogic method Jacotot and his students had discovered that all intelligences are essentially of the same nature and that learning and understanding are nothing more than the act of translating, with no knowledge required other than that which is on the written page: or, 'the true movement of human intelligence taking possession of its own power' (1991 10). Further evidence to support this experiment was that the non-explicatory method is the way that children learn how to speak, as well as the way in which Jacotot's friends and colleagues had taught themselves a wide variety of subjects. All that one needed was the desire to learn: 'The method of equality was above all a method of the will. One could learn by oneself when one wanted to, propelled by one's own desire or by the constraint of the situation' (1991 12). The constraint of the situation in this case had been the will not of the student but of the master/teacher, who had created a situation in which students learn, determined not by the master's own knowledge of the subject but the students' desire to learn, creating a scenario where wills connect, providing what Jacotot/ Ranciére describes as 'intellectual emancipation'. In this case, the matter is not about comparing pedagogies, as if one is better than another, but, rather, how to verify a process of liberation: as a form of teaching oneself, or 'universal teaching' (1991 16). This method can be applied to all sciences, including subjects one knows nothing about.

In this process the role of the teacher is to find ways through which the learning of the student, 'the work of his/her intelligence can be verified' (1991 29) through the effects of what is an immaterial process, which cannot be measured. The teacher does this by asking questions 'in order to be instructed, not to instruct' (1991 29) – hence the phrase, 'ignorant schoolmaster'. Ranciére/Jacotot define intelligence as: 'the power to make oneself understood through another's verification' (1991 72-3). Intelligence then is not the proclamation of some universal truth, but to speak, listen, paint and write in ways that are susceptible to on-going translation, or the capacity of one speaker, painter or poet to confront another in ways that they might understand. Ranciére/Jacotot refer to this not as expressing an absolute truth but as speaking in 'veracity' (1991 57).

Be clear, Jacotot is not saying that equality of intelligence exists, rather that it *might* exist and the purpose of his educational experiment is to verify this supposition. It is this power of the *might* (speculation) that 'makes a society of humans possible' (1991 73). So that the issue is not proving that all intelligence is equal, rather 'It's seeing what can be done under that proposition' (1991 46).

Ranciére's book appears to be a paean to auto-didactivism, but the book is more than how to do self-directed learning. *The Ignorant Schoolmaster* moves far outside the classroom and the relationship between the student and teacher to become a treatise on political society, involving a discussion relating to the state, citizenship, rhetoric (political speaking), general assemblies and other institutions, as well as the use of violence, as a microcosm of 'the very workings of the social world' (1991 15). For Jacotot/ Ranciére the social world is based on the collective fiction of inequality and the irrationalities of what Ranciére refers to as 'A Society of Contempt' (Chapter title 75-99): a contempt for the principle of the recognition of equality, as against what might make a society of humans possible. Jacotot/Ranciére counter this with reason and rationality: the ability to 'rave' (199 94), which is the recognition of 'the equality of intelligent beings' (1991 97) by which Ranciére means 'that every man is born to understand what any other man has to say to him knows intellectual emancipation' (1991 97).

Here the book is very clear that for Jacotot this process occurs at the level of the individual, not the state or class or even society; rather, only individuals can emancipate each other: '*at the level* of people's intelligence' (1991 99). The only institution that is recognised in this exposition is 'the family' (1991 98): 'Universal teaching belongs to families' (1991 103): 'no party or government, no army, school, or institution, will ever emancipate a single person' (1991 102). For Jacotot, 'Every institution is an explication in social act, a dramatisation of inequality' (1991 105).

From this appeal against explication as teaching method, Ranciére/Jacotot are able to extrapolate from practices in the classroom to society as a whole: 'Explication is not only the stultifying weapon of pedagogues, but the very bond of the social order' (1991 117). The idea that by following the teacher at some point in the future you will be like the teacher is a moment that never arrives; referred to as delay or 'lag' (Ross 1991 xx). So much so that 'Progress is the new way of saying inequality...Progress is the pedagogical fiction built into the fiction of the society as a whole' (1991 119). 'Progress....is humanity pedagocised' (1991 120). By which he means society has been made infantile, which is then called, among other things, continuing/adult education, or lifelong learning (1991 133).

So, Jacotot/Ranciére argue, 'An enormous machine was revving up to promote equality through instruction' (1991 134) but this resulted in its opposite: 'the effacement of equality under progress, of emancipation under instruction' (1991 134). However, even within this pedagogised society emancipation is possible at the level of society. 'Whoever forsakes the workings of the social machine has the opportunity to make the electrical energy of emancipation circulate' (1991108). And, in this way, to 'make them conscious of their intellectual power' (1991 108). Although individualised, there is a general social dimension beyond the institution that points to a more general abstract process of socialisation. This can be seen in Jacotot/Ranciére's attachment to the principle of 'panecasticism', by which he means 'in each intellectual manifestation there is a totality of human intelligence' (1991 136). This is the substance of Jacotot's panecastic principle: *everything is in everything* (1991 26), or 'the finger of intelligence in every human work' (1991 41). The result is 'a new consciousness, of an overtaking of the self that extends each person's "own affair" to the point where it is part and parcel of the common reason enjoyed by all' (1991 38-9). So there is a social dimension after all, where the panecastic is defined as: 'the *totality* of human intelligence in *each* intellectual manifestation' (1991 39) or as 'a community of intelligence' (1991 58). The social is not an institution but a process of socialisation beyond the limits of current forms of social institutions, as a sort of non-institution. I will develop this point later with regard to setting up new forms of social institutions, specifically the co-operative university.

The point here is that Ranciére is pointing beyond current institutions to new forms of social institutions, which he refers to in later work as being underpinned by a communist sensibility: not only is everything in everything, but everything for everyone and nothing for ourselves. This communist principle is seen in the way in which Ranciére seeks to develop an alternative social history of labour.

Bringing Dead Labour to Life
Ranciére set out his project to recover a social history of workers' resistance, freeing himself from the influence of Althusser and what Althusser saw as the failure of May '68:

The May explosion, in which student action acted as a detonator for a mass strike, had overturned Marxist schemas of class consciousness and action. The great Althusserian project of a struggle of science against ideology clearly turned out to be a struggle against the potential strength of a mass revolt. The inability of the far-left groups to build a revolutionary workers movement in the wake of the May revolt forced us to measure the gap between the actual history of social movements and the conceptual system inherited from Marx.

It was on the basis of this twin situation that I embarked in 1972 on a research project that aimed to retrace the history of working class thought and the workers' movement in France, in order to grasp the forms and contradictions that had characterised its encounter with the Marxist ideas of class struggle and revolutionary organisation. (Ranciére 2011b 7)

Ranciére's ideas had evolved from a seminar he ran at University Paris 8 (St Denis) on workers' practices (Ross 2002 124) that became a research group, *Les Revoltes Logiques*, with its own journal, and through other publications including *Proletarian Nights* and *The Philosopher and His Poor*. This involved nothing more than a fundamental reappraisal of Marx's theoretical and political project through a detailed encounter with working-class history seen from the perspective of workers themselves and not elitist professors of political philosophy. This was a blast at what Ranciére considered not just Althusser's but Marx's implicit scientism, culminating in an important exposition on the nature of politics itself (Ranciére 1999).

Proletarian Nights is based on archival research by Ranciére, giving space to nineteenth- century French workers to tell their own stories in ways that undermine the caricatures/assumptions of social and labour history, revealed not simply as locksmiths, shoemakers and tailors, but as worker-intellectuals finding time to write and think as poets, artists, metaphysicians, philosophers, humanitarians, aesthetes and flaneurs; and in ways that challenged the accepted boundaries in the social sciences between worker and bourgeois cultures: in particular between intellectual and manual labour. The real lives of workers at night and away from work are presented as a subversive response to the prevailing ideologies; not workerist but with a culture of 'difference' (Reid 2012 xxix), which sometimes included a future based on the nobility of working trades not subsumed in the homogeneity of proletarianism. Presented as a form of 'countermyths' (Ranciére 2012 x) and a way of 'overcoming the order of things' (Ranciére Preface 2013 x), *Proletarian Nights* is written more as literature than social science. The book does not impose any consistent philosophical position on the nature of work and the working class but allows the workers to speak for themselves, in a way that 'deconstructs notions of "working-class" interest and identity' (Larson 2013 2), avoiding the classical interpretation of factory workers set in the context of capitalist production processes and class struggle. What the book reveals is the lived experience of workers at work and away from work as well as their dreams and aspirations (Larson 2013, Ross 2002), together with the mundane reality of their everyday lives in an increasingly bourgeois world; or, as Ranciére would later describe it, 'where everywhere is bourgeois' (Ranciére 2003 118). The *'Proletarian Nights'* of the title is the time when workers re-appropriate aspects of their own lives, against the fatigue of work, in ways which do not 'demand the impossible, but to realise it themselves' (Ranciére quoted in Larson 2013 3). This is what revolution really looks like, to reveal itself by its very nature in ways that we have not yet been able to comprehend (Reid 2012 xxxv). This research, together with the journal *'Les Revoltes Logiques'* (1975-81), sought to publish labour history as 'an alternative historical memory – not that of the Academy or parties – based on thought that comes from below' (Reid 2013 xix). This rewriting of the history of labour from below provides the basis for what would later become Ranciére's treatise on labour in capitalist society.

This alternative approach to labour is set out clearly in *The Philosopher and His Poor* in the section *'Marx's Labour'*, where Ranciére stresses the lived experience of individuality as opposed to party, class or other forms of workers associations, captured and contained by sociological categories or concepts. He had already started this intellectual work in *The Ignorant*

Schoolmaster, which proposes the deconstruction of manual and intellectual work into the equality of all of the intelligences; and, in *Disagreements and Ten Theses* where he lays out his political philosophy on politics and the police.

The Law of Value

Ranciére makes a strong connection between Althusser's scientism and the manner of Marx's theoretical and political project. He sets this out in *The Philosopher and His Poor* (2003) where he again confronts the issue of the relationship between science-knowledge and power (Davis 2010 18). Ranciére situates Marx as if he were a player in Plato's Republic: a society led by a dominant caste of philosophers, as 'a political model of philosophico-pedagogical-tyranny' (Davis 2010 18): a world ruled by educators and a particular form of self-perpetuating education practice which maintains the lower orders, workers and soldier-guardians, in a condition of subordination to the philosopher-kings, which Ranciére argues has no rational basis, and can be otherwise described as 'Plato's Lie' (Davis 2010 19).

At the heart of the matter for Ranciére is Marx's relation to labour, set out in the section *Marx's Labour* (55-154). Ranciére finds the basis for Marx's scientific elitism in what he sees as his contempt for the working class, whose motivations are reduced by Marx to 'the pure drive of animality' (Ranciére 2003 72), as well as their inability to behave in the way Marx requires. Paradoxically, rather than communism being a spectre in the future, artisans and tradesmen are already forming themselves into worker associations, what Ranciére calls the 'paradox of communism' (2003 82), where workers gather to do something other than be workers, in which 'brotherhood...[becomes]...a fact of life' (2003 82).

Ranciére's reading of Marx, through Althusser, means there is little room for human agency or subjectivity. In Marx's schema workers can be emancipated by following the logic of the historical development of the forces of production 'only at the price of abandoning their competence and freedom as artisans for the frenzy of the bourgeois factory' (2003 66). The lack of any working-class agency is set against the overwhelming dominance of the process of production, which 'is the essence of every activity, the measure of labour, war and thinking, and it knows only transformations' (2003 71). Ranciére recounts these transformations not as the result of class struggle, but 'the force of...[the bourgeois]...spirit in perpetual determinations along with all the old decay' (2003 93), as Marx puts it in *The Communist Manifesto*. The proletariat has then failed to rise to their historical destiny (90), characterised by a 'lack of status' and 'pure passivity' (2003 93).

And so, as a result of the failure of the workers' revolution, Ranciére argues, Marx retreats into a world of science, writing *Capital* which, in the absence of the revolution, 'concentrates the cutting edge of contradiction, which is forever socially postponed and always politically stolen away' (2003 103), carrying with it the possibility of being able to 'bring the proletariat into being as the pure subject of the destruction of capital' (2003 104). For Ranciére, Marx's work is not just unfinished, but is 'systematically incomplete' (2003 116), along with its many controversies, for example the meaning of labour, as a concept that can never be completely understood.

But, be clear, if Ranciére is critical of Marx's scientism, he is not critical of his theoretical exposition. What is particularly interesting, in terms of unlearning the law of labour and the question of how revolutionary teachers teach, is Ranciére's ringing endorsement of the labour theory of value.

Ranciére returns in *The Philosopher and His Poor* to his exposition of the commodity-form that he set out in his chapter for Althusser's *Reading Capital*: 'Capitalist production and even simple commodity production carry in themselves the explosive power of the identity of opposites' (2003 114) and quoting Marx:

'"the relative form and the equivalent form are two intimately connected, mutually dependent and inseparable elements of the expression of value; but, at the same time, are mutually exclusive, antagonistic extremes – i.e., poles of the same expression"'; before continuing 'Once he [Marx] has established the equivalent form of the commodity is the *exclusive* form, the game is over' (2003 114). Ranciére recognises this contradiction does not prevent capital from escaping the logic of its own destiny, for the time being, which means that the science of the proletariat cannot be brought to its conclusion, just yet.

What most disturbs Ranciére is that the use of science as a revolutionary tool undermines the power of practice: 'science does not teach its usage' (2003 119), rather it guides in matters of interpretation: 'Marx's theory is not a guide for action: be it violent or peaceful' (2003 120). So that, in the end, 'everything is a matter of individuals' (2003 120) which is the starting point for Ranciére's theory of equality and intellectual emancipation, by which we can become '*historical agents*' and no longer 'the simple "bearers" of social relations' (2003 121).

There are more than traces of Marx's value theory of labour in Ranciére's methodology, which can be uncovered through a symptomatic reading of Ranciére (Neary 2019). These traces point to Ranciére's account of Marx's methodology in his chapter on the value-form in *Reading Capital*. The assumption about the equality of the intellect is an abstract determination that is based on the principle of equivalence, as an impersonal form of social domination. While, as we have seen, the principle of equivalence, or exchange value, in *Capital* exists as a form of structuring determination, the principle of equivalence for Ranciére exists as a form of emancipation (Neary 2019). There is a tradition of value theory, known as autonomist Marxism, which inverts the possibility inherent in the capital relation to express this process of emancipation as self-valorisation; or, a moment when the contradiction of value is turned against itself.

Harry Cleaver (n.d.) describes this process of self-valorisation, when autonomist Marxism:

> changed its meaning from the expanded reproduction of capital to the autonomous, self-determination or self-development of the working class. The new use of the term was designed to denote working-class self-activity that went beyond being merely reactive to capital, e.g., fighting back against exploitation, to denote working-class self-activity that carried within it the basic positive, creative and imaginative reinvention of the world.

This critical application of the value-form can be seen in Postone's reappraisal of Marx, not 'a critique of capitalism not from the *standpoint* of labour, but a critique of labour in capitalism' (1993 5). Not self-valorisation, but a new form of social wealth when people appropriate their own powers that have been alienated by capitalism, particularly the power of knowledge, which has become a key factor in the capitalist process of production. This is a key learning principle for any strategy for teaching and learning for revolutionary teachers.

Police, Politics and Society

Ranciére goes on to develop these ideas about pedagogy and power into a treatise on political society through the use of concepts of emancipation, democracy, equality and the law of Police – all key issues for Student as Producer. At the core of his exposition are workers and the nature of work. He sets out this thesis on emancipation in ways that are key for Student as Producer, not least the way in which emancipation is counter-posed to the law of Police:

> Emancipation is a process rather than a goal, a break in the present rather than an ideal put in the future. It means first

breaking with the law of the police, where everybody is in his own place, with his own job and his own culture, her own body and her own forms of expression. Social emancipation was first made of individual breaks with the kind of 'identity' that pinned workers down to 'their' place and 'habitus'... Emancipation first meant reframing their own existence, breaking with their workers' identity, their workers' culture, their worker's time and space.

(Blechman et al 2005 292-3)

There is a very direct relationship between the way in which Ranciére understands emancipation and his radical concept of democracy understood as resistance to power. For Ranciére, 'Politics is not the exercise of power' (Ranciére 2010b 27), nor is it a theory of power; it is, rather, active resistance to power, out of which a new form of political subjectivity will emerge. He is against the current so-called political system of modern democracy, which is characterised by the rule of the masses by state-centric governments made up of oligarchies and experts. Ranciére is clear, in order for there to be politics 'there must be a rupture in this logic' (Ranciére 2010b 31) on which this system is based. This is more than simply the redistribution of power; rather a rupture in the idea that there are already pre-constituted political groups to which this power could be distributed, e.g., the proletariat or some other disadvantaged alliance.

He relates all of this to the concept of equality that he set out in *The Ignorant Schoolmaster*, now theorised in relation to the law of Police. Politics becomes the logic of the assumption of equality set against the logic of police order or inequality. Politics is 'democratic in this precise sense: not in the sense of institutions, but in the sense of forms of expression that confront the logic of equality with the logic of police order' (Ranciére 1999 101).

For Ranciére there is a very direct relationship between the

State and Police grounded in relation to work and occupation:

> The police is thus first an order of bodies that defines the
> allocation of ways of doing, ways of being, and ways of saying,
> and sees those bodies are assigned by the name to a particular
> place and task; it is an order of the visible and the sayable
> that sees that a particular activity is visible and another is
> not, that this speech is understood as discourse and another
> as noise. It is police law, for example, that traditionally turns
> the workplace into a private space not regulated by the ways
> of seeing and saying proper to what is called the public
> domain, where the worker's having a part is strictly defined
> by the remuneration of his work. Policing is not so much the
> 'disciplining' of bodies as a rule governing their appearing, a
> configuration of occupations and the properties of the spaces
> where these occupations are distributed.
> (Ranciére 1999, 29)

Democracy then for Ranciére is dissensus rather than consensus:

> This is what dissensus means...Political dissensus is not a
> discussion between speaking people who would confront
> their interests and values. It is a conflict about who speaks
> and who does not speak, about what has to be heard as the
> voice of pain and what has to be heard as an argument on
> justice. And this is also what 'class war' means: not the conflict
> between groups which have opposite economic interests, but
> the conflict about what an 'interest' is, the struggle between
> those who set themselves as able to manage social interests
> and those who are supposed to be only able to reproduce
> their life.
> (Ranciére, 2011c 2)

In later work he describes this state of affairs, specifically in relation to the production of knowledge, as communism, or as he puts it, 'communism without the communists' (Ranciére 2010a).

In *Communism without Communists* (2010a), Ranciére sets out his treatise on communism, which he describes, following Badiou, as 'the hypothesis of emancipation' (2010a 167), or a universality constructed by practices of emancipation. He grounds these practices in the work of *The Ignorant Schoolmaster* as 'the intelligence of anybody...or the appropriation of intelligence which is...the verification of the potential of the equality of intelligence' (2010a 168). Ranciére shows clearly how this process can be socialised, beyond Jacotot's insistence on the emancipation of the individual, which Ranciére defines now as 'the communism of intelligence' (2010a 168). This might mean transforming workshops into a public space or 'to take on the task of governing a city which its rulers have deserted or betrayed' (2010a 168) as a form of 'egalitarian invention that demonstrated the collective power of emancipated men and women' (2010a 169), like a social body, beyond the sterile Marxist debate between spontaneity and organisation. Ranciére complains again about a type of Marxist teleology, where communism emerges as the outcome of the evolution of the social relations of production. For Ranciére the problem with this account is that it is based on the impotence of proletariat predicated on 'the disempowerment created by the historical process' (2010a 171). The only knowledge of the process is given to those 'who are not caught up in the grip of the machine, namely the communists as such' (2010a 171). Ranciére proposes instead a communist hypothesis which is based on 'the collectivisation of the power of anyone' (2010a 171), or, in a panacrastian moment, 'collectivising the power of the equality of anyone with everyone' (2010a 173).

He concludes: 'The only communist legacy that is worth examining is the multiplicity of forms of experimentation of the capacity of anybody, yesterday and today. The only possible form of communist intelligence is the collective intelligence constructed in those experimentations' (2010 176), which, as he admits, is very close to his own definition of democracy. What he means by this is that 'The future of emancipation can only mean the autonomous growth of the space of the common created by the free association of men and women implementing the egalitarian principle' (2010a 176). The point is to invent new forms of the future that have not yet been imagined. So 'the rethinking of communism entails above all the investigation of the potential of collective intelligence intrinsic to the construction of those forms' (2010a 177). Whereas I have suggested other work by Walter Benjamin is not dialectic enough, this non-functionalist account of revolutionary is profoundly dialectical.

Writing in response to the proposition that there is a previously unacknowledged underlying theme to his writing, in this case work and workers rather than the value-form (Deranty 2012), Ranciére is prepared to admit that workers and the dignity of work does retain a centrality in his publications (Ranciére 2012). In agreeing to this concession he does suggest a form of activity that might consolidate the type of political strategies put forward by value-form theorists (Postone 1993, Dinerstein 2015) who call for a revolt against the subjectivity of capital and the domination of its abstract social mediations. He refers to this type of activity as 'the power to do nothing and to want to do nothing' (Ranciére 2012 216), as a lesson for 'the class of workers in the new society' (2012 216). In other words, 'the pleasure to do nothing...at the heart of the assertion of the workers reign' (2012 216). This strategy can be recast within the framework of Adorno's negative dialectic and the value-form in ways that link to and add critical capacity to Holloway's critical theory of power and the capitalist state and Postone's critique of labour in capitalism. Remember, Adorno argued that the negative can never be negative enough (1990 159-60). Doing nothing for the new reading of Marx does not mean workers reign in a new society; but, rather, the abolition of a society based on capitalist work. And so the emancipation of the intellect and of knowledge can be recast as doing nothing – do nothing that is instrumental for capital. Or, nothing doing. This is an important lesson for us all to learn, and the essence of any pedagogy that refers to itself as critical.

Lessons from Ranciére for the Revolutionary Teacher

Specifically, Ranciére promotes the power of a practical critically reflective Marxism, not dominated by elite theorists but emerging out of the activity (praxis) of workers themselves, with specific reference to Marx's value theory of labour, especially in his early work. Of particular interest to Student as Producer is that this practical activity can create new knowledge as a form of collective critical intelligence or the emancipation of the intellect. This relationship is not direct but mediated by what Ranciére/ Jacotot refer to as *the thing in common*, expressed as *dissensus*; which Student as Producer conceives as the collective process of the production of critical practical knowledge. Ranciére argues for Marxist theory based on the acknowledgement of real power relations: class struggle in practice not class struggle in theory, and how capitalist social relations can be transformed by a pedagogical process in which the intellectual has a role to play. New intelligences emerge out of workers'·practice, rather than the exploiters' interest. A key theme for Ranciére is: what is it to be a Marxist working in academic labour today, where Marxism is a theory of critical critique, or a theory of emancipation rather than 'theory's police'? Ranciére's work is based on the capacity of workers to realise their own interests. While he is against a labourist notion of worker resistance he does not deny the power of the law of value, and indeed, is a pioneer in the development of value-form Marxism (Neary 2019). Ranciére is clearly a communist, understood in terms of the relationship between democracy and the law of value bringing together the key themes of this book as set out in the keynote lectures for the

Reinvention Centre conference in 2007.

Ranciére makes a strong claim about the extent to which intellectual emancipation as a form of democracy works as an antidote to Police. I will develop this idea of dissensus as the logic of not-Police, which I refer to as Authority and Authorship, at the end of this book. It is the role of revolutionary teaching to summon up ways to conjure this collective critical intelligence not only within the classroom and education institutions but at the level of political society. This is what Ranciére refers to as communism without the communists. And, above all, do nothing that is instrumental for capitalism, as the basis for a radical epistemology.

Paulo Freire: The Word, the Context and the Critique

Paulo Freire is perhaps the leading figure in critical pedagogy, whose most influential book is the *Pedagogy of Oppressed* (1970). Written while working as an educator in Chile, the book describes how, by the practice of dialogic teaching, the oppressed might be liberated through a form of political literacy: not reading the word but reading and translating and transforming the world. Completed while working in Chile on adult literacy programmes with indigenous people, peasants and workers, the book is grounded in European political philosophy and radical liberation theology (Taylor 1993, Irwin 2012, Darder 2018). The theoretical sophistication of his work means it is open to a range of interpretations. I want to argue that orthodox Marxism is one of the main influences on Freire's work. Freire was not always a Marxist, but became a Marxist during his career as a radical educator. In what follows I will trace Freire's career as a revolutionary teacher, as an exemplar of critical theoretical pedagogic practice, so as to see what lessons the revolutionary teacher has to learn from him.

Brazil

Paulo Freire (1921-97) first emerged as a radical educator in north-eastern Brazil during a moment when literacy education was regarded as the cornerstone of national economic development in 'Third World' countries, 'the undeveloped South', where learning to read and write was seen as a way to promote capitalist modernity; although not in all cases, for example Cuba, where literacy was the basis of a revolutionary society (Kirkendall 2010). It was the political space between reform and revolution, where a particular form of social transformation was made possible by enhancing the literacy capacity of oppressed populations, that defined Freire's career as a critical pedagogue (Kirkendall 2010, Irwin 2012).

It was during the period between the late 1950s and early 1960s that interest in adult education in Brazil intensified as part of its transition to becoming one of the most industrialised countries in Latin America. This increasing industrialisation and associated growth in urbanisation, including Freire's hometown of Recife, brought a maturing working-class political awareness and potential for social unrest, linked to developing rural movements for land reform. An important motivation for literacy training was containing the emerging political opposition, supported by the US and its client organisations, e.g., the UN and UNESCO. Freire worked, by his own admission, for organisations that sought to limit the critical consciousness of workers and rural dwellers, although he attempted, within the limits of the ideology of 'national developmentalism', to develop 'pedagogical consciousness' through Christian and other non-Marxist methods (Kirkendall 2010 17). These methods were based on the principles of dialogue and democracy: by the 'creation of education for democracy' (2010 22), as a framework for political engagement in everyday life. It was at this time that Freire gained a national reputation for working with a range of literacy and popular education groups, including the Popular

Cultural Movement and at the University of Recife where he was employed, making allies with the student movement, e.g, the University National Students (UNE) - Volante: 'Flying Students', as part of a newly-emerging independent left in Brazil. His work at the national level was recognised when in 1963 he was made Head of the National Commission on Popular Culture by the government of President Joao Goulart, to design and deliver literacy programmes as part of a nationwide adult education campaign (Kirkendall 2010).

Freire's work in Brazil had been part of a growing movement for workers' and peasants' education in the 1960s imported from immigrant Spanish workers and exiles from the Spanish Civil War. This approach to adult education was influenced by the 2nd Vatican Council,that opened the Catholic Church to the progressive pedagogic approach of Liberation Theology and Popular Education (O'Cadiz et al 1998).

Despite him reiterating his Catholic humanist roots and refusing to support Cuba, Russia or China, the US government and other domestic opponents identified Freire's work as communistic. It was not surprising that, following the Military Coup in 1964, Freire and those who used his literary methods were accused of attempting 'to '"communise" Brazil' (Kirkendall 2010 56). As part of a military crackdown, Freire was imprisoned by the army-led regime for 70 days, after which time he left the country, spending a short time in Bolivia, which experienced a coup soon after he got there, before arriving in Chile in 1964.

Chile

Paulo Freire (1921-97) arrived in Chile in 1964 with his hopes for democratic educational reform in 'smithereens' (Freire 2014 27). Chile seemed like paradise. Eduardo Frei, the Christian Democrat, had just been elected president and there was 'a climate of euphoria in the streets' (2014 27). For Freire, this felt like a 'revolution in freedom' (2014 28), bringing many leftists to Chile: intellectuals, students and union leaders from all over Latin America. Santiago, the capital city, provided a context for practical action and theoretical discussion about socialism, guerrilla theory, liberation theology, metaphysics, love and death and revolution.

Freire had come to Chile with a reputation for teaching successful mass adult literacy programmes. His vision was teaching the poor to read the world, not just the word, through a process he described as 'conscientization': developing a critical consciousness among learners about their place in the world and how to liberate themselves and transform the world around them. He was against didactic teaching, the 'banking method' as he called it, which he saw as a form of oppression. He favoured dialogic teaching based on problem-based enquiry, in a context where teachers have much to learn from their students without losing their authority or intellectual leadership. The curriculum would be built on themes and issues that the students identified, supported by reading and other materials suggested by the teacher, with the extensive use of drawings and images to stimulate discussion. Freire did not invent these teaching methods; he was carrying on ways of teaching that had been developed by Latin American Trade Unionists, revolutionary priests in Brazil and political refugees from the Spanish Civil War (Austin 2003).

Freire arrived in Chile when a national literacy programme campaign was already underway, linked to a wider experiment in social democracy that extended to land and other social reforms. Freire quickly found employment on this programme, working with radical associations, including *Movimiento Independente Revolucionario* and *Movimiento de Accion Popular Unitaria*, who were involved in creating what Freire called 'political pedagogy' (2014 29) and 'democratic popular education' (2014 31). This was at a time of rising militant working-class activity in Chile including the occupation of factories and state repression, e.g.,

Puerto Montt in 1969 where police killed occupiers (Austin 2003). Freire eventually fell out with the Frei government whom he thought were more interested in their own political survival than popular revolution and left the country before his work was complete.

Freire learned much from his students, colleagues and the political context during his time in Chile. What is certain is that 'Chile from 1964-70 endures as the engine room of Freirean intellectual history' (Austin 2003 66). If the Chilean poor learned how to read the world, Freire learned how to be a Marxist. This is clear from his seminal text, *Pedagogy of the Oppressed* (1970), written while in Chile, where his Marxist orientation is there for all to see, and which only became more pronounced in later work (Freire 1983). In the final pages of *Pedagogy of the Oppressed*, he maintains that liberation lies in workers becoming 'owners of their own labour' for the 'authentic transformation of reality' (Freire 1970 164), and where anything else is 'palliative solutions' (1970 164).

Not Always a Marxist

While Freire's early writing: *Education: the Practice of Freedom* (1974) shows signs of Marxist influences, notably through references to Erich Fromm and the radical psychoanalytic movement, combining Marx and Freud, the other influential work he cites in *Education: the Practice of Freedom* is very much *contra* Marx. These critiques of Marxism include the virulent anti-Marx of Zevedei Barbu (1914-93); Karl Jaspers (1883-1969) who had, it was claimed, an irrational hatred for Marx, and Karl Popper (1902-94) for whom Marxism was an unfalsifiable non-science. Other anti-Marxists cited were Mounier (1905-50), whose concept of 'personalism' attempted to provide an alternative political vision to liberalism and Marxism, regarding the person as the main reality-principle; and Seymour Martin Lipset (1922-2006), who was not so much anti-Marx as filled with a desire to prove Marx wrong. Lipset pointed out that the socialist revolution had failed to take place in the US, refuting Marx's claim that revolution will occur in the most technologically advanced countries.

One of the most significant influences on Paulo Freire was Simone Weil (1909-43). While an anti-Marxist, her work very much affirmed the dignity of labour, and in ways that make a very direct connection to higher education:

> Large factories would be abolished. A big concern would be composed of an assembly shop connected with a number of little workshops, each containing one or more workmen, dispersed throughout the country. It would be these same workmen, and not specialists, who would take it in turns to go and work for a time in the central assembly shop, and there ought to be a holiday atmosphere about such occasions. Only half a day's work would be required, the rest of the time being taken up with hobnobbing with others similarly engaged, the development of feelings of loyalty to the concern, technical demonstrations showing each workman the exact function of the parts he makes and the various difficulties overcome by the work of others, geography lectures pointing out where the products they help to manufacture go to, the sort of human beings who use them, and the type of social surroundings, daily existence or human atmosphere in which these products have a part to play, and how big this part is. To this could be added general cultural information. *A workman's university would be in the vicinity of each central assembly shop.* It would act in close liaison with the management of the concern, but would not form part of the latter's property.
> (Weil 2003 73-4, my emphasis)

Weil has an ambivalent approach to Marx and Marxism, in some ways similar to readings of Ranciére. She congratulates

Marx on having provided 'a first-rate account of the mechanism of capitalist oppression; but so good that one finds it hard to visualise how this mechanism could cease to function' (Weil 2013 39). Her main point is that Marx provides no clue as to how that subordination can be overcome, in which the working class is nothing but 'a passive instrument of production' (2013 19). Weil's prescription, like Ranciére's in *The Philosopher and His Poor*, is to make:

the individual, and not the collectivity, the supreme value. We want to form whole men by doing away with the specialisation that cripples us all. We want to give to manual labour that dignity that belongs to it as of right...by placing it in contact with the world through the medium of labour... to give back to man, that is to say to the individual the power which it is his proper function to exercise over nature, over tools, over society itself; to re-establish the importance of the workers as compared with material conditions of work.

And quoting Marx back to himself...'by transforming the means of production...which at present serve above all to enslave and exploit labour, into mere instruments of labour freely and co-operatively performed' (Weil 2013 18), all of which is characterised by 'the unity of mental and intellectual labour' (2013 20).

While Freire's early work was grounded in some anti-Marxist literature, his later work, as we shall see, was to take on a much more Marxist standpoint. This is clear from his concluding remarks at the end of the *Pedagogy of the Oppressed*, where he affirms the power of organised labour, as a foundation for his work in Africa and Brazil, and in later writings reflecting on his life's work. He left Chile in 1969 to take up the role of Head of the Council of Churches in Geneva and before Salvador Allende, the first democratically elected Marxist president, took office in

1970. Before further exploring Freire's work it is worth tracing the political developments in Chile after Freire left, as they clearly demonstrate the emergence of a political project that frames one of the central antagonisms of this book: neoliberalism.

From Pinochetism to Thatcherism

If Freire had walked into an already existing progressive literacy campaign in Chile, it intensified after he left the country in 1969. The newly-elected Marxist government of Salvador Allende, 1970-73, set up the National Workers Education Campaign with literacy established as a key principle on the way towards socialism, with workers and *campesinos*, including women and indigenous peoples, at the centre of social transformation, all of whom were recognised as 'a protagonist in a process of revolutionary change in society' (Austin 2003 139). This was to be part of a 'transition from an economic subject to a political subject, of re-appropriating an education with the goal of transforming it into the education of a popular historical project' (2003 132). Adult literacy was now 'a potentially revolutionary weapon' (Austin 2003 xxxii). This was part of Allende's much wider programme of educational reform in Chile, including the democratisation of teaching; a state system of formal schooling, the National Unified School; a policy to eradicate poverty among children and making universities more accessible. In all of this the elimination of literacy was key, in ways that are linked to other transformations of society and the state; and, particularly, 'sensitising students to the role of productive labour in the revolutionary transformation of a socialist society' (2003 137).

It is not possible to know what might have been achieved if the programme had been allowed to proceed, but it was violently shut down following the Military Coup on 9 September 1973, led by General Augusto Pinochet. Many of those involved in the educational programmes were persecuted, tortured and assassinated by the new regime of state terror (Austin 2003).

The military dictatorship replaced the National Workers Education Campaign with a programme of educational reform based on an authoritarian approach to education and literacy limited to instrumental and functional employment skills, reinforcing uncritically gender and ethnic stereotypes, based on the domestication of women, consumerism, individualism and religious themes. The colleges and universities were 'purified': subjected to militarised occupation with directors of adult education sacked and replaced with military junta appointments. In all of this the role of the state appeared to be reduced, as part of a privatising, marketised regime, in what came to be known as the first neoliberal experiment in social engineering (Taylor 2006). The military junta introduced their own national literacy campaign in 1976, recuperating the language of freedom and self-discovery, but within a framework of free-market economics. Trained teachers were replaced by volunteers, and relationships between teachers and students were now formalised around 'learning contracts' and education technology, with a talking up of the advantages of distance learning. The result was 'the collapse of all that had been achieved' under Frei, Freire and Allende (Austin 2003 219).

The neoliberal model has now been adopted by countries around the world, and particularly in the UK for education and other forms of social engineering. What has come to be known as Thatcherism should actually be referred to as Pinochetism.

In other work I have explored the politics of Salvador Allende as a source of inspiration for the student movement in Chile (Simbuerger and Neary 2015).

Africa

In 1975 Freire was invited to Guinea-Bissau by Luis Cabral, the brother of Amilcar Cabral (1924-73) the Marxist revolutionary and national guerrilla leader. Amilcar Cabral set up the African Party for the Independence of Guinea and Cape Verde (Partido

Africano de Independencia do Guine e Cabo Verde – PAIG)
in 1956. He led the war of liberation against the Portuguese
colonial power, during which time he became the de facto leader
of the parts of the country that his guerrilla army occupied
during the conflict (Chabal 2002). Amilcar Cabral was clear
about the importance of education and other social factors for
the revolution: 'With hospitals and schools we can win the
war' (Chabal 2002 114). Cabral viewed education as 'a political
weapon and teachers as important political actors in the struggle
to achieve liberation' (Chabal 2002 117). A system of education
provision was established, 'organised around the principles
of student participation, responsibility and productive work'
(Chabal 2002 117). The provision of a progressive education
programme was an important part of the new government's
strategy for nation-building. Cabral was assassinated in 1973
only months before Guinea-Bissau and Cape Verde declared
their independence from Portugal.

Freire wrote a book about his experiences in Guinea-Bissau:
Pedagogy in Process: The Letters to Guinea-Bissau (2016). Once
again, in this book, we see the importance he attached to the
process of dialogical learning:

> In defining what should be known must count on the
> involvement of the learners as part of the plan. This means
> that the dialogic relation, as a seal of the act of knowing,
> between active teachers and learners is not the result of
> some objective of learning proposed by the professor to the
> learners but arises in response to the definition of what needs
> to be known.
> (Freire 2016 92)

What is so significant about this book with regard to my claim
that Freire's work is influenced by Marx is that the capitalist

process of production is central to the dialogical pedagogic event, now framed with regard to education and literacy within a 'total plan for society' (2016 5). For Freire the revolutionary transformation of society: [It]...demands increased production. At the same time it requires a reorientation of production through a new concept of distribution. A high degree of political clarity must underlie any discussions of what to produce, how to produce it, for what and for whom is it to be produced' (2016 9). As Freire went on to elaborate: 'It implies the reorganisation of the means of production and the involvement of workers in a specific form of education through which they are called to become more skilled than production workers, through an understanding of the process of work itself' (2016 9).

Key to all of this in 1975-6 was the plan to integrate school activities with forms of productive labour, combining work and study to bring about a unity of theory and practice; and, in so doing, not just teach workers employment skills, but an understanding of the process of production itself, so to educate a revolutionary society of workers:

If production is governed by the well-being of the total society, rather than by the capitalist, private industry or the state, then the accumulation of capital – indispensable to development – has a totally different significance and goal. The part of the accumulated capital that is not paid to the worker is not taken from him but is his quota toward the development of the collectivity. And what is to be produced with this quota are not goods defined as necessarily saleable but goods that are socially necessary. For this it is essential that a society reconstruct itself in a revolutionary manner if it intends to be a society of workers...'
(2016 94)

The literacy project in Guinea-Bissau was a failure. Bowers

(2007) accused Freire of a crass lack of cultural sensitivity in his work, without reference to the traditions and customs of Guinea-Bissau. Bowers argues his teaching methods were based on a westernised understanding of the independent autonomy of the student framed around an acceptance of classical liberal theory, which is itself the product of a particular form of industrial society. The narrow understanding of learning and knowledge takes no account of different forms of learning and knowledge, which are rooted in community and custom and the tradition of populations in the non-westernised 'third world' (Bowers 2007). Linda Harasim argues the failure was due to a lack of trained teachers in Freire's methods and the absence of the high-level support needed for teachers, as well as the fact that the peasants were being taught to read and write in Portuguese rather than their own indigenous languages; nor was there the political motivation among the peasants to support Freire's 'ideological and pedagogical populism' (Harasim in Kirkendall 2010 110, Harasim 1983). The decision to use Portuguese rather than Creole was seen as one of the main reasons why the literacy programme failed. It is worth noting that Freire had 'always advocated teaching the working vocabulary of the students themselves' (Kirkendall 2010 111). On a wider canvas, the success of the war of liberation did not develop into a strong framework for the regulation of the new nation-state. The failure of the literacy campaign must be seen in these geo-political terms (Kirkendall 2010).

Nevertheless, the project points to the level of ambition that is necessary for revolutionary teaching – as a general form of non-state centric political settlement: not just teaching and learning, but a new form of society, taking into account the specificity of a culture to be maintained, but also the reactionary universalism of capital which needs to be overcome.

Back Home: Brazil

Paulo Freire returned to Brazil in 1980 after spending 16 years in exile. Following his return he worked with other leftist academics, politicians, trade unionists and activists to establish the Workers Party (*Partido dos Trabalhadores*: PT), a grassroots democratic political movement that emerged as the main opposition to the military dictatorship. The first elections after the end of the dictatorship were held in 1985 with the Workers Party being eventually voted into power in 2002/3 under the leadership of President Luis Lula. Freire became Secretary of Education in Sao Paulo, where in 1989 he set up a national education programme based on his ideas (O'Cadiz et al 1998).

The project was to establish the Popular Public School. Key to this approach was to 'break from the politics of grandiose campaigns, isolated pedagogical experimentalism, or formulaic solutions to the problems of public schooling' (1998 28). The approach to education was based on Freire's pioneering work around the concept of *conscientizacao*, from lessons learned from the history of the promotion of Popular Education in Latin America and the Workers Party's own socialist policies for workers and the poor, including formal and non-formal approaches to education.

An important aspect of the vision for the Popular School (*Escola Publica Popular*) was the *Movement for the Reorientation of the Curriculum* (MRC). The MRC was based on a Freirean programme of 'interdisciplinarity, generative themes, critical consciousness and democratisation of education' (1998 1) with a new vision for the public school and its role in society, as a social movement in schools linked with other social movements in Brazilian civil society.

The point and purpose of the MRC and PT (Workers Party) was 'not to immediately dismantle the bourgeois-capitalist state but to construct a Popular Democratic Government that can begin to seek viable alternatives to the existing capitalist social formation and now defunct models of anti-democratic socialism' (1998 25). Note well, this strategy is much more than about teaching and learning, but is concerned with education at the level of political society.

The aims of this programme were to increase access to schooling, democratise decision making, improve the quality of teaching, provide education for young people who work as well as adults, and to develop 'critical and responsible citizens' (O'Cadiz et al 1998 72). At the core of this political/education programme was the desire to empower students and teachers for the benefit of poor and working-class communities. The education system that Freire and the PT inherited from the military dictatorship was characterised as having high levels of failure, low enrolment, high drop-out rates and was under resourced, all of which pointed to a deteriorating public education system. The Popular Public School project aimed to dismantle the structures of power and privilege that had been erected by the former military regime, including programmes of national developmentalism as well as the 'slavocratic' empire of the colonial period (O'Cadiz et al 1998 80). Under the new scheme schools would be democratised through the creation of a school council, representing all of the interests within the school; this enhanced democratic approach meant, for example, that the school principal was to be elected.

In line with the politics of the project, MRC was not presented as an already prescribed programme, but, rather, as a framework to critically evaluate teaching and learning in schools and colleges. The approach was exemplified by the Interdisciplinary Project (Inter Project): an attempt to create a 'new pedagogic paradigm' to democratise school decision making, through critical dynamic reflective professional practice based on teachers' activities (O'Cadiz et al 1998 107). This approach was based on a theoretical and practical educational framework that had been developed in Brazil and elsewhere in Latin America by

Freire and other radical educators. The approach was based on the collective construction of curriculum through participatory decision making, while respecting the autonomy of schools based on already existing 'valid practices and local experiences' (O'Cadiz et al 108).

Each school and college was to engage with the project in the following way: get involved with the Inter Project scheme or devise their own programme; establish the local context within which they are working; study the reality of the school; decide on the school's generative theme or organising principles; agree the content of the curriculum as well as the methods arising out of the generative themes; and then design activities and exercises through which students applied the knowledge they had produced.

The Interdisciplinary Project (IP) presents Student as Producer with a fully-functioning working model for how revolutionary teachers teach, so it is worth giving it some detailed attention.

At the heart of the IP programme lay some core principles: the reconceptualisation of the knowledge-making process, a redefinition of the content included in the school curriculum and how the content is used, the transformation of the relationship between teachers and students, as well as a radical change in the role played by schools in the lives of its students and local communities, so that 'teachers and students engage in a mutual exchange of knowledge and understandings based around their socio-cultural reality' (O'Cadiz et al 1998 129). The curriculum was to be developed using Freire's concept of 'generative themes' grounded in the everyday life of students and teachers, within an interdisciplinary framework, not simply that knowledge production is collective and inter-related, nor even how to diminish the rigid boundaries between different subjects; but, rather, from a more critical perspective about how and for whose interests knowledge is produced. The intention was to replace the deteriorating education system with a process of knowledge production where power relations have been liberated and new ways of knowing have been established for the radical transformation of society. A major aspect of this approach was the promotion of interdisciplinarity, which becomes the 'substitution of a fragmented science for a unified Science' (1998 89), in what was to be 'a "multifaceted" view of the totality of our reality' (1998 89). The key for this approach to education is to find the structuring principles, generalised procedures and 'unifying principles' that are valid in all sciences, and the arts and humanities, and not only for the natural sciences (1998 117). This approach to curriculum development has a strong theoretical underpinning that 'incorporates critical theory in the development of a "critical science of the curriculum"' (1998 89).

In a very Freirean flourish this process is presented in PT-MSE documentation as 'a dynamic and permanent act of knowledge centred in the discovery, analysis and transformation of reality by those who live it' (O'Cadiz et al 1998 90). Where the relationship between the student and teacher is now expressed as a 'dialogical relationship', as well as being democratic and co-operative, providing the opportunity for teachers and students to learn from each other. These relationships were to be supported by a process of teacher professional development in a way that impacts on the development of policy formation by drawing on teachers' knowledge and experience: 'as a learning process and the collaborative construction of knowledge among students and teachers' (1998 99).

The project ended in 1992 when the Democratic Socialist Party (PDS), a conservative political party that came from the political wing of the dictatorship (1965-79), won the local municipal elections. The PDS replaced Freire's model of the Popular Public School based on the principles of the pedagogy of the oppressed with a neoliberal version of Total Quality Control of school education in the interests of employers and capitalism. The work done by the Freire's education reforms can claim successes, but its outcomes are the product of the enormous challenges it faced. The assessment by O'Cadiz et al (1998) is written in a way that avoids 'grand conclusions' (1998 233) and from the standpoint of the teachers. Teachers felt that 'the fact they could introduce their own texts and materials to teach their own curriculum was a major liberating experience for many teachers, even those who resisted the Project's more political purposes' (132-3). Teachers developed a higher sense of creativity as reflective practitioners. No significant or enduring changes were achieved, but even when reforms were poorly or not completely implemented, they did give students, teachers and administrators 'the opportunity to reflect on and transform the nature of their individual and collective reality' (1998 133).

In statistical terms there was an almost 10 per cent rise in pupil retention rates between 1989 and 1991 and a 12 per cent rise in student enrolment at the primary level. There was an improvement in teachers' pay and working conditions, with teachers who worked with poor students in *favelas* and inner-city areas receiving extra pay, up to 50 per cent of their salary, although still not high by international standards.

The programme was presented not as a template, but as a general framework with organising principles for educators to consider. There were, as you might expect, ideological objections to the scheme, but it did not require teachers to favour a left-wing political position for them to be a part of the project. It did unleash a large amount of requests for material support and other resources that the state education administration found overwhelming, and some teachers wanted to be told what it was they had to teach: 'to have the curriculum handed to them in a ready to teach fashion, which went against the Project's very principles' (1998 239). There was the problem of combining democracy with bureaucracy and ensuring administrative efficiency, and there was some resentment against the left-wing character of the project, especially in well-resourced schools.

Other teachers and administrators felt it was too ambiguous and that there needed to be more of a basic structure communicated to teachers. O'Cadiz et al 1998 tell us that it was not easy trying to construct a curriculum around a non-didatical model for teaching when this is what staff had been used to all of their professional lives. And, some subjects were more able to do this approach than others, e.g., history and geography, rather than maths. Some teachers felt that there was a tendency to focus on the problems of everyday life, which can be a bit miserable. Taking all of this together, the project was plagued by superficial and reduced understandings of what was at stake. Other teachers saw a transformation in their professional identity, becoming producers of knowledge with their students:

> We know of some teachers that underwent a radical change in terms of their attitude towards their students. They always transmitted knowledge in a structured manner, suddenly they experienced a dismantling of that structure and perceived that this authoritarian method of simply transmitting subject matter had nothing to do with educating…that it was necessary to hear the student, that the student also brought knowledge.
>
> (1998 244)

This review of the IP project is very interesting as it fits with some of the findings of Student as Producer at Lincoln, even if Student as Producer is on a much smaller scale (Neary et al 2015). While there was a positive attitude by academics and students to Student as Producer at Lincoln some colleagues wanted more explanation and instruction about the theory and practice of Student as Producer and others were unhappy about its left-wing orientation (Neary et al 2015).

An important lesson for revolutionary teachers is that there is another level of struggle: not just at the level of the institution but at the state level, so we need a theory of not just power but a theory of the state, including the questions what are the limits and possibilities of state reform, and how to get beyond the state? As well as a recognition of the need to engage with other social movements outside education institutions and to learn from them, even when there is 'a conflictual dialogue among educators, learners and communities' (O'Cadiz et al 246). A very important lesson then is not to be afraid of the dynamic conflicts – they are the motors of change. For Freire, it is necessary 'to remain aware of tensions, not only as a safeguard for democratic practice but also because such an outlook is necessary for building co-operative and participatory democratic alliances' (1998 24). But let us be clear, this was a landmark educational project, so we can gain strength from the fact that a public revolutionary education programme is possible as the basis for a new politics of education to build on and develop.

The key issue here is that revolutionary teaching needs to be part of a movement at the level of society, and not simply the result of teachers in the classroom attempting to change the world, and that revolutionary teaching needs to be linked to other radical social movements and joined up politics.

Pedagogy of Hope

At the end of his career, Freire gets to revisit his earlier work. In *Pedagogy of Hope*, written in 1992/2017, he looked back on the assumptions of his most seminal text, *Pedagogy of the Oppressed*.

Pedagogy of the Oppressed was a book of its time, written during great social upheaval and colonial struggles, in Latin America and Africa. In *Pedagogy of Hope* (2017) he is still committed to critical pedagogy by which he means where 'the object of knowledge is the very act of learning' (2017 70), where 'the professor teaches the student to learn' (2017 70), in a process where 'educands become ever more critical subjects' (2017 71) driven by the curiosity of teachers and students. There is much idealist thinking in *Pedagogy of Hope*, with hope itself described as an 'ontological need' on which to base class struggle (2017 3) written in 'rage and love' (2017 4).

While Freire has a critical view of dogmatic Marxism, as well as all forms of authoritarianism, the work is still firmly grounded in the theoretical Marxism that he developed in *Pedagogy of the Oppressed*, where the oppressed is a class issue, derived out of class struggle, within a framework of the capitalist social relations of production. The book's reference list is very Marxist: Karl Marx, Agnes Heller, Gyorgy Luckas, Erich Fromm, Jean Paul Sartre, Karl Kosik and Antonio Gramsci, as well as others who were engaged critically with Marxism on the topic of labour, Simone Weil, Hannah Arendt, and colonialism, Frantz Fanon and Maurice Merleau-Ponty. Freire sees social transformation in ways that are profoundly Marxist, as the result of social and economic struggle carried out between classes, and more than that: struggle is 'a historical and not metaphysical, category' (2017 33) in the context of 'a certain socio-economic, political system – gotten to an understanding of the social relations of production, gotten to an understanding of class interests and so on' (2017 40), which can be considered in culture circles and group discussion.

Freire is strong on the notion that the working class 'continue to learn, in the very practice of their struggle, to set limits to their concessions – in other words, that they teach the dominant classes the limits within which they themselves may move' (2017 82-3). Indeed, 'relationships between classes are a political fact, which generates class knowledge and that class knowledge has the most urgent need of lucidity and discernment when choosing the best tactics to be used. These tactics vary in concrete history, but must be in consonance with strategic objectives' (2017 83), so that, 'to say that socialism lies pulverised in the rubble of the Berlin Wall, is something in which I, for my part, do not believe' (2017 83).

For Freire, Marx is relevant now and needs to be recovered: 'reseen' (2017 79). To say, as Freire does, that the class struggle is not the motor of history does not mean that class struggle is not important, rather not to reduce human behaviour as 'a pure reflex of socio-economic structures' (2017 80). He goes on to say 'it is impossible to understand history without social classes, without their interests in collision. The class struggle is not *the* mover of history, but is certainly one of them' (2017 81), which includes dreaming for socialism, even: 'Dreaming is not only a necessary political act, it is an integral part of the historico-social manner of being a person' (2017 81). Dreaming the end of authoritarian regimes 'is a kind of ode to freedom, and which....offers us the extraordinary, if challenging, opportunity to continue *dreaming* and fighting for the socialist *dream*, purified of its authoritarian distortions, its totalitarian repulsiveness, its sectarian blindness' (2017 86). This is a critical rather than dogmatic Marx as the basis for his 'political pedagogy' (2017 87), or even a form of political cosmology: 'Class struggle is a historical category, and therefore has historicity. It changes from space-time to space-time' (2017 83).

The limit of Freire's Marxism is that this is very much a democratic socialist project, by which workers take ownership of the means of production, but the law of labour itself is not transformed in any practical or even theoretical way. There is nothing in Freire on the value-form. Like Benjamin, Freire is not dialectical enough, i.e., there is no way of expounding the heat of class struggle or the way that labour melts.

And what of the University and higher education? He describes the University as the 'circle of knowledge' (2017 180) in a manner that mirrors the Humboldtian model for higher education:

The circle of knowledge has but two moments, in permanent relationship with each other: the moment of the cognition of existing, already produced, knowledge, and the moment of our own production of new knowledge. While insisting on the impossibility of mechanistically separating either moment from the other – both are moments of the same circle. I think it is important to bring out the fact that the moment of our cognition of existing knowledge is by and large the moment of instruction, the moment of the teaching and learning of content; while the other, the moment of the production of new knowledge, is, in the main, that of research. But actually, all instruction involves research, and all research involves instruction. There is no genuine instruction in whose process no research is performed by way of question, investigation, curiosity, creativity: just as there is no research in the course of which researchers do not learn – after all, by coming to know, they learn, and after having learned something, they communicate it, they teach. The role of any university, progressive or conservative, is to immerse itself, utterly seriously, in the moment of this circle. The role of a university is to teach, to train, to research.

(2017 180)

Freire develops these ideals more concretely in the book about higher education based on his Marxist understanding of class: *Paulo Freire on Higher Education: A Dialogue at the National University of Mexico.* The book was written by Miguel Escobar, Alfredo L Fernandez, Gilberto Guevara-Niebla with Paulo Freire in 1994.

Freire argues the university cannot be the revolution, which can only be made outside of the formal institutions of education. This raises profound questions about the nature of revolutionary teaching and its relationship to already existing institutions, challenging us to reinvent the university as a transitional institution for revolutionary science.

He is clear: 'the university cannot be the vanguard of any

revolution: this is not the nature of the institution. Like the church' (1994 62). And, key to all of this, is the question of science and knowledge and how it is produced, leading to the practical and theoretical problem of how to create a revolutionary 'Freirean epistemology' (1994 121).

Freire proposes an academy at the level at which the working classes are operating, whereby they 'must take their own alienation into their own hands, questioning themselves about alienation' (1994 55).

Freire considers this in terms of a transitional pedagogy. Here he is speaking about a society in transition to revolution and the role of education to create an ideology that fits the revolutionary situation as part of a movement for revolutionary transition: 'the new, revolutionary education does not yet exist, and cannot exist' (1994 42); but, one thing is for sure: bourgeois education is no longer acceptable as it has nothing to do with the new revolutionary society. So not a revolutionary pedagogy; rather, a 'transition pedagogy' (1994 42). But how to construct this within formal rather than non-formal institutional structures; this is a key question for Student as Producer and revolutionary teachers.

Freire has important things to say about understanding Marx in a Marxist manner that are both dialectical and historical. He argues against taking power and in favour of reinventing power through a reconsideration of the nature of political parties, linked to social movements: '...one of the basic themes of the end of the century is not the issue of taking power in itself, as much as the reinvention of power, and this includes the dialectical comprehension of the role of political parties' (1994 40). This is close to Holloway's notion of how to change the world without taking power (2002). Holloway argued that the revolution was not the proletariat taking control of the state, but labour abolishing the social relations out of which the capitalist had been derived to establish a new form of communist social wealth.

Like Ranciére, popular education and political education is

emerging out of social movements...it is 'necessary to look beyond and discover the intimacy and the dynamics of those movements (women, gay rights, ecology in 1970s), the appearance of a new popular education. To a great extent the new popular education, the politics of this education, are being born in those movements and not in our seminars and our books' (1994 39). So revolution is not possible through education 'education is not the lever of transformation, of revolution, and yet, revolution is pedagogic' (1994 34).

Freire reminds us of the danger of recuperation, telling us he no longer used the word 'conscientization' after 1987, by which he means not giving up what lies behind the activation and understanding of the process but certainly the word itself (Freire 1994 46). While, all of the time, alongside the risk of recuperation is the possible 'joy' of being 'authenticated' (1994 49) by the way in which historical events unfold.

Lessons from Freire for the Revolutionary Teacher

Freire is identified in the book as a sophisticated social theorist, and one who regarded Marxism and the theory of class struggle and the power of labour as a fundamental aspect of social revolution. He was a major figure in the development of literacy programmes around the world, based not on reading the world but transforming the world. His approach to teaching was dialogical rather than dictatorial. Freire did not theorise labour as a real abstraction, choosing to deliver a motivating message through more idealist abstraction, e.g, the pedagogy of *hope*. I shall elaborate on the power of the idea of hope when read through a materialist version of the labour theory of value (Dinerstein 2014). The powerful message from Freire is to take the theory and practice of revolutionary teaching outside of the classroom and to use it to formulate educational policy to challenge the capitalist state, until the moment when the capitalist state withers away. He shows the importance of operating at the local and national state and internationally, linked always to the classroom in a way that is sensitive to the context. He reminds us of the dangers of recuperation and to always remember the violence and brutality of the capitalist state. And, finally, the need for a new form of social institution based on a reinvention of the concept and practice of power and its relationship to knowledge: not the university, but a notion of higher education that reinvents the link between research and teaching.

Although Freire does not theorise his concept of hope in terms of a new reading of Marx it is possible to consider the relationship between hope and the value-form in terms of the kind of historical materialist analysis suggested by Student as Producer. Ana Dinerstein (2014) adds substance to the claim that 'autonomy is politically relevant as the art of organising hope' by linking hope and the 'not-yet', a concept she gets from Ernest Bloch and the value-form (2014 204). Dinerstein's conceptual revolution and the foundation for her concept of what she refers to as prefiguration is to make a clear practical political link between the value-form and hope. She substantiates her theoretical exposition with reference to empirical case studies, which include Argentinian experiences of dignified work and the movement of popular justice in Argentina in 2001/2; a review of the Zapatistas' armed uprising in Chiapas, Mexico, challenging and reinventing revolutionary traditions in the 1990s and an account of indigenous popular movements in Bolivia in 2004-5. She refers to this theorisation within practice as 'non-facticity' (2014 207), as 'the key to grasp the process of prefiguration and the nature of excess produced by the politics of autonomy' (2014 207). In capitalist production surplus value is generated through the imposition of a particular labour process. This surplus value can only be realised in the future, when the quantity of abstract social labour is confirmed in exchange of commodities for money. The value-form constitutes capitalist society but always in a way that is not-yet. While the purpose of this process is the production of surplus value, another as yet unrealised outcome is the social movement of struggles or 'anti-value in motion', or 'doing' as human creativity 'in the form of being denied'. Human doing constitutes the basis of a concrete utopia but it is always in the form of the not-yet. In this sense value and hope exist as 'unrealised materialities' (2014 209). 'They are both mysterious' (2014 209). As she puts it: 'Value requires to be socially validated and attains concreteness only through the form of money. Hope is an emotion of the cognitive kind that guides action and is materialised in concrete utopia' (2014 209).

Freire, together with a critique of the law of value, makes a powerful analytical device for the revolutionary teacher, and part of the foundations for an institution or non-institution grounded in revolutionary teaching.

Paula Allman: Revolutionary Teacher in the Classroom

Paula Allman (1944-2011) was an academic, activist, teacher and Marxist scholar who sought to develop a revolutionary education practice in post-compulsory education as part of a global movement for communism. She has been described as 'one of the best critical education scholars on the planet' (McLaren Foreword xviii Allman 2010).

Born in Chicago in 1944, she came to the UK in the 1970s to take up a post-doctoral fellowship at the University of Nottingham, after having been awarded her PhD from Florida Atlantic University for work on Jean Piaget, the liberal-humanist psychologist. Her specific area of expertise was the education of adults and lifelong learning (Cunnane 2011). Her interest in Marx and the critical pedagogy of Paulo Freire and Antonio Gramsci developed after coming to England where she was inspired and motivated by her students, her experience as a classroom teacher and her political activism (Allman 1983). This commitment to revolutionary theory went on to provide the basis for her revolutionary teaching practice, her writing, publishing and editorial work. Allman saw herself as an academic activist involved with creating alternative policies for radical education. She had connections with the left-leaning Institute for Education Policy Studies and was a member of *Red Chalk*, a group of prominent radical educators, including Peter McLaren, Glenn Rikowski, Caroline Benn, Dave Hill and Mike Cole. In addition, she was the first co-chairperson for the Nottingham Campaign for Nuclear Disarmament and a member of the education subgroup of The Socialist Movement.

Paula wrote her theory of revolutionary education through a systematic reading of the work of Karl Marx – including key political and historical texts, as well as his major works on critical political economy. She read this work alongside the writings of two iconic figures in Marxist critical education, Paulo Freire (1921-97) and Antonio Gramsci (1891-1937). What is distinctive about Allman's work is the way in which she brought her theoretical expositions to life in her own actual teaching practice: through a philosophy of 'critical/revolutionary praxis' in the classroom (Allman 2010 167).

She published three substantive books on Karl Marx's social theory and critical pedagogy: *On Marx: An Introduction to the Revolutionary Intellect of Karl Marx* (2007); *Revolutionary Social Transformation: Democratic Hopes, Political Possibilities and Critical Education (2001)*, and *Critical Education Against Global Capitalism: Karl Marx and Revolutionary Critical Education* (2010).

The *Introduction to the Revolutionary Intellect* book is a primer to Marx's work, setting out clearly, 'the real genius of Marx's thought' (2007) against ideas that have been erroneously attributed to him by traditional versions of Marx and writing that is antagonistic to his work, with a focus on capital and capitalism, consciousness and education.

Her teaching style was not a dry translation of Marx's

greatest works in the classroom. She had been a swimming teacher and wanted to infuse learning with joy, humour, fun and light-heartedness, as well as with a 'love for humanity' (Allman 2010 187), not possessive love but a profound love, enabling her students 'to be more fully human' (2010 188).

Her overall aim was to create 'authentic social transformation' (Allman 2001 1) for 'socialism/communism' (2001 2), as she describes it, which she understood not as a blueprint for action or as a framework to impose her version of actually existing socialism/communism; but, critically and classically in Marxist terms, as 'the movement that abolishes the present state of things' (Marx 1846 13); and, abundantly, for a communism defined as, following Marx, 'from each according to his [her] ability, to each according to his [her] need' (2001 23). For Allman these revolutionary principles of critique and abundance are present within the current conditions of capitalist society, but have not yet emerged as an alternative generalised social form.

A distinctive feature of her writing is that it is based on a close reading of 'what Marx actually said' (Allman 2001 29), so as to provide a reading 'without interruptions' (Allman 2010 3) across the range of Marx's published work: *The Communist Manifesto, The Gotha Programme*, four volumes of *Capital* as well as *Resultate* and *The Grundrisse*. Taken together her work sets out a challenging encounter with Marx's social theory in the context of critical education studies. Allman's work reminds us that a key lesson for the revolutionary teacher is to study the original texts. Allman's early writing on Marx is informed by a range of Marxisms, both orthodox and humanist, although her later work makes strong connections to the version of value-form theory that informs Student as Producer. I shall argue that her later work does not shake off the limitations of these orthodox and humanist assumptions. Nevertheless her later Marxism has much to offer in relation to other value-form theorists and subversive Marxist scholars. This milieu of value-form theorists that inspire her work is not a formal group, but they are sometimes defined as 'capital relation' theorists or Open Marxists, providing a 'new reading of Marx' or 'value-critique' theory (Neary 2017a). This is the reading of Marx from which the theory and practice of Student as Producer is derived. These theorists include Isaak I Rubin (1886-1937), Roman Rosdolsky (1898-1967) and from among contemporary theorists, including Simon Clarke, Werner Bonefeld, John Holloway, Ana Dinerstein, Robert Kurz and Moishe Postone.

Her interpretation of the essential aspect of the value-from approach, in contradistinction to mainstream Marxism, is that the organising principle of capital is not that its economic base supports a complex legal and ideological superstructure; but, rather, capital is interpreted as a theory of value-form, where the main categories of political economy, the commodity and money, as well as the categories of political jurisprudence, private property and the state, are forms of the capital-labour relation. The economistic base-superstructure reading of Marxism, which she is against, characterises capital as a series of external relations with a focus on alienation and exploitation of workers by bosses, enforced by a state apparatus that has been captured by political elites. Contrary to this orthodox approach, the value-form reading of capital looks for the internal or *inner* or immanent connections which lie inside the structures of capitalist society: commodities, money and the state, all of which can be derived from the inner structure of the commodity-form: the relation between use value and exchange value with which Marx begins his exposition of *Capital Volume 1* chapter 1 page 1.

A key expression of this unity of opposites is the capital-labour relation. This relation is inherently antagonistic, leading always and everywhere to struggle and resistance. It is the nature of capitalist process of production and the exploitation on which it is based that creates the on-going antagonism, or 'unity of opposites' (Allman 2010 39) between workers and their bosses.

Allman is keen to point out that this antagonism is not the result simply of competing class interests, but that class interest is itself a product of the capital-labour relation or the law of value, and, in this way, makes her own contribution to value-form theory. She stresses throughout that this is not an issue merely of ownership, but, rather, about the social relations of capitalist production. What is distinctive about her work is her attempt to break out of a 'traditional Marxism' based not on the politics of distribution and ownership but with a focus on the politics of production. For Allman the antagonism between capital and labour is not resolvable through the redistribution of resources, but depends on the abolition of the capital relation: 'not limited/ reproductive praxis but critical/revolutionary praxis' (Allman 2001 85). This key to transformation is the power of labour as the 'restless negatives' (Allman 2010 224), an expression she gets from the dissident Marxist, CLR James (2010 2 225 footnote 2).

Allman is particularly interested in the work of Moishe Postone, a key inspiration for Student as Producer, with whom she finds many affinities with her own scholarship. Writing through his work she wants to stress the significance of abstract labour as a dynamic movement of impersonal social domination and mediation out of which is derived the institutional forms of capitalist social life, e.g., money and the state. Like Postone, Allman works through Marx's exposition of the value-form, its abstract and concrete nature, to reveal the substance of value as abstract labour, measured by time for the purposes of valorisation: the expansion of capital. She traces the different forms through which valorisation is realised: absolute and relative value, the specificity of labour-power as a unique commodity that produces more than its own value as the basis for exploitation and surplus value accumulation, as well as the way in which money as the universal equivalent falls out of this process, historically and logically, as the universal equivalent through which value is realised in the process of exchange. She traces, after Marx, the move from formal to real subsumption to the point where capital in general is the basis for global capitalism. She is careful to emphasise the way in which capitalist wealth produces scarcity in a system of production that could meet human need and the needs of the environment if properly planned (Allman 2010). What is so helpful for the question of how revolutionary teachers teach is that Allman formulates her approach to critical education or revolutionary critical education, as she calls it, through value-form theory. Her work is also important because of the manner in which she seeks to develop a revolutionary theory of consciousness as a key issue for critical pedagogy, developed in what she refers to as 'Marx's...theory of consciousness' (Allman 2001 35). This raises an important question about how do Marxists consider their own role and function working within a capitalist form of higher education. However, as I shall show, there is a gap between her value-form theory and her theory of consciousness which undermines the power of her revolutionary teaching.

Critical Theory of Consciousness

A key point for Allman is that structures and institutions of capitalist society refer not only to money, the state and commodities, but to the nature of human life: being and consciousness itself. This theory of critical consciousness is a key issue for how revolutionary teachers teach.

As a psychologist, Allman is very interested in Marx's 'revolutionary theory of consciousness' (2010 5). In *Revolutionary Social Transformation* she frames this in relation to 'human consciousness and our need to understand how it is constituted and how it can be rendered more critical' (2001 2). She sets revolutionary consciousness alongside communication, as the need to 'strive to improve this ability to listen and to speak with both our hearts and our minds and to empathetically and systematically question what both we ourselves and others think' (2001 6), so as to be able to 'create social and economic justice on a global scale' (2001 8). Allman's revolutionary theory of consciousness is based on a method that she refers to as 'dialectical conceptualisation' (2001 61). She counterposes dialectical conceptualisation with bourgeois social science, which looks for ways to categorise things in groups, leading to a celebration of complexity, chaos and fetishised thought. She conceptualises the fetishism of knowledge as the basis for Marx's critical understanding of ideology, as the basis for our failure to understand the emancipatory potential of human life.

Allman recovers Marx's materialist theory of consciousness by making a clear connection between theory and action through which to develop critical/revolutionary praxis. For Allman, Marx's 'theory of consciousness is actually a theory of praxis – that is, a theory of the unity between thought and action' (Allman 2010 154), or a kind of critical practical activity that is self-conscious of the context in which practice takes place, so as to ensure revolutionary social transformation. In this case the production of knowledge is not detached from social reality, as it is in bourgeois social sciences, and reified into subject disciplines, all of which capture the fragmented nature of the world but fail to grasp the totality of the capital social relation out of which they have been derived (Allman 2010). Another key problem for Allman is ideology, which she argues distorts understandings about the dialectical nature of reality, as 'a defective way of thinking' and 'the opposite of science' (2010 42). The power of ideology is based on the power of fetishism, as if the power of things is gained from an innate quality of the thing itself separated from the social world, rather than things being derived out of a social process that can be transformed through human activity. She makes a link with Piaget's work which, she argues, 'comes close to being a psychological translation of Marx's theory of consciousness' (2010 153). She uses the example of the cognitive development of children, when, according to

Piaget, active learning becomes internalised in the mind of the child as a developing mental process.

For Allman, the purpose of revolutionary critical education is to overcome ideological thinking 'by developing the ability to dialectically conceptualise the world' (Allman 2010 156). This requires, Allman argues, a revolutionary theory of consciousness. She is concerned with the failure of resistance to capitalism, which, she argues, 'will go on so long as critical action for social transformation remains underdeveloped' (Allman 2001 80), and, therefore, the need, in this moment, to create the space for the emergence of the revolutionary teacher, to facilitate a revolutionary critical consciousness: 'some of those involved must have the critical understandings that will enable them to pose critical questions to the others at appropriate times' (2001 82), and that 'these people must initiate and engage in quite different, totally transformed educational relations… [which]…cannot be delivered "to" people or "for" people but only established with them' (2001 82).

Allman then goes on to justify this claim with an appeal to the very undialectical communitarian philosophy of Charles Taylor in his book *The Ethics of Authenticity* (1991) based on social justice and a moral and ethical framework. This is not the basis of revolutionary teaching, but is based on a strong appeal to liberal ideals.

She makes an important connection between the work of Paulo Freire and Antonio Gramsci. Freire, as I have done in this book, is considered in terms of his Marxism, although she does not elaborate on the nature of Freire's writing in relation to Marx's social theory. She wants to emphasise the condition of Freire's understanding of 'the oppressed' in class terms, as a restless negative against the oppressor (Allman 2001). She writes how Freire challenges the naive consciousness that sustains the rule of the oppressor, which can be countered by revolutionary teachers working to develop 'a critical dialectical consciousness, a critical praxis, but this pertains as much to the leaders or educators as it does to the people, even if the former have a "theoretical", conceptual and analytical head start' (2001 91). She stresses the basis of Freire's critical education as the humanisation of our species-being, drawing on Marx's early work based on 'the natural destiny of humankind' (2001 92). She tells us that this forms the basis of what Freire refers to as 'conscientisation'. This account of Freire's Marxism by Allman is not presented in relation to value-form theory or by emphasising the social form of labour in capitalist society.

A key point is that she stresses the significance of refunctioning the relationship between students and teachers, who in the current arrangement form a dialectical contradiction, through a dialogic relation that demonstrates commitment to each other in a way that generates trust. The revolutionary project is the struggle to establish the unity of the teacher-learner in each person, without relinquishing the authority of the teacher (Allman 2001). This can be done as the fundamental issue is not simply the relationship between student and teacher but their relationship to knowledge: therefore, revolutionary teaching becomes the reconnection of the act of acquiring knowledge with the act of producing knowledge. The key then is not simply the relation of the student and teacher to each other, but rather their relation to knowledge, as a radical epistemology, or a means by which we begin to learn, and the springboard for the creation of new knowledge or a deeper understanding of the world which we will need for 'revolutionary transformatory praxis' (2001 98). All this takes place through dialogue, as a form of collaborative communication based on a commitment to the question under review and to each other in a way that generates trust. Here the key question is not what we think, but is based on a critical question: *why* we think, as a way of problematising knowledge, and as a way of understanding 'ideological contamination' (2001 100). This is what Allman describes, after Freire, as a 'cultural revolution' (Allman 2001 101). This involves authority and leadership carried out by radical educators who work with and learn from the people, but not in an authoritarian way, including a recognition of the oppressor within ourselves. This cultural activity needs to be prefigurative: humanised, democratic and socialist. So, Allman claims Freire as a Marxist, not through a discussion of Freire's account of relationship between labour and capital, the labour debate, nor the value-form; rather, her reading of Freire's Marxism is based on an analysis of class struggle as a political power relation (Allman 2001).

Another strong influence on her work is Antonio Gramsci, from whom she gets her philosophy of praxis, a radical education project based on a dynamic reading of ideology as a way of understanding the structure of society as a project for radical transformation. In her early work Allman talks about 'organic intellectuals' (Allman 2001 112), a central idea of Gramscian teaching, where teacher-intellectuals emerge from out of the radical milieu of which they are already a part, but not in her later writing. Her work on Gramsci is less assured than her account of Freire, spending time dealing with the ambiguities in his work, providing her own explanation and justification. She wants to stress the similarities between the work of Freire and Gramsci, including the method of critical analysis that underpins Gramsci's work to establish a critical conception of the world. She points out the very similar understanding of the reciprocal relationship between student and teacher as the basis for a new theory of knowledge. She makes clear the political nature of Gramsci's project based on a commitment to the working class and through the formation of alliances with other social movements inspired by the example of worker councils and other democratic political parties of the working class. For Gramsci, and for Allman, the proletariat are the revolutionary class, along with others who 'could potentially be drawn into the capital-labour relation...[and thus]...potentially capable of creating a new form of society and thus bringing about the abolition of capitalism'(Allman 2010 213). She sees this in terms of a class relation, in opposition to capital 'to renew people's hopes for a socialist future and to also renew and re-energise their solidarity and commitment to struggle for that future with a greater strength in numbers than they have ever had in the past' (2010 224).

Allman wants to recover the concept of class as a way of connecting with millions of workers who, she maintains, now more than ever in human history, are subsumed within the capital-labour relation and the process of valorisation and, therefore, are capable of forming alliances against capital; as she puts it: 'never have the truly progressive forces for epochal change been greater' (Allman 2010 223). This is a powerful analysis but, due to its positive affirmation of the working class as the subject of revolution, misses the point of Postone's negative critique of labour.

What is required, she argues, is an international movement of critical educators imbued with the ethics of compassion and social justice, solidarity and informed by the philosophy of critical education. For Allman, this can be a real live prefigurative experience of struggle out of which to build a new social order.

What makes Allman's work so appealing for Student as Producer is that her sophisticated theoretical interpretation of Marx's society theory is grounded in her classroom teaching.

In the Classroom

A very important aspect of Allman's writings for Student as Producer is the way in which she connects her theoretical work with her own teaching practice in higher education. This approach to critical education aims to prepare her students to be able to shape and determine their own personal and social destinies collectively, critically and creatively, 'to be collectively and critically in control of their future conditions of existence rather than being determined by them' (Allman 2010 167), as well as embracing and internalising the principles that guide this approach, based on groups getting together 'focussed on an issue or a problem that was being widely experienced by themselves and others' (2010 169). The strength of critical revolutionary education, she argues, is that it offers 'an abbreviated experience of pro-alternative and counter-hegemonic social relations within which they [her students] can learn to read the world critically and glimpse humanity's possible future beyond the horizon of capitalism' (2010 203), enabling people to 'live the no' (2010 203), and, therefore, work together to establish 'a counter capitalist, pro-humanity form of worldwide togetherness' (2010 204).

Allman sets out very clearly the way in which she uses Freire's work as an inspiration for a teaching programme, a Diploma in Education, in the Department of Adult Education at Nottingham University. The account of her teaching practice on this programme is written from her memory and through critical reflection.

She is keen to emphasise that her approach to teaching is based on the work of Freire, which Allman had developed in her own way. The course was organised around the principles of coherence, authenticity, trust and honesty, which, she argues, need to be applied to the whole process of teaching.

The students she taught were generally working in public sector jobs, and other types of formal and informal education provision, including community and voluntary organisations, and they were from all over the world. The course was taught to full-time and part-time students, on a day release (for 2 years, part-time) and 2 days of the week (for one year, full-time).

The programme ran all day from 10.30-5.30. This included time for going to the library and for tutorials, dialogue, silent reflection, study circles, collective forward planning, as well as some flexible time, always keeping strictly to the timetable. The course included a field trip with an evaluation at the end of the course. There was a study weekend before the beginning of term two on Freire's philosophy of education, during which time learner-teachers did experience a 're-birth' (Allman 2010 184) enabling them to function as more effective teacher-learners.

One piece of work was a collective project, with a grade given to each member of the group. The first project was planning, organising and hosting a conference on 'Adult Education for Social Action'. This was successful, but she says it was too much work. In future she arranged less ambitious activities, e.g., group writing projects. She records that students felt this aspect of the course to be of great value. The course was supported by student and teacher reunions and newsletters.

She set up this course when she was a new member of staff and the only woman academic in the department. There were tensions with older and more conservative staff. She had support from students, evidenced by positive course evaluations. The course ran for 12 years. The number of students on the programme was limited to 20. The course selection process, carried out by individual interviews and group activities, was followed by a pre-course orientation day, where those selected could meet each other and sample the course, before the students made their final commitment to taking up a place on the programme. She justified the process and the programme in these terms:

The entire process is important...Freirean education cannot possibly work by imposition, and by this careful procedure from interview through pre-course orientation, we were doing as much as we possibly could to assure ourselves and the entire learning group that we were all committed, at least in principle, to trying to learn together in an alternative, unconventional and what we hoped would become a revolutionary way.

(2010 178)

The programme was based on a clear social science approach to education, but without too much theoretical difficulty. The work of the group was based on generative themes they developed themselves, which were then supported by relevant reading the teachers collected. This is a key task for the educators: what is chosen and why by the teachers must be made clear to the students. The themes were not predetermined; by generating themes together the students and teachers learned about each other.

The themes tended to be around 'community, education and disadvantage'. One theme became the focus for discussion each week, and was then supported by the readings to deepen their understanding. The purpose was 'to co-investigate the generative words and themes that constituted our curriculum' (Allman 2010 179). Each student was also a member of a study circle, decided on by teachers so no one gets left out. These study groups met at lunch and when they felt it necessary, and chose their own activities, for example, reading, or study visits or topics for discussion. The most important function of the study circle was to support each other's learning, giving the 'members of the study circle a collective sense of responsibility and interest in each other's work, thus breaking down the individuated and isolated way in which such work is usually produced' (2010 180).

Allman is keen to stress that they were not writing a curriculum together; it was not a negotiated curriculum:

Negotiated curricula...are something entirely different from the selection process we used. We were not simply trying to put together a syllabus that would hold some element of interest to everyone involved, or working out some sort of compromise that would be relevant to a particular group. We were trying to "read the world" critically and thus trying to come to a collective consensus about the themes that would

lead us to this critical understanding.
(Allman 2010 182)

She is clear, this is not based on a humanist psychology, e.g., Carl Rogers or Abraham Maslow, in the sense that it is not negotiated, rather it is prescriptive and directed, so that students can 'read the world critically':

It is prescriptive to say that the world needs transforming and that education must play a role in this. And Freirean educators must use the authority that comes from their own critical 'reading of the world' and their understanding of Freire's philosophy of education if they are to enable (and sometimes this involves direction) others also to engage in critical/revolutionary praxis. Of course, Freirean educators, because of their transformed relation to knowledge – their epistemological position – prescribe and direct with humility and with a spirit of mutuality that would be impossible to convey had they not undergone the necessary transformations. Therefore, when they prescribe and direct, they are doing so from the basis of an alternative philosophical position, and thus what they are doing cannot be equated with traditional or conventional modes of direction and prescription.
(Allman 2010 190)

And:

It also became clear to me that non-prescriptive and non-direction are impossible. They are even present, despite their purveyor's intent in the most facilitative, non-prescriptive, non-directive forms of progressive teaching because any form of laissez-faire or, for that matter, relativism is just another form of uncritical/reproductive praxis. No matter how unintentional, this is a prescription for domestication –

that is, educating people to accept and adapt successfully to capitalist reality. Understanding all of this, however, comes with fully understanding what Freire means when he says that all education is political – it either has the potential and the intent to liberate all those involved in it or it domesticates both teacher and learners.

(Allman 2010 190)

During this course Allman herself was transformed from a left of centre political position to a more radical orientation. But the course itself, she is keen to stress, was not designed to radicalise the students, rather students must choose their own way, although most students did move to the left, but respect was shown for those that did not.

By 1993, working in a difficult external political context and an intellectual environment of postmodern negativity and scepticism, her adult education programme struggled to survive: student numbers declined, there was a lack of support for the course in her department, she was under pressure to restructure the course as credit bearing modules incompatible with Freirean education, and she lost the support of senior colleagues. In 1996 she took a sabbatical leave, became ill and depressed and retired in 1997. Her writings about this period are important as she reveals the emotionality of teaching, in a mixture of 'sheer joy' and sadness (Allman 2010 197). She writes eloquently and movingly about Freire's approach as a philosophy to education and not a method, and the ways in which a teacher has to live this philosophy, to continue learning and question what one knows. She talks about the problem of Freire in formal educational contexts, arguing that critical pedagogy is more suited to informal education. Critical education takes time, to counter the idea of training for the market with that of education. Allman writes of the pleasure of reading other people's accounts of education that she has inspired.

This is a compelling account of one woman's struggle to establish a critical education programme. In the end she frames the basis of her programme as a series of principles: mutual respect, humility, openness, trust and co-operation; commitment, vigilance; honesty truth and an 'ethics of authenticity' (Taylor 1991); as well as passion. Her revolutionary pedagogy involves critical, creative and hopeful thinking; transformation of the self and the social relations of learning and teaching; democratisation, along with an unquenchable thirst for understanding or genuine critical curiosity; solidarity, as well as a commitment to the project of humanisation. As she argues: '...it is only critical education that embodies these aims and principles and thus offers an abbreviated experience of the future reality we are striving for that will be able to prepare people who are capable of and committed to revolutionary social transformation' (Allman 2010 170).

Along with the practice of reading Marx without a filter or interruption as the basis for her *revolutionary critical education* her work is informed by communitarian philosophy (Taylor 1991), radical liberalism (Giroux) and theology. As she puts it, somewhat ironically, her work as a revolutionary pedagogue led her to 'a deeper relationship with God, whose love and wisdom fuel my criticality and my hope and to whom my gratitude is boundless' (Allman 2010 ix). I will look at the role of God and critical pedagogy when I review the work of one of the main members of Allman's milieu, Peter McLaren, later.

There is no account of the extent to which her version of revolutionary pedagogy was addressed at the level of the institution as a way of transforming institutional culture.

Consciousness as a Socially Constituted Activity: A Critique

This is a powerful exposition, yet despite the sophistication of her value-form reading of *Capital*, her account of consciousness remains one dimensional and under-theorised. Remember Allman is by training a psychologist, and for psychologists consciousness remains a tautological idea: the explanation of consciousness is revealed by reference to the concept of consciousness itself (Vygotsky 1986). She does not refer to the writings of Lev Vygotsky (1896-1934), which is a limitation of her work given his significance as a revolutionary Marxist psychologist (Newman and Holzman 1993). Rather, she draws on the liberal-humanist Jean Piaget, the subject of her PhD thesis, as a way to illustrate her particular Marxist approach to psychology. Nor does she refer to Alfred Sohn-Rethel (1899-1990) who theorised consciousness as a critical epistemology through an understanding of capitalist exchange relations. Sohn-Rethel's work is referenced by Postone (1993) along with his limitations. Sohn-Rethel sought to uncover the mystery of human consciousness by embedding it with a Marxist theory of capitalist exchange and historical materialism. The strength of Sohn-Rethel's work is that he explains consciousness as a social and historical phenomena that can be derived from the social relations of capitalist exchange. The limits are, according to Postone, that he restricts his analysis to capitalist exchange in a formulation that naturalises the social relations of capitalist work, thus undermining the very logic of what he is trying to explain (Jappe 2013).

But while Allman situates herself near to Postone's theoretical understanding of Marx, Postone is very critical of the type of approach to critical education which she is promoting: what he refers to as 'avant-garde pedagogy' (1993 39). Postone grounds the development of consciousness through the elaboration of Marx's labour theory of value, providing a critique of the kind of approach that characterises Allman's work. Postone argues that for this form of avant-garde pedagogy '...only consciousness which affirms or perpetuates the existent order is socially formed'. The approach suggested by Allman appears to put itself outside of the social relations of capital, or as he maintains: 'critical, oppositional, or revolutionary consciousness must be rooted ontologically or transcendentally – or, at the very least, in elements of social life that are purportedly noncapitalist' (Postone 1993 38).

Postone's point is that 'the possibilities for critical distance and heterogeneity are generated socially within the framework of capitalism itself' (Postone 1993 38). Consciousness is constituted by the contradictory process out of which it emerges, thus demonstrating the relationship between 'critical theory and the emergence of capital negating needs and oppositional forms of consciousness on a popular level' (1993 38).

He goes on to provide a devastating critique of critical pedagogy:

> Such a reflexive social theory of subjectivity contrasts sharply with those critiques that cannot ground the possibility of fundamentally oppositional consciousness in the existing order, or do so only objectivistically, implicitly positing a privileged position for critical thinkers whose knowledge has inexplicably escaped social deformation. Such approaches fall back into the antinomies of Enlightenment materialism, already criticised by Marx in his 'Theses on Feuerbach', whereby a population is divided into the many, who are socially determined, and the critical few, who, for some reason, are not. They implicitly represent an epistemologically inconsistent mode of social critique that cannot account for its own existence and must present itself in the form of tragic stance or avant-garde pedagogy.
> (1993 38-9)

This is not a credible position for the revolutionary teacher to find themselves: outside the social relation that forms a central part of any critical elaboration of capital, as Marx uncovered.

Global Movement

In the longer term, Allman's solution to what should and must be done is based on establishing a critical education group that will develop into an international movement. This grand ambition is linked with a down to earth practicality: 'I am suggesting that, at least initially, this alliance might begin as a relatively small grouping, so long as it was as international as possible in composition' (Allman 2010 205). This group, or '"seed" alliance' (2010 207), would not function as a Marxist vanguard, although many might be Marxists. They would provide 'an overview of what is going on elsewhere' (2010 206) for other grassroots groups. There would be a focus on use values, rather than exchange values and 'so far as possible, the alliance would function outside market relations' (Allman 2010 206). Once the larger movement takes off, all can be up for election. These are offered as suggestions to get the process of world revolution started.

For Allman revolution is in the future: the struggle is something that has still to be initiated through the formation of a new social movement with 'a realistic alternative vision' (Allman 2010 134). She finds inspiration for resistance in the Zapatistas in Chiapas, Mexico in the mid-1900s and the anti-globalisation movements that kicked off in Seattle in 1999. She feels the Zapatistas are showing signs that 'people are beginning to think more critically and creatively about how to challenge capitalism effectively' (2010 144). They are doing this through radical democracy and autonomy, defined as that which 'affirms people's freedom and capacity to freely determine themselves in their own spaces, and at the same time to determine with other people and cultures forms of communion based on intercultural dialogue' (Allman 2010 145). She maintains the Zapatistas share affinities with critical education, although this point is not elaborated. However, she warns, 'Of course, critical education on its own is clearly not the solution, but without critical education there will never be authentic revolutionary social transformation' (2010 147). She complains about radical liberal scholars: Susan George, Noam Chomsky, David Held, Samir Amin, who fail to name the enemy and retain 'a tacit acceptance of capitalism and its handmaiden liberal democracy' (2010 127).

Nevertheless, these critiques are part of what she acknowledges as 'people in increasing numbers are for various reasons expressing their desire for change' (Allman 2010 119), but, she argues, 'so far their focus has been on results, or problems rather than the causes' (2010 119), or 'a gap between wanting change and knowing what needs to be changed' (2010 119). This gap in knowledge, or the fetishisation of knowledge (ideology), is to be filled by critical educators who 'can play an important role in helping people develop a more accurate comprehension of the real causes of the problems they are experiencing' (2010 120), so that it is 'increasingly urgent for critical educators to seize the initiative' (2010 120).

Allman is not without a sophisticated awareness of revolutionary subjectivity that lies beyond the industrial working class, and has a critical sociological understanding of social class, after the Marxist historian, Edward Thompson, where class is not a pre-ordained group; but a relation in the 'making' (Allman 2010 35). She does feel that more people are now within the category of productive labour and, therefore, the numbers of the revolutionary class are expanding, but 'there remains the problem of critical awareness of self-consciousness' (Allman 2010 133) along with 'the development of a critical consciousness' (2010 139). So, in order to make revolution happen, you need a revolutionary theory and critical educators are the ones to provide it.

The problem with her revolutionary theory is the way in which she constitutes her theory of consciousness and the role of the critical educator. In the absence of any critical or negative impulse, and despite her reference to 'restless negatives', Allman has to create a functionalist role for the enlightened radical educator, in precisely the way Postone described and criticised in relation to critical pedagogy. This critique by Postone of critical pedagogy is based on the same theoretical principle as his critique of Lukac's affirmation of the proletariat as the revolutionary subject. Allman makes Postone's point for him. She writes:

Revolutionary critical adult education also has the equally pivotal role of unleashing the critical and creative potential that resides within us all so that we can become the creators and recreators of our collective conditions of existence and thereby people *capable of developing our own and others'* humanity in a profoundly positive direction. (Allman 2010 xv)

So, the question remains, as it did for Marx in his *Theses on Feuerbach* (1845), in a world made up of revolutionary educators of the type promoted by Allman, who educates the educators?

The Hillcole Group

Red Chalk and the Hillcole Group is an embryonic form of the world movement of leaders in critical pedagogy that is suggested by Allman.

Allman was part of the Hillcole Group, founded in 1989, as an association of leftist academics involved with the Institute for Education, London. The aim of the group has been to improve the quality of schooling and teacher education, against education policy being implemented by neoliberal politicians. The group published *Red Chalk: On Schooling Capitalism and Politics* (2001) and members of the group run the *Journal for Critical Education Policy Studies*. Dave Hill, editor of the journal and founder member of the group, states how revolutionary teachers should teach in schools:

There are individual and small group actions over school democracy, and over issues of equality within the subject curriculum and hidden curriculum. But, radical teachers also need to organise on a mass solidaristic basis, with a critical awareness of the bigger picture of capitalist exploitation and schooling as economic, cultural and yes, ideological reproduction. They need to become critical transformative intellectuals, working for equality within and outside the classroom, aware of the economy destroying, human alienating, commodifying and essentially class exploitative nature of national and global capitalism. It's not just the ideological struggle, the cultural struggle. Teachers, cultural workers, need to be activists as part of the working class movement, active in the material struggles of teachers, and of those of other groups of workers...it's not enough just to work within education. The struggle is wider; the role has to be wider, and co-ordinated, organised.
(Dave Hill 2001 56)

This group is closely affiliated to a group of radical educators in the US, including those involved with the journal *Critical Education*, the Institute for Critical Education Studies and the International Conference for Critical Education. Published books by the group include an edited collection by Curry Mallot, John Elmore and Mike Cole published in 2013:*Teaching Marx: the Socialist Challenge*. While not intending to be prescriptive this book gives concrete examples of how Marxism can inform and enhance the curriculum as an inspiration to revolutionary teachers.

Soft Machine
Glen Rikowski is a leading Marxist scholar of education and a member of Allman's milieu. He has provided the most developed theoretical account of labour as a critical category in

an educational context. For Rikowski, 'education and training... produces labour-power' (2002 205). He formulates the problem in terms of the concept of labour-power as it relates to value-form theory, and, specifically, the ways in which human life is constituted as human capital in the process of education and training. Rikowski points out that education and training are implicated in the social production of labour-power and that it is the nature of this implication that establishes their capitalist form, i.e., makes it possible to refer meaningfully to 'capitalist' education and training. And, not just in terms of labour-power, but the way in which human life is 'screwed up' by capital, as a form of 'personhood' (2002 196), affecting not just our ability to work but our 'mental and physical capacities' (2002 196). However, Rikowski argues, while labour-power takes a specific social form as human capital, 'Labour power is capitals' weakest link' (2002 189) and, therefore, 'education and training should be at the forefront of thinking regarding oppositional strategies to capital's social domination, and also be a core concern of Marxist theory' (2002 189), in the context of a discussion about revolutionary critical pedagogy. So, 'the effectiveness of critical or revolutionary pedagogy', Rikowski argues, is one of the key questions facing Marxists and anti-capitalists today: 'It has the potentiality for disrupting the smooth flow of labour-power production and reconfiguring labour-power for the prospect of social transformation' (2002 190). Rikowski wants to put the issue of 'the social production of labour power at the heart of contemporary education and training policy' (2002 202) and to recognise and confront the education project to reconstitute human life as human capital, or, 'the human as a form of capital' (2002 205). He identifies the capitalist education project as the basis for educational institutions' obsession with 'employability' and their insistence that students be 'work ready' as a way of understanding, following Walter Benjamin's *The Life of Students*, how capitalist education contaminates the curriculum in schools, colleges and universities.

Rikowski argues it is possible to confront this issue not simply through the enlightened attitudes of critical educators, as Allman's work implies, but as a result of the social form of labour in capitalism. For Rikowski labour-power is the 'impossible commodity' by virtue of its immanent contradiction, its non-identity with itself, as use value and exchange value, in ways that mean the contradiction can never be fully resolved. His work mirrors the pioneering theoretical work carried out by Paula Allman on value-form theory. In this way he makes clear the contradiction that exists as the inner connection of the commodity-form should be the focal point for a critical political education. This critical attitude is already immanent in the moment of what is being reproduced, as a function of capital's own contradictory tendencies. And so, for Rikowski, 'labour-power is capital's soft machine' (2002 205), i.e., its weakest point.

From Pedagogy of Love to Pedagogy of Hate

Peter McLaren is another member of the Hillcole Group. Like Allman, he has a preoccupation with theology. We have seen how Allman writes about her commitment to God as an important aspect of her critical pedagogy, a feature she shares with Paulo Freire. Allman says about her religiosity, 'it is perhaps an irony in the case of Marx and Gramsci, but of course not Freire, that they also led me to a much deeper and important relationship with God, whose love and wisdom fuel my criticality and my hope and to whom my gratitude is boundless' (Allman 2010 ix). She does not go on to elaborate this point. Peter McLaren has written a book about his commitment to Jesus in *Pedagogy of Insurrection: From Resurrection to Revolution* (2015) and his dedication to Christian Socialism. McLaren's writings are, like Allman's, based on a mixture of Marxisms, although as with Allman, an exposition of the value-form is central to his analysis. For McLaren, Jesus's life forms the basis for a commitment to social justice and love and communism based on redistribution of resources. There are problems with Jesusism as a revolutionary principle, not least the fact that social transformation is limited to the politics of redistribution and lack of historical evidence (Neary, 2017b).

For Student as Producer, grounded as it is in Adorno's negative critique, the revolutionary teacher is not fired by love, but, rather, a radical hate for what the world has become: love-hate need to constitute each other for the magic of the negative dialectic to work (Neary 2017b).

Pedagogy of Insurrection already includes references to hate, usually as a malevolent force and, therefore, to be avoided, although McLaren does hate technology. Yet, in a chapter on Che Guevara, hate is given its voice as a principle of revolutionary struggle: 'Hatred is an element of struggle' (2015 211). McLaren at one point gives himself up to the logic of love-hate dialectics: 'Hatred can be the only proof that we love someone' (2015 211). McLaren frames this discussion about hate around the concept of violence through a discussion of Walter Benjamin's notion of 'divine violence', as interpreted by Slavoj Zizek (2008). For McLaren divine violence is 'the refusal to compromise' and 'a violence that refuses a deeper meaning; it is the logic of rage, a refusal to normalise crimes against humanity, either by reconciliation or revenge' (2015 211). McLaren follows Jesus, who chose the path of non-violence, arguing 'all acts of violence generate forms of evil' (2015 213) and that violence can never establish the Kingdom of God.

This discussion about violence and hate is compelling, but McLaren's account of Benjamin on violence is not what Benjamin means by political violence (Benjamin 1986/1921). As we saw in Chapter 2 on the Police-State, Benjamin regards political violence as workers' activities that have the potential for revolutionary change, e.g., strikes. The capacity to decide what constitutes political violence depends on a pedagogical process of deep contemplative reflection, what Benjamin calls 'educative power'. Educative power is not an absolute principle, or objective assessment, or 'a criterion of judgment' like the commandment 'thou shalt not kill' (1986/1921 298), but a 'guideline' for those who have to take responsibility for such activities. Educative power is 'critical, discriminating and decisive' (1986/1921 299-300), providing the conditions by which state power can be abolished and replaced by a revolutionary society. Educative power is then a type of 'radical doubt... [or]...fundamental critique' (Benjamin 1996 41), that Benjamin had referred to as a key aspect of intellectual life that is missing in his Life of Students in German universities. This version of political violence does not promote mortal combat or any particular form of intervention, so, like Ghandi, might mean the withdrawal from political life (Zizek 2008). Zizek, thinking about his own academic profession, argues that sometimes it is better to do nothing, rather than engage in 'pseudo-activity...to mask the nothingness of what goes on...academics participate in meaningless debates...Sometimes doing nothing is the most violent thing to do' (Zizek 2008: 183 [epilogue]), and could involve 'withdrawing to a solitary place to learn, learn, learn' (2008 7).

Learn, Learn, Learn is a good lesson for the revolutionary teacher. Do nothing. Learn. Learn. Learn. Do nothing. Teach. Teach. Teach.

I will return to the concept of doing nothing and educative power at the end of the book in my discussion of Strike prime and in relation to Authority and Authorship as a form of not-Police.

What is to be learned from Allman's version of revolutionary teaching?

Paula Allman reminds us of the power of reading the primary texts unfiltered and uninterrupted as a way of substantiating our revolutionary teaching. She argues in favour of a dialectical reading of Marx and in particular the contradictory struggle between capital and labour as the basis for human emancipation. As we saw from a critical engagement with her work, this reading requires critical self and social reflection as a way of avoiding the idealism of liberal humanism, as the seductiveness of this idealist theory can undermine the importance of what her version of revolutionary pedagogy has to say. Allman is important because she connects the reality of critical theory and practice with her own emotionality, as anxiety and pain of higher education, as part of what Hall (2014) calls 'the anxiety machine'. An important element of the pain is the struggle to connect theory and practice in ways that are not instrumental for capital, and to deal with the critique when it comes, even and especially from people with whom you have connected your work. Moishe Postone, who Allman claims affinity with, is very critical of her approach to critical pedagogy as a form of pedagogical avant-gardism.

Revolutionary Teachers and Radical Epistemology

Each of these revolutionary teachers have developed a form of radical epistemology based on an approach to the production of knowledge grounded in a critique of capitalist society. In the next chapter I will develop the lessons learned from Benjamin, Postone, Ranciére, Allman and Freire, together with my own work with others, to seek to answer the question: How Do Revolutionary Teachers Teach? I will do this in relation to work I have been doing with others to create a co-operative form of higher education, a co-operative university, making a link with the concepts of democracy and the law of value that were established as framing devices in the first chapter of this book and throughout the book, as the basis for revolutionary teaching.

5. The Co-operative University: Democracy and the Law of Value

Corbynism

What was so remarkable about the General Election result of 2017 in the UK was the number of young people, 58 per cent of 18-24 year olds, that had come out to vote for the Labour Party (Allsop et al 2018). These young people had been attracted by the manifesto pledge made by the leader of the Labour Party, Jeremy Corbyn, to provide free higher education and other progressive social policies. The promise of free education had been made during the previous General Election in 2010 by the then leader of the Liberal Democratic Party, Nick Clegg, before he reneged on his promise when the Liberal Democrats went into a government coalition with the Conservative Party. The sense of betrayal felt by the students had fuelled the impassioned protests against fees and cuts that are described in the beginning of this book. Nick Clegg lost his parliamentary seat in the 2017 election. Despite this previous betrayal of students by politicians this time it was going to be different.

The argument of this book is that reforms, which emerge out of formal democratic processes that do not impact on the law of labour, are not going to have any significant impact on the domineering processes of capitalist social reproduction. This does not mean that reform should not be attempted, but that it should be done with a long-term revolutionary goal in mind.

Young people were not supposed to be interested in politics; remember how Mark Fisher described his students in *Capitalist Realism* (2009); they were said to be suffering from 'reflexive impotence' and 'depressive hedonia' made miserable by the pursuit of pleasure and addicted to the Control Society (2009 21): 'They know things are bad, but more than that, they know that they can't do anything about it' (2009 21). But, in the 2017 election, massive numbers had turned out to vote, and had been part of the large crowds that Corbyn had been attracting to his political rallies around the country. He had credibility with young people, appearing at music concerts where they chanted his name: 'Oh Jeremy Corbyn'. This appeal continued after the election when he went on stage at the Glastonbury music festival, reading out a poem by Percy Shelley, *The Mask of Anarchy* (1819), from which the Labour Party election campaign slogan was derived: 'For the many not the few'.

My argument in this last section of the book, supported by others including Michael Chessum, is more fundamental than young people were attracted to Corbynism; rather, young people, and in particular students, had, in a sense, created Jeremy Corbyn. This is following an argument developed by George Ciccariello-Maher who maintains in his book *We Created Chavez: a People's History of the Venezuelan Revolution (2013)* that it was the social movements in Venezuela that had brought Chavez to power (Simbuerger and Neary 2015). It was the students and young people in the UK, starting with the protests and riots in 2010-11, who had kicked off the political process that brought Corbyn to political prominence. Corbyn, indeed, presented himself not as a personality politician but as the figurehead for the social movement Momentum, that developed out of the student protests and other campaigns, e.g., the Anti-War movement, to support him and his brand of Labour politics (Myers 2017, Seymour 2017). So what does all of this have to teach the revolutionary teacher and unlearning the law of labour?

Corbyn had fought the election on a manifesto based on his socialist principles as a long-time radical left-wing MP, radical by UK standards, following years of neoliberal policies by the major political parties. He personified the fact that 'After decades in which the market had been unchallenged, Keynes and Marx were back in fashion and the political and corporate elites destabilised' (Milne 2012 xx). Corbyn and Momentum and the political involvement of young people emerged as a way to respond to the crisis of social democracy brought about by deindustrialisation, the shockwaves of the financial crash in 2008 and the politics of austerity. The campaign was framed around the manifestations of this crisis and was evident in the Labour Party Election Manifesto, which concentrated on reinvestment in public services, nationalisation and work creation schemes (Labour Party 2017). Although the policies in the manifesto were not that radical, what lay behind them was a more radical strand of Labour Party thinking. One issue that was prominent during the election and which has been gaining increasing significance is the crisis in the world of work, not just as unemployment and a lack of work but in the nature of work itself (Pitts and Dinerstein 2017b).

This radical rethinking included a report, which promoted the practice of co-operatives based on the power of the people, although this was not given much prominence in the manifesto or in debates since the election (Labour Party 2016). The issues that lie at the heart of thinking about the future of the world of work are very pertinent to the way in which revolutionary teachers teach. One of the most prominent thinkers in this area and whose work is influential in Labour Party circles is Paul Mason, freelance journalist, writer and broadcaster.

Mason, as we saw in earlier chapters, had been a reliable witness at the student demonstrations, giving an account on TV, in print journalism, books and drama. He had linked the student protests to the Arab Spring, foregrounding the importance of network technologies. In his book *Post Capitalism: a Guide to our Future* (2016) he establishes information technology as the basis for a post-capitalist society. For Paul Mason 'capitalism is already past its best' (Mason 2016 ix), his vision of the post-capitalist future is based on a critique of political economy using a version of Marxist economics which foregrounds Marx's labour theory of value as a device to understand capitalism where, he argues, its imminent if not already demise is the ground on which a new economic system can be built. The strength of Mason's argument is that capitalism is examined as a whole system that has lost the capacity to reproduce itself. Mason's arguments fit with the approach on which Student as Producer is based, although they differ in some material aspects discussed below.

Mason argues for a movement for social transformation based on advances in information technology, as part of the transition to a post-capitalist society, the basis of which can be found within the already existing capitalist system. In post-capitalist society the ubiquity of information technology reduces the need to work, because commodities are now free to share and to be commonly owned. This is characterised by the rise of peer productive ways of working, e.g., co-operatives and communes as 'outbreaks of liberated freedom that redefine human behaviour' (Mason 2016 xxi), and the basis for what he calls 'the postcapitalist project' (2016 xvi). He characterises this as the rise of networks over what had previously been power hierarchies. He identifies what amounts to nothing less than 'a new agent of change in history: the educated and connected human being' (2016 xvii). He is clear about the historical role of the working class as a point of resistance to capitalism and the significance of the state in building regimes of accumulation. But, for Mason, this new agent of change in history has replaced the working class who have now been defeated as the revolutionary subject, allowing for the emergence of a new frictionless group, 'a new generation of networked people understand they are living through a third industrial revolution...reproducing a networked lifestyle and consciousness at odds with the hierarchies of capitalism...[with an]...appetite for radical economic change' (2016 213).

What is important for my argument is the significance Mason gives to knowledge as the key to the future. He bases this argument on the section on the 'Fragments of Machines' in Marx's *Grundrisse*. Mason follows Marx with the argument that knowledge has been transferred into machines which now have the power to satisfy the needs of people who will no longer be required to work long hours to produce the necessary goods and services for themselves and society.

Mason references Peter Drucker in emphasising the role of the new knowledge worker. Drucker is an important source because of the significance he attaches to knowledge workers for a post-capitalist society, as 'the production of knowledge by means of knowledge' (Mason 2016 140), through 'the universal educated person' (2016 113). Mason does not discuss this in relation to university or higher education although he does suggest the need to 'create a global institute or network for stimulating the long-term transition beyond capitalism' (2016 272). In this transitional process there would be a role for the state which would need to 'wither away', becoming less powerful until its 'functions... [are]... assumed by society' (2016 290). In the meantime the state would persist, in whatever political form is appropriate for an economy that 'includes capitalist and postcapitalist structures'... [as an]...'enabler and coordinator' (2016 274) to drive the transition to a new economic system.

Pitts (2017) recognises the extent to which this new thinking has permeated Labour policy forums that feed the Labour Party's approach to what is being described as a new industrial revolution, which includes a new settlement between leisure and work in a utopian vision of society based on an automated worklessness. Pitts argues that Mason's theory of value sits too close to the economistic/orthodox labour theory of value where value is a quantity of labour to be measured, rather than the synthetic principle for a particular form of society; driven by the dynamic logic of abstract labour that rests on the exploitation and brutalising of society as a whole. Pitts contests Mason's economics with a model of value-form theory that is close to the version of Marx on which Student as Producer is based. For Pitts, Mason is too affirmative of capitalism, not critical enough. For Pitts, Mason's argument makes no real challenge to the fundamental social relations of capitalist production, i.e., they are affirmed rather than negated as the basis for the reorganisation of society (Pitts, 2017). Pitts and Dinerstein (2017a) argue for a different model of social development organised not on work-based futurological schemes, but new forms of social reproduction. They argue that these new forms, of what they call '"concrete utopian"' alternatives...[can]...'create the capacity to reshape the relationship between individuals, society and the rule of money, value and the state rather than reinforce it' (2017a), and are already in existence. These include 'new commons in housing, food and environment that reclaim unused public space for community orchards, for instance, or acquire unused office space to convert into mixed use housing' (Pitts and Dinerstein 2017b 424).

This futurology is pertinent to the central debate of this book: how do revolutionary teachers teach, pointing out ways to deal with the collapse of the world of work, in a manner that foregrounds the significance of knowledge as a factor in the production of capitalist wealth, and, as the basis out of which a post-capitalist society can be engineered. Among the central ideas are the concepts of peer production and co-operative working which lie at the core of the Student as Producer project. In 2011 the concept and practice of Student as Producer was extended to consider the idea of setting up a co-operative university. What distinguishes this project from Mason's version of post-capitalism is that the theory that supports the co-operative university is grounded in a value-form theory of labour and the need to get beyond social relations based on notions of capitalist wealth.

In the next section I will explore in more detail the idea of the co-operative university, not as a solution to the crisis of market economics but as a moment in transition towards a revolutionary society: a type of revolutionary reformism and a new form of social institution. I will discuss this by returning to a discussion of Clover's Riot-Strike-Riot, arguing in favour not of Riot prime, like Clover, but Strike prime; not to defend capitalist work, but as a way of overcoming capitalist work and creating a new form of social wealth. At the end I will return to one of the main themes of the book, the science of Police, to consider how such a form of social institution could be defended. I will explore this notion of defence by offering a new communist science of police: not-Police, as a form of Authority and Authorship, after a contemporary reworking of Roman philosophy and Walter Benjamin's *Author as Producer*. All of this is grounded in a Marxist theory of law written by the Russian Soviet legal theorist Evgeny Pashukanis, based on the notion of social defence and unity of purpose.

Co-operation and Higher Education: The Co-operative University

There is very considerable synergy between the values of co-operation and the co-operative movement and the idea of a university. Indeed, the Co-operative College, the main institution for promoting co-operative education in the UK and around the world, has been calling for a co-operative university for over 100 years: 'What we want and seek to obtain is a co-operative journey that will end in a co-operative university' (Rae 1909 29, quoted in Woodin 2017 34). More recently the idea of establishing a co-operative university has been promoted by the co-operative movement (Yeo, 2015, Swain 2017).

Dan Cook (2013) in *Realising the Co-operative University*, sets out the case for establishing a co-operative university based on legal arrangements, financial matters and with a range of possible business models, pointing out the similarities between the culture of co-operative enterprises and academic practice. He starts from the position that: 'Co-operative principles are academic principles. There is arguably a close alignment between co-operative principles and mainstream academic values' (2013 19). A co-operative is 'an autonomous association of persons united voluntarily to meet their common economic, social and cultural needs and aspiration through a jointly owned and democratically ran enterprise' (International Co-operative Alliance 1995 [ICA]). The values of the worldwide co-operative movement, which totals over one billion members, are: self-help, self-responsibility, democracy, equality, equity and solidarity. The values are the basis for a set of co-operative principles: voluntary and open membership, democratic member control, member economic participation, autonomy and independence, education, training and information, co-operation among co-operatives and concern for community.

It is possible to recognise the contemporary university within this co-operative framing, especially the collegiate Oxbridge model, although co-operative values and principles are much less evident in the more corporate post-1992 models based on chief executive and senior management teams (Bacon 2014, Hall and Winn 2017). While democratic decision making is in short supply in the post-1992 university, it could be greatly enhanced by promoting more neo-collegiate models. There is a view that universities lose much leadership and organisational capacity by not including highly-skilled and intelligent staff in decision making, leading to staff dissatisfaction and lack of motivation (Bacon 2014). A key principle co-operatives and universities share is the emphasis on education and co-operative learning. Other shared principles are that in spite of the pressure on universities to act like competitive businesses there is a need for universities to co-operate in ways that create research capacity through research and teaching networks, as well as an interest in their communities through public engagement and science. Cook reports that a model for such a university has already been suggested as a Trust University (Boden et al 2012), and references Mondragon University in Spain as an already existing exemplar of co-operative higher education. Cook's conclusion is that the idea of a co-operative university is not radical but 'realistic and desirable' (2013 57) and 'in many ways the higher education sector already is co-operative' (2013 59).

Co-operativism, the University and the Value-form

Joss Winn's work situates the idea of the co-operative university in terms of the framework of this book: the university and the law of value. For Winn (2015a) in *The Co-operative University: Labour, Property and Pedagogy. Power and Education,* the university is an edu-factory that can only be fundamentally understood through an analysis of labour, value and the commodity-form, as a critique of the political economy of higher education. Winn sets out the capitalist value-form in a way that supports the critique of labour that has been the argument in this book. He does this alongside the principles and practices of Student as Producer as the pedagogical basis for a co-operative university. He extends this analysis in relation to worker co-operatives in general and the co-operative university in particular. The worker co-operative is not an alternative to capital, but a type of social institution that has emerged historically and logically out of the increasingly capitalist socialised model of production. This is a very important point, as Marx argued: 'Co-operation remains the fundamental form of the capitalist mode of production' (Marx 1976: 454). The principle of co-operation is not an anathema to capital, quite the reverse, it is the direct result of the capitalist labour process. The worker co-operative is the historical and logical extension of capitalist production. Winn develops the argument through an analysis of the legal form of capitalist enterprises. The current epitome of capitalist organisation is the joint stock company, a private concern representing 'the abolition of capital as private property within the capitalist mode of production' (Marx 1991: 567). The purpose of a joint stock company is to generalise or socialise the profits and the risks of capitalist enterprises among shareholders, not including workers, whose wages do not usually extend to the capacity for trading in stocks and shares. Winn reminds us that Marx argued that the joint stock company is a 'necessary point of transition' from capitalism to communism. Worker co-operatives attenuate this movement of transition as they are based on a model of social property and common ownership, contra private and public models of equity that characterise joint stock companies. The essence of common ownership is that workers of the enterprise collectively own the assets of the enterprise for the benefit of the members and the co-operative movement. Winn argues: 'Common ownership of the means of knowledge production among scholar-members of a co-operative university would therefore be a significant step towards an institutional form of academic labour that is not alienated from its product in the way that private property enforces' (2015 48).

Winn sets out a number of propositions by which the transition to a co-operative university might occur: *conversion* – a process by which existing universities take on co-operative values and principles; *dissolution* – co-operative principles are developed within a university through curriculum development, e.g., research activities as well as co-operative cafes and co-operative housing provision; and *creation* – in the form of new co-operative experiments. Winn finds inspiration for the model at the University of Mondragon, as an already existing co-operative university, pointing out its strengths but also its limitations, not least, the extent to which it is a real alternative to 'the entrepreneurial university' (Wright et al 2011), the possible limits of workplace democracy, and the division of working classes between the favoured groups who own worker co-operatives and those workers employed in the corporate business model (Kasmir 1996); and, he is careful to recognise the inherent limits of co-operativism as forms of worker self-exploitation. Nevertheless, in spite of these limitations, there is much to be gained with worker co-operatives as an 'immanent critique' (2015 45 quoting Shukaitis 2010 63) of capitalist work. Winn finds an account of the problems of co-operatives and a solution to these problems in Egan (1990) who argues 'the potential for degeneration [from worker controlled enterprises to capitalist firms] must be seen to lie not within the co-operative form of organisation itself but in the contradiction between it and the capitalist environment' (1990 81). I would want to stress, following Egan, that the potential of worker co-operatives relies on class struggle at a more general level beyond the institution: 'it is only by linking co-operatives with class struggle that the former have a chance to flourish (relatively speaking) within capitalism' (Egan 1990 75). Class struggle enhances co-operativism and solidarity as part of an international organisation in the context of other political struggles.

Winn (2015b) further substantiates his argument in *Writing about Academic Labour*, where academic practice is to be seen as a form of academic work. Winn does this through an exposition of Marx's labour theory of value. Winn's approach to Marx is informed by the work of Postone: 'not a critique of capitalism from the perspective of labour, but a negative critique of labour in capitalism' (Postone 1993 5). Winn argues that focusing on academic practice as a form of academic labour and dealing with labour through Postone's negative critique provides the possibility to develop a form of resistance to the alienating effects of academic work. He argues that a focus on academic labour through a value-critique can overcome the sense of helplessness in the face of the rise of neoliberalism engendered by academic research into education that struggles to find ways to resist the culture of neoliberal performativity. Winn cites the work of Stephen Ball (2003) 'The Teachers Soul and the Terrors of Performativity' as an example of this type of helpless analysis.

Making use of Marx's theoretical method of abstraction, Winn argues it is possible to uncover the valorisation process which lies beneath the form of institutional appearances, namely the performativity of capitalist work. To support this argument, Winn provides a review of Harney and Moten's 'Doing Academic Work' (1998) to further develop the relation between student and academic labour in the process of valorisation, a function which they identify as 'student as producer' (1998 172). I did not know Harney and Moten used the term student as producer before we used the term Student as Producer at Lincoln, although, as I show, they use the term in a more limited way, referring only to the practice of teaching and not research. The main point is the extent to which students are already involved as producers and consumers in the capitalist valorisation process, not recognised in the current HE regimes, i.e., 'the actual practice of academic labour in capitalist society as a "social world of making and sharing knowledge" where both academics and students co-operate in the "production, circulation and realisation" of the knowledge commodity' (Winn 2015b 9 quoting Moten and Harney 1999 26). Winn makes the point again that this co-operation between students and academics in the university edu-factory exemplifies the co-operative nature of capitalist production. The way in which Harney and Moten use the concept student as producer is limited to an account of the teaching process and does not extend to research activity:

Many of us know academic workers who are dedicated to helping students analyse and critique society where the object of that critique is actually existing capitalism. The academic workers are admirable for their faith in the human nature of these students and for their understanding of the subject of any such critique (what we would call socialism). Such workers are capable of viewing students as a social group, based on age, race, income, or their superficial place in the education system. They may attempt to teach anti-racism, feminism, anti-imperialism, or pacifism. But it is necessary to be rigorous in critiquing the analysis that informs this position. The production of knowledge requires the student as producer. The student must manipulate the raw material of thought. She must expend labor time in this process. She must and she does add something to the product that the academic worker has not, no matter how insignificant, for the commodity to be formed. She is, therefore, a worker in the production of the teaching commodity. Now it is possible for an academic worker to hope for an agency from students not based on their position as workers, as one can hope for such agency among people in general. But it does not seem to us possible to devise a strategy for that agency which does not recognise, first, that the very act of strategising implicates the students as workers and, second, that any strategy ignorant of these material conditions of production is at least incomplete. (Harney and Moten 1998 172).

This all points to the need for new models of democratic education organised directly through the co-operation of academic and student labour; models of practice which aim to re-appropriate what Winn following Marx refers to as the 'general intellect' (Marx 1973 706) as well as 'mass intellectuality' (Hall and Winn 2017). We saw the concept 'general intellect' in our discussion of Postone's point about the revolutionary capacity inherent in non-alienated forms of human knowledge (1993 131). Mass intellectuality refers to 'the same knowledge's immanent (negative) and prefigurative (positive) critical and reconstructive potential for new forms of human sociality' (Hall and Winn 2017 3).

The possibility to create a co-operative university in the UK has been enhanced by changes in higher education law: the Higher Education and Research Act 2017, which makes it possible for alternative forms of higher education to be established. The potential for a co-operative university has been further enhanced by the emergence of new forms of co-operatives: social or multi-stakeholder co-operatives that are made up of a wider constituency than consumer or worker co-operatives: in this case academic workers, students and external partners (Neary and Winn 2019).

Student as Producer and the Co-operative University

Winn's research, building on the concept and practice of Student as Producer, has provided the basis on which to further consider co-operative higher education. The research was grounded and gained credibility through Winn's association with the Social Science Centre (SSC), Lincoln, a co-operative organising no-fee higher education in the city of Lincoln, England, since 2011. I worked closely with Joss Winn and others to set up the SSC as well as on a number of research projects.

The SSC was a co-operative organising free higher education in the city of Lincoln, England. It was formed in 2011 by a group of academics and students in response to the massive rise in student fees, from £3000 to £9000, along with other government policies that saw the increasing neo-liberalisation of English universities.

The SSC was established in order to provide higher education in Lincoln, a small city in the east of England, for people who were unwilling or unable to take on the burden of massive debt to pay for a university degree (SSC Collective, 2013). The Social Science Centre was inspired by the social centre model of community organisation that had been developed in Italy in the 1970s and had been taken up by some organisations in the UK, e.g., SUMAC and The Cowley Club in Brighton (Chatterton et al, 2010). The Social Science Centre was distinguished as a social centre by its focus on organising higher education. It became a co-operative because that seemed to be the most appropriate form of organisation for its purposes. As we have seen there are many similarities between co-operatives and the academic values which underpin the collegiate model of higher education: democratic, consensual decision-making processes and with a membership structure of governance (Cook 2013). The founders of the SSC felt it was important to develop the SSC within a recognised legal and bureaucratic framework with radical pretensions to express their commitment to create a new form of social institution based on a model of the co-production of knowledge (Roggero 2011). The view was that this form of institutionalised practice gave the SSC a life of its own beyond the involvement of any individual member, including its founders.

Some members of the SSC had already been involved in developing the radical pedagogic model of teaching: Student as Producer, at the University of Lincoln. The Student as Producer model, as discussed earlier, is a form of research-engaged teaching that had been adopted by the University of Lincoln, where some members of the SSC work (Neary and Winn 2009, Neary and Saunders 2016). Research-engaged teaching means that the curriculum is organised around research and problem-solving activities, rather than a model where lecturers transmit knowledge to students.

At the core of this approach was the recognition that students were already making an important contribution to academic life as a form of academic labour that was going unrecognised and uncompensated (Winn 2015). There was a strong democratic aspect to Student as Producer, with the idea that organising teaching in a collaborative and co-operative manner could underpin the creation of a democratic university in opposition to the neoliberal model of university education that was dominating higher education in England.

The Social Science Centre ran a series of educational courses on the social science imagination, the history of co-operative education, as well as documentary photography and poetry projects. The courses were developed and taught in a collaborative and co-operative manner between students and teachers

(Saunders 2017). Each course was led by a teacher and a student. To express the democratic sensibility that underpins the SSC the terms 'students' and 'teachers' were not used, but all members were referred to as 'scholars'. Courses were taught for 2 hours on a week-night once a week for 10 weeks. The approach to teaching was inspired by critical pedagogy and popular education. The centre ran a programme of public lectures as well as conferences on such topics as war and the media, the problems of economic growth, racism and fundamentalism in cities, Lincoln and the built environment, sustainable environmental planning, safe spaces in dystopian sites, and sessions on colonial, settler and indigenous knowledges. There were monthly planning meetings to manage the affairs of the co-operative, as well as an Annual General Meeting every year.

The SSC did not have degree-awarding powers, but provided the opportunity for scholars to work at a level that is equivalent to a university degree, including postgraduate, and to be able to have an intellectual life collectively with other people. There was no fee to take part in the teaching sessions and none of the members were paid for the work that they did at the centre. Members paid a subscription based on what they could afford in money or by some other payment in kind. The SSC did not have large running costs, operating with a turnover of approximately £2000 per annum. There were usually about 20 members, which was the number originally envisaged by the founding group, as well as associate members not involved in the day to day running of the centre and its activities who act as critical friends and supporters all around the world.

The SSC had no institutional connection to any higher education provision, but was linked to other alternative providers, including the Free University of Brighton, the Social Science Centre Manchester, the Ragged University and People's Political Economy in Oxford. The SSC felt a strong connection and resonance with the history of adult and community education.

It was originally envisaged when the SSC was set up that other higher education co-operatives could be established using the SSC model. That has happened, with the SSC Manchester formed in 2015 on a very similar co-operative arrangement, running programmes on Brexit and Donald Trump. The membership of the SSC Lincoln reflected the demographic of the city, with a mixture of gender and ages, although most were mature students. A major consequence of the rise in fees in England has been the collapse of the involvement of older students in adult and higher education. The participation of this group of people at this level of education had once been a progressive feature of the education system in England.

The SSC saw itself as a local provision based in the city of Lincoln. The SSC did not have its own building, but made use of the local public facilities: libraries, cafes, community centres, pubs, museums, art galleries and parks. Some members liked to say the SSC occupied the city (Neary and Amsler, 2012). The SSC had a website but there was no web-based teaching (http://socialsciencecentre.org.uk).

An important aspect of this provision was to critically reflect on the activities of the SSC. Members were concerned about the nature of what they were providing: was the SSC a genuine alternative or was it a place to discuss what an alternative might look like? To what extent was the SSC replicating the hierarchies of academic power relations in another form outside of the university? How could they make a meaningful connection to real issues that affect people living in the city?

Maintaining the SSC in the social and political context of the time was difficult; much of the organisational work was mundane and could be very time consuming. This could be compensated for when sessions went well, and there was much to be gained from the friendships and sense of solidarity that had been built up over the years, as well as the sense of renewal when new members joined (Ross and Noble 2019).

Members of the SSC have written extensively about the work that they did in a series of publications. There is now a considerable body of work on Student as Producer, charting how it was developed as an original idea and the basis for organising teaching and learning across the University of Lincoln (2013, Neary et al 2015), the intellectual ideas on which it is based (Neary 2010, Neary 2012a, 2012b, 2012c, 2015, 2016) as well as its transition from a project inside the university to a local city-wide co-operative for higher education. Members of the centre have written collective pieces about the SSC (SSC Collective 2013, Wonkhe 2017). There are a number of essays that critically reflect on the SSC as a reformist or revolutionary project (Saunders 2017, Neary 2014) and the function of community organisation as a type of radical practice (Amsler 2017) as well as papers on academic labour and co-operative leadership (Winn and Hall 2017, Hall and Smyth 2016, Winn 2015a, 2015b).

The SSC has been written about by journalists in the higher education press (Bonnett 2011, Bonnett 2013), and in The Guardian (Swain 2013, 2017), as well as PhD research projects (Earle 2015, Saunders 2019) and as the subject for undergraduate dissertations (Macrae 2016). Academic papers have explored the extent to which the SSC is a radical alternative for higher education (Cole and Maisuria 2017, Pusey and Sealey-Huggins 2013) and the SSC and Student as Producer have been the topics for interviews in publications about radical forms of academic practice (Withers 2013, Class War 2013). References to the SSC appear in a range of publications, for example in The Debt Resistors' Operations Manual (Graeber, Ross and Caffentzis 2014).

An enduring matter for activity that regards itself as revolutionary is the problem of pseudo-activity. To what extent did the Social Science Centre, and like-minded projects, replicate the instrumental logic of capital, while claiming a revolutionary alternative? The way to deal with this matter is to focus on the process of mediation that underpins the logic of capitalist social relations, between labour and capital, and work towards dissolving the capital relation. This process of dissolution of the capital relation is the essence of Student as Producer.

The Social Science Centre closed at the end of February 2019. This was their farewell statement, posted 16 February 2019:

Dear Members, Friends and Followers of the Social Science Centre,

The Social Science Centre is closing at the end of February 2019. Since 2011, we have organised and run free, co-operative higher education courses and community projects in the city of Lincoln. The SSC was created as both a critique of and an alternative to the dominant model of higher education in the UK, and has been inspirational for many of its members and followers. It has created many spaces for intellectual life, learning, solidarity and friendship within the city and enabled many of us to follow new dreams. Running such a project has required considerable time and commitment from us all, and been challenging at times, and we have reached the limit of what we are able to achieve in this organisational form. The ideas that have underpinned the SSC, and co-operative higher education generally, are being developed elsewhere. A Co-operative University with degree-awarding powers is now being established in England and will open in 2019. The SSC was free and relied on voluntary labour; the Co-operative University will charge students £5,500 in order to access government funding and workers will be paid. Although one project is charging a fee and the other was free, both projects, following the historical aim of the Co-operative movement, intend to develop a new form of common wealth. We look forward to working with you in the city of Lincoln and elsewhere on other projects.

Yours in hope and solidarity.

Beyond Public and Private

The SSC created a base from which to develop further research into the development of co-operative higher education. This has included work to develop a conceptual framework for higher education: *Beyond Public and Private: a Framework for Co-operative Higher Education* (Neary and Winn 2017a). This research established a set of key principles on which to consider this framework: *knowledge* – the production of knowledge and meaning by the organisation as a whole; *democracy* – the levels of influence on decision making; *bureaucracy* – not only administration but a set of ethical and moral principles on which administration is based; *livelihood* – working practices that support the capacity to lead a good life and *solidarity* – sharing a commitment to a common purpose inside and outside of the institution.

This research is grounded in a version of Marxist critical theory, a value-form analysis that informs the approach of this book. The basis of this theoretical approach is that struggle is derived out of the contradictory processes that maintain capitalist productivity, while at the same time creating the conditions which can overcome capitalist social relations for the benefit of people and the planet, vitalising new forms of social institutions (Holloway 2005). Working with a design student Joss Winn developed a poster to visualise this approach, which we describe, after (Dyer-Witheford 2015) as 'the value vortex' (see image below). The vortex image graphically illustrates, in an abstract style, the way in which the contradictory relationship between labour and capital acts as the organising principle for capitalist civilisation, spinning out into a range of forms that express the dialectical contradiction. Our image relates specifically to the co-operative university and higher education. The revolutionary principle at the core of the vortex is the possibility of re-engineering the contradiction so that capital becomes subordinate to labour for communism not capitalism (Neary and Winn 2017a)

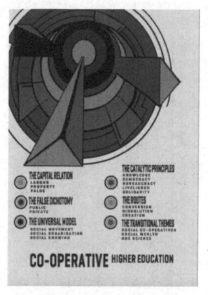

VORTEX IMAGE
Designed by Sam Randall

Further research (Neary, Venezuela Fuentes and Winn 2017) has involved visiting already existing co-operative organisations: a co-op school, there are about five hundred in the UK; a worker co-operative wholesale food retailer with 70 members; a major high street retailer owned by its employees; and an already well-established co-operative university, the University of Mondragon in the Basque country in Spain. One of the main lessons from this research was to affirm the strategy of working within and against institutional and social contradictions. This was put very clearly by the former assistant head principal of the co-operative school that we visited: 'It is actually at this point of heightened tension and conflict that the objective can be co-constructed and substantial transformation take place. This is important as it informs us that we should accept the conflict and tension rather than seeing it as a dysfunctional measure of the democratic work we are undertaking' (Jones, 2015, 82).

Taking this work forward, members of the SSC have been part of a working group made up of academics, activists and students, led by the Co-operative College in Manchester, the major promoter of co-operative education in the UK and internationally, to create a co-operative university with degree-awarding powers in England. As stated earlier, the Co-operative College in Manchester has had the ambition to establish a co-operative university since 1909. This project has been made possible by recent changes in higher education legislation in England to promote the involvement of alternative higher education providers. The intention of the government is to use this legislation to challenge the public service based model of higher education in England through the enforcement of neoliberal principles. The new co-operative university seeks to disrupt this neoliberal vision for higher education with a new university based on democratic and co-operative principles. Recently, there has been a change in the political mood in the UK, led as a political project by the Labour Party away from the politics of austerity, which includes a no fees model of higher education, and with ideas for public provision based on 'people power', including co-operatives (Labour Party 2016). The plans for a co-operative university feel like members of the SSC and the Co-operative College project are very much a part of this political change, although this political transformation is by no means assured (Neary and Winn 2019).

The project for a co-operative university has become an urgent necessity to support academics who have been made redundant after their teaching programmes were shut down. Three co-operative enterprises have been established by academics previously employed at Ruskin College, Oxford, to run courses for local trade unions, at Leicester Vaughan College, which will provide local adult education courses, as well as lecturers and students from Hull College who have set up the Feral Art College. These co-operatives will constitute the new co-operative university, forming a network of independent and autonomous co-operatives providing a range of different subject courses. The model for this federated network of co-operative providers of higher education is the Mondragon University governance structure, although the new co-operative university in the UK would initially be on a much smaller scale, initially teaching about 200 students.

Revolutionary Reformism: a Moment of Transition

A real live issue that members of the Social Science Centre and those involved with the co-operative university project are very aware of is to what extent this work constitutes revolutionary teaching or a form of opportunism and adaptation (Hanson 2017). Those involved in these co-operative higher education projects represent a broad spectrum of progressive political opinions. For those of us whose work is grounded in Marx's social theory, one fruitful approach is to consider the co-operative university as a moment of transition to communism.

The early co-operators well understood the co-operative movement as a form of revolutionary transition: from what they referred to as association, through co-operation, to communism. George Holyoake, one of the founding intellectuals of the co-operative movement (1817-1906) saw: 'Communism...a more enlarged and comprehensive form of co-operative life' (Gurney 1988 55). And: 'The Rochdale Pioneers founded a new form of co-operation: their inspiration was Communistic...their object was the emancipation of labour from capitalist exploitation. They had no idea of founding a race of grocers but a race of men (and women). Communism suffered incarnation in their hands, and the new birth was the co-operative store...' (1988 63-4).

Gurney reminds us that the co-operative movement was 'an oppositional and emergent culture' (Holyoake quoted in Gurney 1988 64).

There is some debate in the literature about the extent to which Holyoake advocated the abolition of capitalism or a way for capitalism to be humanised (Blaszak 1988). Blaszak argues that Holyoake was not the enemy of capital. For Holyoake workers were capitalist-labourers who sought to acquire capital for themselves, as self-employed workers; the main difference being that a co-operative is a 'co-operative company in which labour hires capital' (Holyoake in Blaszak 1988 58).

Holyoake was a contemporary of Marx who had a great deal to say about co-operatives. In Marx's Inaugural Address to the International Working Mens' Association he refers to co-operative enterprises as 'great social experiments':

The value of these great social experiments cannot be overrated. By deed instead of by argument, they have shown that production on a large scale, and in accord with the behests of modern science, may be carried on without the existence of a class of masters employing a class of hands; that to bear fruit, the means of labour need not be monopolised as a means of dominion over, and extortion against, the labouring man himself, and that, like slave labour, like serf labour, hired labour is but a transitory and inferior form, destined to disappear before associated labour plying its toils with a willing hand, a ready mind, and a joyous heart.
(Marx 1973 10)

For Marx co-operatives emerge out of the contradictions of capital and point towards its transcendence, but – and this is an important but – they are not the means by which this transcendence takes place, which requires connection and engagement with class struggle.

Reform or Revolution: How Do Revolutionary Teachers Teach?

A core issue for the revolutionary teacher is the relationship between reformism and revolution. The debate between reform and revolution, along with the associated issues of opportunism and adaptation, is a classic debate in revolutionary politics. Rosa Luxemburg (1871-1919), the Marxist revolutionary political activist and writer, took a radical line against reformism, including co-operatives, although she recognised the need for a politics of transition: 'Between social reforms and revolution there exists for social democracy an indissoluble tie. The struggle for reforms is its means; the social revolution, its aim' (Luxemburg 2006 3).

And, furthermore, she argues: '...there can be no time when the proletariat, placed in power by the force of events, is not in the condition, or is not morally obliged, to take certain measures for the realisation of its programme, that is, take transitory measures in the direction of socialism' (Luxemburg 2006 63).

Luxemburg favours the mass strike, not as a technical form of struggle decided by leaders of the labour movement from the subjective position of what is desirable, 'but only by objective investigation of the sources of the mass strike from the standpoint of what is historically inevitable' (2006 108), not based on the 'abstract logical analysis' (2006 108) of committees, but 'pulsating flesh and blood which cannot be cut out of the large frame of the revolution but is connected with all parts of the revolution by a thousand veins' (2006 134). This is a political event 'which can have sense and meaning only in connection with definite political situations' (2006 108). And to be clear: 'the mass strike does not produce the revolution; but the revolution produces the mass strike' (2006 141).

Other seminal work on this matter by Ralph Miliband and

Marcel Liebman in *Beyond Social Democracy* (1985) discusses reform or revolution from the perspective of the limits of parliamentary democracy in the UK. Since the First World War social democracy has been based on a project to gain a better deal for the working class within capitalism, with the state playing an important role in the distribution of resources in an equitable manner along with planning and managing capitalism linked to national interest to support the idea of 'capitalism with a human face'. This has led to many advancements for working people but has sought to limit the scope of political activity to parliamentarianism and trade unionism along with a strong criticism of 'leftist activists in the labour movement'. This means that 'social democracy has never posed any real threat to the structure of domination and exploitation of capitalist societies'. However, Miliband and Liebman argue, this does not mean that the working class has been opposed to more radical policies to create a new social order, the support of which has led to political victories. Corbyn is an example of this, perhaps, showing a clear sense of leadership and purpose, rather than 'conciliation and compromise'. The solution is not a vanguard party in a Marxist-Leninist style leading to authoritarianism and suppression of dissidents. Miliband and Liebman propose a 'revolutionary commitment...to a wholesale transformation of capitalist society in socialist directions. But it also involves a "reformist" commitment, in so far as it also seeks all reforms which can be seen to form part of the larger revolutionary purpose.' They refer to this as 'revolutionary reformism', which involves intervening in sites of class struggle, at work especially and during elections, as the development of a significant political culture which may mean that this takes place in the form of a political party. And, in the face of what is bound to be fierce resistance, 'to meet that resistance with every weapon that this requires, including of course the mobilisation of mass support'.

Marx himself recognised the need for transitional

arrangements.

Writing towards the end of his life, Marx set out in empirical terms an outline for a communist society (Berki 1983, Hudis 2013). This was in the form of a critical response to a political strategy to be adopted by the German Social Democratic Party (SPD) following their first political congress in the German town of Gotha from 22-27 May 1875. The aim of the Congress was to unite the German labour movement: the Social Democratic Workers Party of Germany and the General Association of German Workers. Marx's response, written originally as marginal notes to the congress programme weeks before the event took place, is known as the *Critique of the Gotha Programme*.

The Gotha Programme was underpinned by the assumption that the labour of the working class is the source of value and social wealth, which should be distributed in equal measure to all members of society. This would break the dominance of the capitalist class, ending the misery and servitude of workers based on wage slavery and inequality. At the heart of this proposition lay the ambition to establish producer co-operative societies with state support as a way of organising social labour. Marx is writing at a time when co-operative societies had been established in the early nineteenth century around Europe and the US by the labouring classes as a way of taking control of their own work, with workers employing capital rather than capital employing labour, in an attempt at securing economic self-determination. This movement was enriched by socialist and anarchist ideas and intellectuals (Vieta 2014): in the UK, Owen and Holyoake; in France, Lascelles and Proudhon; in Russia, Bakunin and Kropotkin as well as Chernyshevsky and Dmitrieff, and in the US the Knights of Labour and the International Workers of the World (Weir 1996, Wright 2014, Curl 2012, Yeo 1989). Other demands made by the *Gotha Programme* included a secret suffrage for men, a people's militia, restriction on women's and child labour, the freedom of association, freedom of the press and, of interest to revolutionary teachers, free education. So that, through all of this, would be achieved 'the emancipation of labour' (Marx 2018 6).

Marx's critical response in his critique of the Gotha Programme was based on a very different approach to the problem of communism: not the emancipation *of* labour, but the emancipation *from* labour. For Marx communism is not an alternative to capitalism, but emerges from within the social relations of capitalist production 'out of the womb' of 'the old society' (2018 8), whereby a society based on the measure of work in any form is denied.

Marx's trenchant disagreement with the Gotha Programme was based on a number of fundamental points. Firstly, abstract labour: generalised social labour measured by time, not labour, is the substance of value. Secondly, while capitalist society might wish to construct the ideology/idea of labour as a supernatural creative power' (2018 3), as an ideology to give substance to a universal ethic of work and improvement, the glorification of work is actually undermined by the class-based nature of society. In capitalist society the labour of others is exploited by the owners of the means of production, providing wealth and affluence for the owners along with misery and deprivation for workers. These conditions are enforced by the state through the law of private property and the police: 'a state which is nothing but a police-guarded military despotism, embellished with parliamentary forms' (Marx *Critique of Gotha Programme* 2018 19).

For Marx, communism would not be achieved through one leap, but as a process of transition, from a lower to a higher state of society. During the lower stage labour would not yet have been abolished, but workers should be recompensed for their direct labour time based on what they have contributed to society. While this transitional stage outlined by Marx gets away from the exploitation of labour it still relies on the connected processes of exchange and equality as well as a principle of right, all of which provide the basis of a marketised capitalist society. The transition to a higher stage is an historical process, which would emerge automatically from the lower stage once 'the material conditions of production are the co-operative property of the workers themselves' (Marx 2018 11). This would lead automatically to a shift in focus from the distribution of what had been produced to the process of production itself. This focus on production would be further enhanced through the development of co-operative enterprises. Marx was in favour of co-operatives, but not those supported by the state:

> That the workers desire to establish the conditions of co-operative production on a social, and first of all on a national scale in their own country, only means that they are working to revolutionise the present conditions of production, and has nothing in common with the foundation of co-operative societies with state aid. But as far as the present co-operative societies are concerned they are of value only in so far as they are independent creations of the workers and not the proteges either of the government or of the bourgeoisie. (2018 17).

This focus on co-operative production would dissolve the division of labour as well as the distinction between mental and manual labour, so that labour is transformed 'from a mere means of life' to 'the prime necessity of life'. In this arrangement recompense and reward is not based on the proceeds of labour according to rights and equality, but, rather, 'from each according to their abilities, to each according to their needs' (Marx 2018 10).

For Marx, the capitalist state, whatever its democratic pretensions, is only ever 'a police-guarded military despotism' (Marx 2018 19), in which democracy is within the limits of what is 'permitted by the police' (2018 19). This aversion to state provision is extended in Marx's critique of free education, which he regards as 'altogether objectionable' (2003 20); rather than the state educate the people 'the state has need...of a very stern education by the people' (2018 21).

So what would a stern education by the people look like? The answer to that question is the same as how do revolutionary teachers teach?

Riot-Strike-Riot: Lessons for the Revolutionary Teacher – Strike-Riot-Strike

I started this book with student protest and urban riots. I want now, at the end of this book, to return to that theme to consider the real nature of Student as Producer. I will do this through an engagement with Joshua Clover's (2016) *Riot-Strike-Riot: the New Era of Uprisings,* as a very useful way of framing this debate. While Clover favours Riot prime over strikes, I will argue in favour of Strike prime as a way of unlearning the law of labour. Strike prime is based on the principle of 'do nothing that is instrumental for Capital' based on a negative critique of labour in capitalism (Postone 1993), to create a new form of communist social wealth, specifically knowledge/social knowing, as the basis for the communist society/ university.

I want to reclaim Strike, in terms of Strike prime. Not Strike in terms of defending capitalist work: labour and the wage, as Clover defines it; but, rather, the abolition of labour and the creation of a new form of social value, or common wealth.

Clover wants to acknowledge the social and political significance of riots, a form of political activity that has intensified since the period he refers to as, after Brenner, 'the Long Crisis'. The purpose of Clover's book is to provide an adequate theory of riot: 'They deserve an adequate theory' (Clover 2016 1). The theory of riot goes beyond the riot itself: 'A theory of riot is a theory of crisis' (2016 1), providing the possibility for new thinking about crisis and how it unfolds. His intention is to uncover *'a practice to which theory is adequate'* (2016 191, author's italics).

Clover sets out to provide an account for the development of strikes and riots through a version of historical materialism. This version of historical materialism grounds strikes as protests to defend wages where the focus is on production (work), and riots as a protest against the price of food and other commodities (the market). He argues that in the pre-Long Crisis period when capitalist accumulation was dominated by productivity growth, strikes were the dominant form of political protest; but now, in an era in which global productivity is in decline, and as capital moves to focus its profit-making activity in the realm of consumption, then the riot assumes major significance. While the riot may involve looting for everyday necessities, it has profound political and even ludic inclinations: 'No one knows what the riot wants. It wants nothing but its own disorder, its bright opacity' (2016 83). The riot is not an event, but a modality or a way of life, as a form of stretched radical co-operation: The 'riot and strike are collective personifications of circulation and production at the limit' (2016 121). But, whereas strikes have predetermined demands, 'unlike the strike it is hard to know when and where the riot starts and ends' (2016 123). One key aspect of the current post-industrial world is that the crisis has produced surplus populations, especially black and racialised groups, for whom not only waged work but even the market is now out of reach. In this new set of social arrangements, the market has been replaced by the state, so that 'the police now stand *in the place of* the economy' (2016 125, author's italics). Riot prime is when the struggles with the market and the economy recede and are replaced with struggle against the state. In this context the revolutionary subject is no longer labour or the proletariat, whose moment passed with the decline in productivity and who was only ever implicated in the capitalist process of growth to defend the wage, but the revolutionary subject will emerge from out of the lumpen, the rabble and the dispossessed.

It is out of this population that the riot is born. To Clover's credit he recognises that this new subject cannot be named a sociological category in advance. Clover argues the way in which the new radical subject emerges is 'to bring forward the real movement within which these social categories develop, change, and elaborate themselves internally and in relation to other social forces' (2016 180).

There is an element of value-form theory in Clover's work, including an account of Police from other value-form theorists, especially Endnotes, a Marxist writing collective. Quoting Endnotes, Clover argues that the police are an internal, integral and dialectic aspect of the riot, in what he describes as 'an economy of state violence' (2016 171):

> The Police, in this sense, are not an external force of order applied by the state to an already rioting mass, but an integral part of the riot: not only its standard component spark-plug, acting via the usual death at police hands, of some young black man, but also the necessary on-going partner of the rioting crowd from who the space must be liberated if this liberation is to mean anything at all; who must be attacked as an enemy if the crowd is to be unified in anything; who must be forced to recognise the agency of a habitually subjected group.
> (Endnotes 2011)

However, this form of agency is not elaborated or discussed, rather reduced by Clover, to a type of unmediated violence: 'The global *class dangereuses* are united not by their role as producers but by their relationship to state violence' (2016 165). It is out of this unmediated violent relationship (terror) that 'the basis for the surplus rebellion and its form...[emerges]...which must exceed the logic of recognition and negotiation' (2016 165). Or, what Clover calls, following Frantz Fanon's strategy for decolonisation in *Wretched of the Earth* (1961), 'an agenda for total disorder' (2016 165). In this violent scenario Clover has it that Police, after Huey Newton, the African-American communist revolutionary, are an 'occupying army' (2016 164).

Clover's historical materialism understands the significance of Marx's labour theory of value, recognising 'value's self-undermining dynamic' (Clover 2016 84), but this is expressed in an orthodox economistic form; like Mason and Benjamin: it is not dialectic enough. Clover does refer to the work of Moishe Postone (1993), who is critical of orthodox Marxism, and Postone's point about the complicit role that labour plays in capitalist accumulation, and, therefore, the labour movement's limited contribution to revolutionary struggle. For Clover 'struggles against capital can only be *against* capital's existence, rather than *for* the empowering of labour' (2016 147, author's italics). Clover uses Postone to support the idea that communism is not a redistribution of resources, but rather is 'the abolition of the economy and the end of the indexical relation between one's labour and any relation or access to social wealth' (2016 148). This argument is the basis of Clover's Riot prime thesis. But Clover does not extend this important insight to Postone's reappraisal of Marx's critical theory. Postone's point is not that the limits of labour mean we move to a focus on circulation and dispossession, quite the reverse, in fact: production is central for Postone, not from 'the perspective of labour, but as a critique of labour in capitalism' (Postone 1993 5), with very important consequences, as we have seen, for the nature of revolutionary subjectivity and the politics and tactics of revolution. It is only through the abolition of labour, and a civilisation based on labour, that capitalism can be transcended and a new form of social wealth established.

There is much to be learned from Clover about the significance of the riot. The strength of the riot is its sheer negativity: 'The riot seeks to preserve nothing, but perhaps for a shared antagonist, a shared misery, a shared negation' (Clover 2016 150). His insights about the racialisation of riots and the killing by the police of black men and women are compelling. And, we are living in a time of civil war. The riot is a pedagogy: a way to 'figure out' the nature of its predicament (155), not just as 'collective action but as class struggle' (2016 159) passed on not by explication or explanation but through 'resonance' (2016 153). But without an understanding of the way in which the value-relation mediates the life-world of capitalist civilisation, and out of which its regulatory instruments are derived, including the police-form and the state-form (Holloway and Picciotto 1977, Clarke 1991), then more terrible violence is very likely to be inflicted on the civilian population as a whole. Clover's Riot prime, for all of its spectacular manifestation, is an expression of 'reduced praxis and pseudo-activity' (Kurz 2007). To use Clover's own words against him, his theory is not adequate to practice.

I want to reclaim Strike, in terms of Strike prime; so Strike-Riot-Strike not Riot-Strike-Riot. Not strike in terms of defending capitalist work: labour and the wage, but in ways that move for the abolition of labour. Not the abandonment of the strike, but Strike prime, by which I mean not the defence of labour and the wage, nor mass strike in the terms envisaged by Rosa Luxemburg, but rather, after Postone, the abolition of capital through a critique of capitalism, not from the perspective of labour in capital but a critique of labour in capitalism. This is not to dismiss Luxemburg, who has pertinent things to say about the real nature of revolution, including its relationship to violence:

History has found a solution in a deeper and finer fashion: in the advent of revolutionary mass strikes, which, of course, in no way replaces brutal street fights or renders them unnecessary, but which reduces them to a moment in the long period of political struggle, and which at the same time unites with the revolutionary period an enormous cultural work in the most exact sense of the words: the material and intellectual elevation of the whole working class through the 'civilising' of the barbaric forms of capitalist exploitation. (Luxemburg 2006 161)

The difference between the mass strike and Strike prime is that Rosa Luxemburg does not recognise the significance of the value-form of labour and the function abstract labour plays in the constitution of capitalist society. She is for the affirmation of labour, rather than its negation. Strike prime is for the abolition of a society organised on the principle of work.

Benjamin (1986 [1921]) has written on the power of the strike, taking his line from George Sorel's *Reflections on Violence* (1908). Benjamin makes a distinction between the political strike and the proletarian, or revolutionary, strike in the context of class struggle. The political strike aims to maintain centralised and authoritarian state power under the control of moderate socialist politicians. The proletarian strike is anarchistic and revolutionary, intent on 'destroying state power…to abolish the state' (1986 [1921] 291). The proletarian strike does not return to work after having won concessions; but, rather, 'to resume a wholly transformed work, no longer enforced by the state' 1986 (291-2). Benjamin is extending his version of proletarian politics to the strike but again his reading of the proletariat is not dialectic enough. Following Lukacs and against Adorno, he argues that sociologists and social reformers cannot think for the proletariat, although this version of the proletariat is profoundly sociological, as a categorical entity that appears to stand outside of the social relations of production as a form of social activity that is already made. This approach to revolutionary politics does not fully develop a Marxist theory of the state, using Marx's method set out in his analysis of the law of value and the commodity-form (Clarke 1991a, Holloway and Picciotto 1977). Clover's theory is not dialectical enough.

My focus on strike is in a moment when the strike is being rejuvenated.

Women's Strike

Strike has already gained a second life – this time as the Women's Strike, in Italy, North and South America and globally since 2016, including *campaneras*, Black and indigenous women, extending the movement of protest to include not just work oppression and exploitation but femicide (Mason-Deese 2018). Only with women can a strike become a General Strike (Mariarosa dalla Costa 1974). The Women's Strike is against all forms of 'sexist violence' (Gutierrez 2018 6/22), identifying labour as a major cause of gender violence and a way for women workers to make common cause; 'to change everything' (Gutierrez 2018 13/22). This approach insists that feminism looks at the way in which capitalism 'extract(s) value from life...puts life at risk' (2018 6/18), and so focuses on 'the reproduction of life itself' (Mason-Deese 2018 6/18), looking to 'redistribute and rearrange reproductive labour' and produce 'a new collective subject' (8/18). The Women's Strike does not define itself as victim but as forms of resistance conceptualised as 'collective self-defense and mutual aid' (Mason-Deese 2018 13/18) 'in defense of life...threatened by capital' (Gutierrez 2018 3/22). This is a structural problem and capital is the structuring principle (9/18). The Women's Strike sees a clear connection between 'dominant masculine rationality' and 'the rationality of capital accumulation' (2018 11/22). The Women's Strike aims 'to create new relations, challenging the inequalities and hierarchies that make gender violence so prevalent, and begin to imagine new ways of structuring society and work' (Mason-Deese 2018 2/18) as a new form of 'popular economy' (Mason-Deese 2018 7/18): 'among women' (Gutierrez 2018 14/22). In this way they mean to add a collective dimension to the #MeToo movement, extending beyond the denunciation of famous men by woman, to find strength in solidarity to resist all male violence against women. They call this a 'politics in feminine' Gutierrez (2018) as resistance to the matrix of 'colonial-capitalist-patriarchal power' (Mason-Deese 2018 15).

The Women's Strike is supported by Silvia Federici (2014). Her approach is based on a critique of mainstream Marxism, where the starting point is the 'waged male proletariat and the development of commodity production' (Federici 2014 12). The strength of this approach is, as is evident from the Women's Strike, that it allows women to find a common cause and collective forms of resistance to the violence imposed by capitalist work. Labour is affirmed as a collective source of strength:

> We name our enormous capacity for reproductive, productive, and affective labor, and through those words we assume our own strength. We assume and exhibit our own force. We weave together the struggle against feminicidal violence with the other multiple and (re)hidden forms of violence that threaten and annihilate our everyday existence, that capture our capacity for enjoyment, that impose a life that has been ripped apart, which we will have to continue nourishing if we do not subvert it. We will not do it: we strike. (Gutierrez 2018 12/22)

Student as Producer supports the Women's Strike as a form of Strike prime, being against the affirmation of labour in any form and for the abolition of capitalist work and social reproduction based not on the law of labour but life-enhancing-life. This revolutionary approach is sustained by a critique of value set out in this book. Gutierrez does reference Dinerstein's value-from theory as the most careful reflection on materialist prefiguration but this is not developed (Gutierrez 2018 20/22). The connection between capitalist rationality and masculine violence is well made but the relationship is not fully established leaving the space for patriarchy to be presented as a transhistorical category, and for the revolutionary struggle to be fragmented as a series of intersections and road-blocks.

Roswitha Scholz (2009) has elaborated on gender relations with a 'new Marxist-feminist framework' giving Postone's critique of value and labour 'a feminist twist'. For Scholz 'gender specific attributes are a fundamental characteristic of the symbolic order of commodity producing patriarchy' (4/12). What appear to be given as feminist attributes disassociated from the masculine subject, sensitivity, emotionality, as well as 'difficiences in thought and character', are lesser forms of valorisation. Masculinity in capitalism is an expression of the real character of capital, brutal and violent, so that 'male gender must be understood as the gender of capitalism' (5). Men and women are the bearers of the social relations of capitalism which through the imposition of value and the law of abstract labour act as an impersonal form of social domination. Reading gender relations in this way must take into account identity politics and the cultural context of each situation. This critique of labour with a feminist twist provides a theoretical framework to consider other forms of identity politics, e.g., racism and antisemitism (Postone 1980).

Strike prime is for a society of abundance: communism (Kay and Mott 1982). There is no affirmation or civilising of capitalism. Strike prime is cast by divine violence, educative power and radical doubt (Benjamin 1921), or the creation of non-institutions (Wilding 2009), or doing nothing: teach, teach, teach, learn, learn, learn (Zizek 2007, Ranciére 1991) and Adorno's negative understanding of the social world against itself, not pseudo-concrete solutions (Kurz 2007). That is what revolutionary teachers have to learn.

Back to Walter Benjamin and Beyond

This book has been written from inside the English higher education system at a time when it has been going through considerable traumatic transition from public provision to financial machine. The move to reinvent the university was taking place before the student protests of 2010 and the summer riots that followed in 2011, but these revolts were catalytic and gave the move to transform the English university energy and dynamism, focusing our minds on the problem of Police.

What I have learned is that the student protests of 2010 achieved a great deal, in very real practical terms that have made the issue of student fees one of the most important political issues for parliamentary politics, and created a political movement in support of the most radical left-wing politician in British politics, Jeremy Corbyn. While all of this points to progressive reforms in education and other social issues, it falls a long way short from any attempt at revolutionising the political process.

For revolutionary inspiration we turned to Walter Benjamin. Walter Benjamin asked the question: how do radical intellectuals act in a moment of crisis? I have rephrased his question in this book as how do revolutionary teachers? This is not a question about merely pedagogical techniques, e.g., operativism and astonishment, although techniques are important; but, more fundamentally, the need to revolutionise the means of capitalist production. The point made by Student as Producer is that in *The Author as Producer*, Benjamin could not answer the question he set for himself, because his understanding of capitalist labour: the proletariat was not dialectical enough. A revolution of the means of production starts from a critique of labour in capitalism: that is what Student as Producer means by unlearning the law of labour, as the basis for revolutionary teaching. This is a practical problem as much as a theoretical problem, based on an approach to democracy grounded in the value-form and reconciled as a type of non-institution: or transitions to communism, like the co-operative university. Postone's critique of orthodox Marxism as well as Lukac's work, on which Benjamin relies, shows the limits of revolutionary transformation based on an affirmative approach to labour. Postone, after his reappraisal of Marx's social theory, provides the theoretical framework to reconsider the real nature of labour and, as a result, how the social relations of capitalist production can be transformed; but he provides no practical suggestion as to how this might take place. In this book I have suggested developing a co-operative university, grounded in a theory of radical democracy and the law of value, as a moment of transition to a new form of radical epistemology, based on what can be learned from revolutionary teachers.

The book critically engaged with three major revolutionary teachers: Jacques Ranciére, Paulo Freire and Paula Allman, setting out key learning points from their theoretical and practical work. These authors were chosen for their capacity to read through Marx's labour theory of value and, therefore, have much to teach about unlearning the law of labour. To pick a central theme from these theorists, each offered a reinvigorated way of considering the politics that underpin Marx's social theory: for Ranciére: *dissensus* – the way in which new forms of social subjectivities emerge out of struggle contra Police; for Freire: *dialogue* – that the world comes to be known and radically transformed through critical debate, social policy and practice; and from Allman's close reading of Marx's texts, the power of the *dialectics*, and, in particular, the struggle of labour against capital, as a form of 'restless negative'.

Democracy and the Law of Value

The central issue identified at the first Reinvention Centre conference in 2007 is the relationship between democracy and the law of value: the value-form. This matter is directly addressed in the attempt to build the co-operative university, not as a qualifications factory, but as a new form of social institution or non-institution even – as a new form of social wealth grounded in social knowing at the level of society: or the communist university. The co-operative university will be democratically run by its members with the transitional intention of abolishing the law of value and creating a new form of social wealth: maybe 'anti-value in motion' (Dinerstein 2015, Dinerstein and Neary 2002). All of this needs to take into account the ubiquity of Police as the imposition of the most institutional of all capitalist forms: labour, or capitalist work.

This taking into account of what is at stake is encapsulated by the concept of Strike prime, not workers acting to defend their jobs, although there are times when this needs to be done, but by abolishing the social relations of capitalist work. I have suggested the co-operative university as a type of revolutionary reformism institution, on the way to communism.

That is how revolutionary teachers teach; but how can this radical epistemology be defended?

Afterword: Authority and Authorship

Not-Police

The police have come in for much scrutiny in this book – as the violent and brutalising Police-State, as occupying an unenviable position between neoliberal policy makers and the public (Bloom 2012), as a force that racially profiles young offenders (Hall et al 2013), as an institution that enforces the law of labour (Neocleous 2000), as a repressive device that decides who has political legitimacy or identity (Ranciére 1999), as well as an integral aspect of state violence and riot (Endnotes 2011). And, even, as the basis for a university curriculum: Police Studies (Wellmon 2015). Now, at the end of the book, I want to consider a radical alternative to Police, through what I am calling Authority and Authorship, after Walter Benjamin and Evgeny Pashukanis, to consider what policing would be in a communist society, as a sort of thought experiment. I will do this using the conceptual framework operationalised in this book as the basis for Student as Producer: a Marxist critique of the commodity-form, now applied to the design of socialist sanctions and defence.

This goes beyond a call for policing to be based on greater social, economic and political equality and for an end to racialised and class-based inequality (Vitale Alex 2017). These are important and necessary demands, but they are unlikely to be realised, as the concepts on which they are based, equality, justice and freedom, are functions of a society based on the logic of the commodity-form: a bourgeois morality grounded in the notion of commensurability producing an inhuman value system, carrying with it, as Ranciére explains, the implicit assumption of an inequality that will be forever maintained.

Much of the theoretical work on socialist sanctions and defence that run counter to the capitalist law of crime and punishment has already been done by Evgeny Pashukanis (1891-1937) after the October 1917 revolution in Russia. Evgeny Pashukanis is considered 'a giant of legal theory' and 'the dominant figure in Soviet jurisprudence in the 1920s and 1930s' (Mieville 2005 75), based on his analysis of Marxism and the rule of law (Pashukanis 1989). Pashukanis has given us 'the most exciting critique since Marx of the critique of law' (Arthur 1989 31). Pashukanis favours a materialist 'revolutionary-dialectic approach to questions of law' (1989 34); not based on class law, or the proletariat, but looking for the sociological roots to expose capitalist law's social and historical derivation as a temporary capitalist/bourgeois arrangement. The task is to create 'a jurisprudence that is equal to its immediate practical task' (1989 48) for a communist society.

Pashukanis asks the question: 'How are we to understand the historical configuration of state and law in social formations where capitalist property (value) has been abolished but where communism has not yet been achieved?' (Beirne and Sharlet 2015). Pashukanis's communist law is not based on class interest: 'a Proletarian or socialist law was a conceptual, and therefore practical, absurdity' (Beirne and Sharlet 2015 24), but following Marx he creates a social theory of capitalist law from an analysis of the commodity-form and the law of value. His theory is referred to as 'commodity exchange theory' in which legal relations are themselves derived from the same set of social relations as the capitalist commodity. He comes to this conclusion after applying Marx's social theory to the legal aspects of capitalist society:

> In as much as the wealth of capitalist society appears as "an immense collection of commodities", so this society itself appears as an endless chain of legal relations. (Pashukanis 1989 85)

What is distinctive about Pashukanis' version of Marx is the focus on the commodity-form as the organising principle of capitalist society. The focus on commodity-form is much closer to Marx's critical social theory in *Capital* and *The Grundrisse* than interpretations which consider Marx's work merely an economic theory, and the working class as the agents of revolutionary transformation, after Benjamin and Lukacs and traditional versions of Marxism (Postone 1993). Pashukanis provides a radical critique of traditional Marxism, contradicting any version of 'proletarian law' (Pashukanis 1989 61) or support for a Marxist-Leninist state. Pashukanis's legal theory was to cost him his life, as it ran counter to the Stalinist version of a worker's state. He was murdered in 1937 by one of Stalin's murder squads.

As we have seen, according to Marx, the commodity-form is a contradictory arrangement, made up of use value and exchange value: commodities must be useful but they are made to be exchanged. Exchange swamps utility (Kay and Mott 1982), forming 'a synthetic whole' (1989 57) as the basis for social relations of capitalist society. This synthetic whole is imposed as an impersonal type of domination by Money and the State as supreme forms of social power (Clarke 1988). This form of domination is characterised by freedom: individuals must have the capacity to exchange commodities, including their own commodity labour- power, and equivalence; commodities have a common denominator, providing the basis for the core principles of capitalist law: freedom and equality, as well as the framework for legal ideology and bourgeois morality (Kurz 2014). While the realm of exchange may appear, as Marx puts it in *Capital*, like 'a very Eden of the innate rights of man', it is conjured from the more exploitative productive arrangements of valorisation.

Despite the power of Pashukanis' theory of law based on commodity exchange, he has nothing to say about the productive relations of work on which it is based, which can be regarded as a weakness in his exposition (Arthur 1989 30). An account that includes capitalist labour processes would recognise that while value is validated in exchange, it is produced in the process of production. Exchange value, the common denominator, is human energy measured in time (Jappe 2017). Workers are paid the full value of their labour-power: a subsistence wage which maintains their condition of needing to work, but not the full value of what has been produced. This is what Marx refers to as surplus value and is the basis of capitalist exploitation. While the employment contract appears to be based on the free will of workers it masks the reality of command and coercion that is a feature of capitalist work. What Pashukanis does maintain is that relations of social domination are imposed politically and legally by the capitalist state, which, acting in the 'impersonal interest of the system' (Pashukanis 1989 137) appears as if it were an independent power. This independence is undermined by its determination to impose the law of value, by any means necessary, through the instruments designed to cope with every emergency: the rule of law, prison and the police.

Dragan Milovanovic (2003) shows how Pashukanis theorised the equivalence implied in commodity exchange relations is manifest in capitalist crime and punishment: 'Similarly, with the violation of law, equivalent exchange materialises itself in the form of equivalent punishment. It is only at a certain stage of economic development – where equivalent exchange dominates – that we also find punishments fully expressed and articulated in the form of equivalent exchange. Ancient law, Pashukanis goes on to say, knew only collective responsibility. Bourgeois-capitalist law, on the other hand, invents the notion of individual responsibility and liability and a "gradation of liability". The equivalence principle becomes dominant: Deprivation of freedom – for a definite term previously indicated in the judgement of the court is the specific form in which modern, that is, bourgeois capitalist criminal law, realizes the basis of equivalent retribution' (2003 xv).

This principle of individualised equivalence is evident by the way in which capitalist law is measured in terms of time equivalents as prison sentences, or fines based on monetary values, and even work as a form of punishment as prison labour schemes and community punishments. The principle of equivalence under the law is derived from the principle of equivalent exchange, just as the freedom ideal is based on the freedom to buy and sell goods in the capitalist market as a bearer of private interest or abstract legal subject. Pashukanis calls this 'a deep interconnection with the legal form and the commodity form' (1989 63).

Pashukanis concludes his general treatise on Marxism and law by stating that abstract notions of crime and punishment will only begin to disappear with 'the withering away of the law altogether, that is to say, the disappearance of the juridical factor from the social relation' (1989 61).

Pashukanis returns us to the Marx of the Gotha programme, where transition bears the scars of the legal form. The full withering away is when 'labour has become not only a means of life but life's prime want' (Pashukanis 1989 63); in other words, not a society labour organised as a labour camp, but another form of social activity 'when the productive forces grow together with the all-round development of the individual, when everyone works spontaneously according to their abilities' (1989 63). The version of the future foregrounds what Marx refers to as 'the social individual' (*Grundrisse* 1993 749) rather than a society based on the interests of the working class or notions of equality.

Bourgeois law should not be replaced by proletarian law, but by another version of social order in which 'the means of production are socially owned and in which the producers do not exchange their products' (1989 61). This impersonal law of equivalence is to be replaced by a form of order where infractions are seen as 'a medical-educational problem' (1989 64): a pedagogical problem based on an ethic of care. The way to do this is to abolish the value-form and, in particular, the abstraction within which all of this is constrained: 'labour in general' (1989 67), i.e., the overwhelming social imperative of capitalist work.

Pashukanis's proposal is to create a society based not on the general interest of capital, and the radical individualism of freedom and equivalence imposed by money, the state and contract law, but on a 'unity of purpose' (1989 81) carried out through technical regulation, grounded in the principle of 'social defence' (1989 185), as various forms of planning and administration. Pashukanis explains there is a difference between the equivalence-based punishment of capitalist law and his notion of social defence. The latter would go beyond the abstract equivalence principles of the former inasmuch as '[i]t would require...an exact description of *symptoms* characterizing a socially dangerous condition and an exact elaboration of the *methods* to be used in each individual case in order to avert the danger to society' (1989 187). In other words, for Pashukanis, the social defence approach must return to the notion of differences, not equivalences, in dealing with those who contravene this new form of social order. From out of this approach will come an ethics of care grounded in an historical materialist version of the social world: not normatively based on social justice or some other liberalised cosmology (Earthcare 2018).

Pashukanis makes the point that in the world of 'legal regulation everything is a conflict of private interests' (1989 81), but a communistic version of the social world conceives of social order as a 'unity of purpose' (1989 81). He further develops his medicalised analogy: in a hospital there are a set of rules for the patient and the hospital with the same purpose of healing the sick person. This can involve some constraint on the sick person, but is a progressive arrangement 'so long as the constraint is viewed from the standpoint of a goal' (1989 81). This is the same goal for the sick person and person doing the constraining. This is not a legal arrangement but 'a technically expedient act and no more' (1989 81). Under this arrangement the regulatory principle becomes a technical function based on a social unity of purpose – as a social goal rather than a collection of private interests, as an act of 'social defence' (1989 185). Punishment is replaced by 'expediency for the protection of society' (1989 185), with a focus on the 'symptoms' which 'characterise the socially dangerous situation' (1989 187) along with an exact elaboration of the methods to be used in each individual case in order to avert the danger to society. 'These rules express in clear and simple terms the goal society has set itself' (1989 187). In the value-form, the social purpose is masked (the expansion of value); although it cannot help but reveal itself: hence capital punishment (Linebaugh 2006). In the new social arrangement not capital punishment but communist care: another form of what I want to call authority when Police has withered away.

The new authority would operate not as technical-administrative planning, as Pashukanis would have it, but as the process of practical *mediation*, not based on compulsion or even consensus, but grounded in lessons learned from revolutionary teachers: through Ranciére's notion of *dissensus*, Freire's *dialogical* teaching and Allman's recognition of the power of the *dialectic*, enabling a system based on needs and capacities to operate according to the principle of social defence, from the standpoint of the social individual. Not the *discretion*, revealed by Neocleous as the basis for Police behaviour, but *dissensus*, *dialogue* and *dialectics*. This new authority and the *dissensus*, *dialogue* and *dialectics* on which it is based, can be set alongside Walter Benjamin's concept of educative power, or radical doubt. Educative power is not an absolute principle, or objective assessment, or 'a criterion of judgment' like the commandment 'thou shalt not kill' (1986/1921 298), but a 'guideline' for those who have to take responsibility for decision making. Educative power is 'critical, discriminating and decisive' (1986/1921 299-300), providing the conditions by which state power can be abolished and replaced by a revolutionary society. This is what I mean by revolutionary teaching and learning.

Authority and Authorship

We can find support for this notion of Authority in Walter Benjamin's concept of authorship, as set out in *The Author as Producer*, while noting its limitations. Benjamin's concept of authorship points away from bourgeois sociological concepts of agency, reaching out to more structural determinations, as the struggle between the proletariat and capitalists; although, as we have seen, this approach is not dialectical enough. For Student as Producer agency needs to be grounded in the version of Marx's value theory of labour presented here as a critique of labour. Benjamin's version of class struggle would lead to what Pashukanis refers to as the absurdity of proletarian law, with all of its negative consequences – as a sort of authoritarian state acting on behalf of the working class. But authorship can be substantiated by divining a more substantive understanding of its own derivation, and, in particular, the concept of authority.

I want to reclaim authority as a critical political category for social theory, taking my lead from Alexandre Kojeve (1902-68). In *The Notion of Authority* (Verso 2014) Kojeve argues that a study of authority is essential before attempting a study of the state. This focus on authority as a critical category means authority does not have to end up as authoritarianism. The concept of authority has gained some recognition in sociology: as charismatic, traditional and legal (Weber 1978), but these categorisations tend towards psychological, cultural and functional explanations, lacking the historical materialism of revolutionary theory (McCulloch 2014, Weber 1978, Agamben 2005).

Hannah Arendt (1954) has done much to restore the concept of authority to political philosophy, finding her inspiration in ancient Rome (Hammer 2002, 2014). Authority is derived from the Roman notion of *auctoritas*, which claims its authority as a form of participatory politics working towards a common aim (Hammer 2014 130). This is contrary to the Greek Platonic variation of authority, the version we saw in Ranciére's account of Pluto's cave, which gives legitimacy to the philosopher king or other sovereign power (the state). For Arendt, the Roman *Auctoritas* is derived from the verb *augere*, to augment, conceived as a type of social partnership based on a 'subjective notion of on-going agreement' (2014 130) and 'settlement' (2014 137). Power is not then fixed but 'a form of authoring or negotiating within history' (2014 131). Auctoritas is 'a public and negotiated power' (2014 133). Arendt tells us that for Roman political philosophy the alternative to auctoritas is 'stalemate or violence' (2014 132).

We can start to reimagine Walter Benjamin's fascination with Klee's Angelus painting, not as Postone describes it as a backward looking facing up to the future, but as a way of grounding revolution firmly in what has already been made: the historical now.

For Arendt in 'What is Authority?' authority gets its legitimation from the past based on the founding principles of the Roman world, as represented by custom and tradition. As she put it:

Authority, resting on the foundation of the past as its unshaken cornerstone, gave the world the permanence and durability which human beings need precisely because they are mortals – the most unstable and futile beings we know of. Its loss is tantamount to a loss of groundwork of the world, which even since then has begun to shift, to change and transform itself with ever-increasing rapidity from one shape into another, as though we were living and struggling in a Protean universe where everything at any moment can become almost anything else. But the loss of worldly permanence and reliability – which politically is identical with the loss of authority – does not entail, at least not necessarily, the loss of the human capacity for building, preserving, and caring for a world that

can survive us and remain a place fit to live in for those who
come after us.
(1954 3)

In this scenario authorship is the spirit or the energy with which
a world is founded and imbued anew as the really existing
derivative of an already constituted political society. Authority
for Arendt is the augmentation of the foundation of society, with
the character of advice that cannot be ignored, requiring 'neither
command not external coercion to make itself heard' (1954
18). The current absence of any sense of authentic authority
is 'because we have no reality, either in history or everyday
experience, to which we can unanimously appeal' (1954 26).
And so Arendt is claiming authority based on the affirmation
of the foundations or the groundwork of the social world. The
point of authority for Student as Producer as the science of not-
Police is that there is a groundwork that can be known, through
reason and science and a radical epistemology. Student as
Producer has established that groundwork as the law of labour,
but, rather than affirming that groundwork, the law of labour
needs to be abolished, in such a way that the problem of power,
as Arendt says, 'needs to be confronted anew' (29). This is the
point Marx made when he described the co-operative movement
as challenging not affirming the groundwork of capitalist social
relations: 'We recommend to the working men to embark in co-
operative production rather than in co-operative stores. The
latter touch but the surface of the present economical system,
the former attacks its groundwork' (Marx, 1866). This attack on
the groundwork can be extended to include men and women
as a 'transforming force', reflecting 'the structural possibilities
for democratic social production found within capitalism' (Egan
1990 72).

And so it is by abolishing the groundwork of capitalist labour
that we can retain 'the human capacity for building, preserving,

and caring for a world that can survive us and remain a place fit to live in for those who come after us' (Arendt 1954 3).

Agamben (2005) emphasises that the act of authorship or augmenting (*auctor*) is not based on individual agency in the sense understood in bourgeois sociology, grounded in entitlements, but occurs in relation to 'formless matter of incomplete being – that must be perfected or made to grow. Every creation is always a cocreation just as every author is always a coauthor' (2005 76). That is, 'not so much the voluntary exercise of a right as the actualisation of an impersonal power in the very person of the *auctor*' (2005 77). This impersonal form of power is not the alienated abstract power of the law of commodity exchange but the power that is grounded in the actions of others: an incomplete being in the act of being created, or, the 'perfect act' (Agamben 2005 78). What is at stake here, in terms of 'the perfect act', is not law but life-enhancing-life, or an 'august life' (2005 83), giving substance to what others have described in critical theory as dignity (Holloway 2002), anchoring struggle not into the future, as hope, but in the historical now; within a moment that is 'already in the process of ruin and decay' (2005 86), against capital's 'killing machine' (2005 86). All of this gives substance to the concept of radical doubt based on a critique of the groundwork of capitalist society, or unlearning the law of labour

And now, finally, in answer to the question, what is it to be a Marxist working in higher education in an English university? The answer is that a critical reappraisal of Marx's theory grounds our enterprise as worker-intellectuals not in a commitment to the proletariat, but, more foundationally, in the struggle to dissolve the social relations of capitalist work. It is this attempt to abolish the capital relation that avoids the charge of pseudo-activism. This is the principle on which Marxist academics can claim Authority and Authorship, alongside others, as the true movement of human intelligence taking possession of its own power. The project is to create a civilisation that is not organised as a labour camp, but one that recognises and reconciles humanity and nature's needs and capacities, learning and teaching each other, as a pedagogy of excess in a world of abundance.

References

Adorno, Theodor (1993) Hegel: Three Studies. Massachusetts and London: MIT Press.

Adorno, Theodor (1998) Marginalia to Theory and Practice. Critical Models: Catchwords and Interventions. New York: Columbia University Press, 259-278.

Adorno, Theodor (2004) Negative Dialectics. London and New York: Routledge.

Alley, Stuart and Smith, Mat (2004) Timeline: Tuition Fees - https://www.theguardian.com/education/2004/jan/27/tuit ionfees.students, accessed 27 December 2018.

After the Fall: Communiques from Occupied California (2011) http://libcom.org/library/after-fall-communiques-occupied-california - accessed 27 December 2018.

Agamben, Giorgio (2005) State of Exception. Chicago and London: University of Chicago Press.

Ainley, Patrick and Allen, Martin (2013) Running Up a Down Escalator in a Class Structure Gone Pear Shaped, Sociology Research Online 18 (1) - https://journals.sagepub.com/doi/abs/10.5153/sro.2867 accessed 27 December 2018.

Ainley, Patrick and Allen, Martin (2010) Lost Generation? New Strategies for Youth and Education. London and New York: Continuum.

Allman, Paula (2001) Revolutionary Social Transformation: Democratic Hopes, Political Possibilities and Critical Education. Westport, Connecticut and London: Bergin and Garvey.

Allman, Paula (2007) On Marx: An Introduction to the Revolutionary Intellect of Karl Marx. Rotterdam: Sense Publishers.

Allman Paula (2010) Critical Education Against Global Capitalism: Karl Marx Revolutionary Critical Education.

Rotterdam: Sense Publishers.

Allsop, Bradley, Briggs, Jacqueline and Kisby, Ben (2018) Market Values and Youth Political Engagement in the UK: Towards an Agenda for Exploring the Psychological Effects of Neo-Liberalism. Societies 8 (4) - https://www.mdpi.com/2075-4698/8/4/95, 7 November 2018

Althusser, Louis, Balibar Etienne, Establet, Roger, Macherey, Pierre and Ranciére, Jacques (1965/2015) Reading Capital: The Complete Edition. London: Verso.

Althusser, Louis (2011/1964) Student Problems. Radical Philosophy170:11-16-https://www.radicalphilosophyarchive. com/article/student-problems, accessed 27 December 2018.

Amsler, Sarah and Canaan, Joyce (2008) Whither Critical Education in the Neo-Liberal University Today. Two Practitioners' Reflections on Constraints and Possibilities. Enhancing Learning in the Social Sciences 1 (2) -https:// www.tandfonline.com/doi/full/10.11120/elss.2008.01020008, accessed 27 December 2018.

Amsler, Sarah (2010) Creative Militancy, Militant Creativity and the New Student Movement. Huffington Post - https:// www.huffingtonpost.com/sarah-amsler/creative-militancy-milita_b_794978.html, accessed 27 December 2018.

Amsler, Sarah (2017) What Do We Mean When We Say Democracy? Learning Towards a Common Future Through Popular Higher Education. Robert Haworth and John Elmore (eds.) Out of the Ruins: The Emergence of Radical Informal Learning Space. Oakland: PM Press, 106-125.

Anderson, Perry (1979) Considerations on Western Marxism. London: Verso.

Arendt, Hannah (2007) Introduction. Hannah Arendt (ed.) Walter Benjamin Illuminations: Essays and Reflections. New York: Schocken Books.

Arendt, Hannah (1954) What is Authority? - https://www. pevpat-ugent.be/wp-content/uploads/2016/09/H-Arendt-what-is-authority.pdf, accessed 22 January 2019.

Arthur, Chris (1989) Editor's Introduction. Evgeny Pashukanis: A General Theory. London: Pluto, 9-32.

Aufheben (2011) Intakes; Communities, Commodities and Class in the August 2011 Riots - https://libcom.org/files/Intakes%20 -%20Communities%2C%20commodities%20and%20class%20 -%20Aufheben.pdf, accessed 27 December 2018.

Austin, Robert (2003) The State, Literacy and Popular Education in Chile. Maryland: Lexington Books.

Bacon, Edwin (2014) Neo-Collegiality: Restoring Academic Engagement in the Managerial University. Leadership Foundation for Higher Education - http://eprints.bbk. ac.uk/11493/1/Neo-Collegiality%20Edwin%20Bacon%20 April%202014.pdf, accessed 27 December 2018.

Bailey, Michael and Freedman, Des (2011) The Assault on Universities: a Manifesto for Resistance. London: Pluto Press.

Ball, Stephen (2003) The Teachers Soul and the Terrors of Performativity. Journal of Education Policy 18 2 215-28.

Barbagallo, Camille and Beuret, Nicholas (2012) The Revenge of the Remainder. Alessio Lunghi and Seth Wheeler (eds.) Occupy Everything: Reflections on Why it's Kicking Off Everywhere. Brooklyn: Minor Compositions - Autonomedia, 46-57.

Bateman, Tim (2012) With the Benefit of Hindsight: the Disturbances of August 2011 in an Historical Context. Daniel Briggs (ed.) The English Riots of 2011: a Summer of Discontent. Hampshire: Waterside Press, 91-110.

Beirne, Piers and Sharlet, Robert (2015) Towards a General Theory of Law and Marxism. Piers Bierne (ed.) Revolution in Law: Contributions to the Development of Soviet Legal Theory, 1917-1938. London and New York: Routledge, 17-44.

Benjamin, Walter (1929) Surrealism: the Last Snapshot of the European Intelligentsia. Peter Demetz (ed.) Walter Benjamin: Reflections - Essays, Aphorisms, Autobiographical Writings.

New York: Schocken Books, 177-92.

Benjamin, Walter (1998) The Author as Producer. Understanding Brecht. London and New York: Verso, 85-103.

Benjamin, Walter (2005) (1932/1999) We Ought to Re-examine the Link between Teaching and Research. Michael Eiland, Howard Jennings and Gary Smith (eds.) Walter Benjamin Selected Writings, Volume 2 Part 2 [1931-4]. Massachusetts: Harvard University Press, 419-20.

Benjamin, Walter (2002) The Arcades Project. Cambridge MA: Harvard University Press.

Benjamin, Walter (2004) The Life of Students. Marcus Bullock and Michael Jennings (eds.) Walter Benjamin Selected Writings 1 [1913-26]. Massachusetts: Harvard University Press, 37-47.

Benjamin, Walter (1978/1921) Critique of Violence. Walter Benjamin - Reflections: Essays Aphorisms, Autobiographical Writings. New York: Schocken Books, 277-300.

Berki, Robert (1985) Insight and Vision: the Problem of Communism in Marx's Thought. Dent: London.

Berlyne, Josh (2016) White Paper: the Government has Given the Students an Even Greater Opportunity for Massive Disruption. The Independent – https://www.independent. co.uk/student/istudents/white-paper-the-government-has-given-the-student-movement-an-even-greater-opportunity-for-massive-a7032761.html, accessed 22 February 2019.

Bhandhar, Brenna (2013) A Right to the University. London Review of Books Blog -https://www.lrb.co.uk/blog/2013/12/10/brenna-bhandar/a-right-to-the-university/, 27 December, 2018.

Blaszak, Barbara (1988) George Jacob Holyoake 1817-1906 and the Development of the British Co-operative Movement. Dyfed, Wales: Edwin Mellen Press.

Blechman, Max Chari, Anita, Hasan, Rafeeq (2005) Democracy, Dissensus and the Aesthetics of Class Struggle: an Exchange with Jacques Ranciére. Historical Materialism 13 4, 285-302.

293.

Blenkinsop, John and Scurry, Tracy (2007) Hey Gringo! The HR Challenge of Graduates in Non-Graduate Occupations. Personnel Review 36 4, 623-37.

Blenkinsop, John and Scurry, Tracy (2011) Underemployment among recent graduates; A Review of the Literature. Personnel Review 40 5, 643-59.

Bloom, Clive (2012) Riot City: Protest and Rebellion in the Capital. Palgrave Macmillan.

Bonnett, Alastair (2011) Are Radical Journals Selling Out? Times Higher Education - https://www.timeshighereducation. com/features/are-radical-journals-selling-out/417988. article?storycode=417988, accessed 27 December 2018.

Bonefeld, Werner Critical Theory and the Critique of Political Economy: on Subversion and Negative Reason. London and New York: Bloomsbury.

Bonnett, Alastair (2013) Something New in Freedom. *Times Higher Education* https://www.timeshighereducation.com/features/ something-new-in-freedom/2003930.article, accessed 27 December 2018.

Boden, Rebecca and Epstein, Debbie (2006) Managing the Research Imagination: Globalisation and Research in Higher Education. Globalisation, Societies and Education 4 2, 223-36.

Boden, Rebecca, Ciancanelli, Penelope and Wright, Sue (2012) Trust Universities: Governance for Postcapitalist Futures. Journal of Co-operative Studies 45 2.

Bowers C. A. (2007) The False Promises of Constructivist Theories of Learning. New York and Oxford: Peter Lang.

Boyer, Ernest (1990) Scholarship Reconsidered: Priorities of the Professoriate. The Carnegie Foundation for the Advancement of Teaching -http://www.hadinur.com/paper/ BoyerScholarshipReconsidered.pdf, accessed 27 December 2018.

Boyer Commission (1998) Reinventing Undergraduate

Education: A Blueprint for America's Research Universities. Stony Brook, NUY. Carnegie Foundation for the Advancement of Teaching - https://eric.ed.gov/?id=ED424840, accessed 27 December 2018.

Brew, Angela (2006) Research and Teaching: Beyond the Divide: Universities in the 21st Century. Basingstoke and New York: Palgrave Macmillan.

Briggs, Daniel (2012) (Ed.) The English Riots of 2011 - A Summer of Discontent. Hampshire Waterside Press.

Brown, Roger and Helen Carasso (2013) Everything for Sale: The Marketisation of Higher Education. London and New York: Routledge.

Budgen, Sebastian (2011) French Lessons: the Struggle Goes On. Clare Solomon and Tania Palmieri (eds.) Springtime: the New Student Rebellions. London and New York: Verso, 183-92.

Burns, Rob (1977) Understanding Benjamin. Red Letters No. 7, 16-33.

Burrow, J (1993) Editors Introduction. Wilhelm Von Humboldt. Limits of State Action. Cambridge University Press, vii-xliii.

Cameron, David (2011(Full Statement on the UK Riots (2011)) The Guardian, 9 August - https://www.theguardian.com/uk/2011/aug/09/david-cameron-full-statement-uk-riots, accessed 19 February 2019.

Cammaerts, Bart, Mattoni, Alice and McCurdy, Patrick (eds.) (2013) Mediation and Protest Movement. Bristol: Intellect Publishers.

Chabal, Patrick (2002) Amilcar Cabral: Revolutionary Leadership and People's War. London: Hurst and Co. Publishers.

Charles, Mathew (2016) Towards a Critique of Educative Violence: Walter Benjamin and 'Second Education'. Pedagogy Culture and Society 24 4, 525-36.

Chatterton, Paul, Hodkinson, Stuart, Pickerill, Jenny (2010) Beyond Scholar Activism: Making Strategic Intervention Inside and Outside the Neoliberal University. Acme: an

International E-Journal for Scholarly Geographies 9 2, 245-75.

Chessum, Michael (2015) How the Student Protestors of 2010 Became the Corbyn Generation 2 October - https://www. theguardian.com/commentisfree/2015/oct/02/student-protesters-2010-jeremy-corbyn-election-labour-party, accessed 5 April 2018.

Ciccariello-Maher, George (2013) who maintains in his book *We Created Chavez: a People's History of the Venezuelan Revolution.* North Carolina: Duke University Press.

Clark T J (2003) Should Benjamin Have Read Marx? Boundary 2: An International Journal of Literature and Culture, 31-49 https:// read.dukeupress.edu/boundary-2/article-, abstract/30/1/31/6148/ Should-Benjamin-Have-Read-Marx?redirectedFrom=PDF, accessed 27 December 2018.

Clarke, Simon (1980) Introduction. Simon Clarke, Terry Lovell, Kevin McDonnell, Kevin Robbins and Victor Jeleniewski Seidler (eds.) One Dimensional Marxism. London: Alison and Busby, 5-102

Clarke, Simon (1988) Keynesianism, Monetarism and the Crisis of the State. Aldershot: Edward Elgar.

Clarke, Simon (1991a) Marx, Marginalism and Modern Sociology, Second Edition. Basingstoke: Macmillan.

Clarke, Simon (1991b) (ed.) The State Debate. Basingstoke: Macmillan.

Clarke, Simon (2005) The Neoliberal Theory of Society. Alfredo Saad-Filho and Deborah Johnston (eds.) Neoliberalism: A Critical Reader. Pluto Press, 50-59.

Class War University (2013) Occupying the City with the Social Science Centre: An Interview with Mike Neary - https:// classwaru.org/2013/09/02/occupying-the-city-with-the-social-science-centre/, accessed 8 November 2017.

Cleaver, Harry (2000) Reading Capital Politically. Chico, CA: AK Press.

Cleaver, Harry (n.d.) On Self-Valorisation - https://la.utexas.

edu/users/hcleaver/357k/HMCDallaCostaSelfvalorization2. htm, accessed 23 April 2018.

Cleaver, Harry (2017) Rupturing the Dialectic. The Struggle Against Work, Money and Financialisation. Chico, CA: AK Press.

Clover, Joshua (2016) Riot-Strike-Riot: the New Era of Uprisings. London and New York: Verso.

Cole, Mike, Hill, Dave, McLaren, Peter, Rikowski, Glenn (2001) Red Chalk: On Schooling, Capitalism and Politics. University College Northampton http://www.ieps.org.uk/media/1021/ redchalk.pdf, accessed 9 April 2018.

Cohen, Paul (2010) Happy Birthday Vincennes! The University of Paris - 8 Turns 40. History Workshop Journal 69 1, 206-24 https://academic.oup.com/hwj/article/69/1/206/553047, accessed 6 April 2018.

Cohen, Stanley (1973) Folk Devils and Moral Panics: the Creation of the Mods and Rockers. London: Paladin.

Collini, Stefan (2012) What Are Universities For. London: Penguin Books.

Cook, Dan (2013) Realising the Co-operative University - a consultancy report for the Co-operative College http:// josswinn.org/wp-content/uploads/2013/12/realising-the- co-operative-university-for-disemmination.pdf, accessed 9 April 2018.

Corbett, Anne (2005) Universities and the Europe of Knowledge: Ideas, Institutions and Policy Entrepreneurship in European Union Higher Education Policy, 1995-2005. Basingstoke: Palgrave Macmillan.

Corporate Europe (2011) Austerity for Ever https:// corporateeurope.org/eu-crisis/2011/09/austerity-forever, accessed 27 December 2018.

Cunnane, Sarah (2011) Paula Allman. Obituary 1944-2011. Times Higher Education Dec 1: https://www.timeshig hereducation.com/news/people/obituaries/paula-allman-1944-2011/418263.article, accessed 19 April 2018.

Curl, John (2012) For All the People: Uncovering the Hidden History of Co-operation, Co-operative Movements and Communalism in America. Oakland, CA: PM Press.

Davis, Oliver (2010) Jacques Ranciére. Cambridge: Polity.

Debord, Guy (1984) Society of the Spectacle. Black and Red Books, US.

Delanty, Gerard (2001) Challenging Knowledge: the University in the Knowledge Society. Buckingham: Society for Research into Higher Education and Open University Press.

Deranty, Jean-Philippe (2012) Work in the Writings of Jacques Ranciére. In Jean-Philippe Deranty and Alison Ross (eds.) Jacques Ranciére and the Contemporary Scene: The Philosophy of Radical Equality. London and New York: Continuum, 187-204.

Deleuze, Gilles and Guattari, Felix (1987) A Thousand Plateaus: Capitalism and Schizophrenia. Minnesota: University of Minnesota Press.

Dinerstein, Ana, and Neary, Mike (2002) The Labour Debate: the Theory and Reality of Capitalist Work. Aldershot: Ashgate.

Dinerstein, Ana (2015) The Politics of Autonomy in Latin America: the Art of Organising Hope. Hampshire: Palgrave Macmillan.

Disobedient Objects Exhition 26 July 2014-1 February 2015 http://www.vam.ac.uk/blog/section/disobedient-objects

Docherty, Thomas (2015) Universities at War. London and Los Angeles: Sage Swifts.

Docherty, Thomas (2011) For the University: Democracy and the Future of the Institution. London: Bloomsbury Publishing.

Dokuzovic, Lina (2017) Struggles for Living Learning. Vienna and London: Transversal Texts.

Dosse, Francois (2011) Gilles Deleuze and Felix Guattari: Intersecting Lives. New York: Columbia University Press.

Dyer-Witheford, Nick (2015) Cyber Proletariat: Global Labour in the Digital Vortex. London: Pluto Press.

Edelman-Boren, Mark (2001) Student Resistance: a History of the Unruly Subject. Abingdon and New York: Routledge.

Egan, Daniel (1990) Towards a Marxist Theory of Labour Managed Firms: Breaking the Degeneration Thesis. Review of Radical Political Economics. 22 4, 67-86.

The Edu-factory Collective (2009) Towards a Global Autonomous University. New York: Autonomedia.

Eiland, Howard and Jennings, Michael (2014) Walter Benjamin: A Critical Life. Harvard: Harvard University Press.

Elton, Lewis (2001) Research and Teaching: Conditions for a Positive Link. Teaching in Higher Education, 6 (2001), 43-56.

Endnotes (2011) A Rising Tide Lifts All Boats: Crisis Era Struggles in Britain - https://endnotes.org.uk/issues/3/en/endnotes-a-rising-tide-lifts-all-boats, accessed 27 December 2018.

Escobar, Miguel, Fernandez, Alfredo, Guevara-Niebla, Gilberto with Freire, Paulo (1994) Paulo Freire on Higher Education: A Dialogue at the National University of Mexico. Albany: State University of New York Press.

Federici, Silvia (2014) 12 Caliban and the Witch: Women the Body and Primitive Accumulation. Brooklyn: Autonomedia.

Feldman, Karen (2011) Not Dialectical Enough: On Benjamin and Adorno: an Autonomous Critique. Philosophy and Rhetoric 44, 336-62.

Fisher, Mark (2009) Capitalist Realism. Winchester and Washington: Zero Books.

Fisher, Mark (2018) Winter of Discontent 2.0 Notes on a Month of Militancy. Darren Ambrose (ed.) K-Punk: The Collected and Unpublished Writings of Mark Fisher (2004-2016). London: Repeater Books, 475-82.

Fleming, Peter (2019) The Worst is Yet To Come: a Post-Capitalist Survival Guide. London: Repeater Books.

Free Association (2011) Moments of Excess: Movements, Protest and Everyday Life. Oakland CA: PM Press.

Freedman, Des (2011) An Introduction to Education Reform and Resistance. Michael Bailey and Des Freedman (eds.) The Assault on Universities: a Manifesto for Resistance. London: Pluto, 1-14.

Freire, Paulo (1970) Pedagogy of the Oppressed. London: Penguin Books.

Freire, Paulo (1974) Education: the Practice of Freedom. London: Writers and Readers Publishing Co-operative.

Freire, Paulo (2016) Pedagogy in Process: The Letters to Guinea Bissau. Bloomsbury Revelations: London and New York

Freire, Paulo (2014) Pedagogy of Hope: Reliving Pedagogy of the Oppressed. Bloomsbury Academic.

Fuller, Steve (2009) The Sociology of Intellectual Life: the Career to the Mind in and Around Academy. London: Sage Publications.

Korsch, Karl (1989) Appendix: An Assessment. Evgeny Pashukanis: Law and Marxism: A General Theory. London: Pluto, 189-95.

Gilbert, Jeremy (2016) The Case for Radical Modernity: https://www.redpepper.org.uk/the-case-for-radical-modernity/, accessed 2 April 2018.

Gillespie, Thomas and Habermehl, Victoria (2012) On The Graduate with No Future. Alessio Lunghi and Seth Wheeler (Eds.) Occupy Everything: Reflections on Why it's Kicking Off Everywhere. Brooklyn: Minor Compositions - Autonomedia, 11-17.

Gough, Marie (2002) Paris: Capital of the Soviet Avant Garde. October 101 Magazine. MIT 53-83.

Gough, Marie (2005) The Artist as Producer: Russian Constructivism in Revolution. Oakland: California University Press.

Graeber, David (2018) Bullshit Jobs: A Theory. London: Penguin.

Graeber, David Ross, Andrew and Caffentzis, George (2014) Debt Resistors' Operations Manual. Oakland, CA: PM Press.

Graham, Steven (2010) Cities Under Siege: The New Military Urbanism. London and New York: Verso.

Gurney, Peter (1988) Georg Jacob Holyoake: Socialism, Association and Co-operation in Nineteenth Century England. Stephen Yeo (ed.) New Views of Cooperation. London: Routledge, 52-72.

Gutierrez Aguilar, Rachel (2018) Because We Want Ourselves Alive, Together We are Disrupting Everything: Notes for Thinking about the Paths of Social Transformation Today. Viewpoint Magazine - https://www.viewpointmag.com/2018/03/07/want-alive-together-disrupting-everything-notes-thinking-paths-social-transformation-today/ accessed 20 February 2019

Haiven, Max (2011) Undead Ideologies: Necro - Neo-Liberalism, Necro-Keynesianism and the Radical Imagination https://maxhaiven.com/2011/06/27/new-polemic-essay-undead-ideologies-necro-neoliberalism-necro-keynesianism-and-the-radical-imagination/, accessed 4 June 2018.

Haiven, Max (2014) Crises of Imagination, Crises of Power: Capitalism, Culture and Resistance in a Post Crash World. London: Zed Books.

Hall, Richard (2014) Notes on the University as Anxiety Machine - http://www.richard-hall.org/2014/07/10/notes-on-the-university-as-anxiety-machine/, accessed 28 December 2018.

Hall, Richard and Smyth, Keith (2016) Against Boundaries Dismantling the Curriculum in Higher Education. Open Library of the Humanities - https://olh.openlibhums.org/articles/10.16995/olh.66/, accessed 28 December 2018.

Hall, Richard (2018) The Alienated Academic: the Struggle For Autonomy Inside the University. London and New York: Palgrave Macmillan.

Hall, Richard and Winn, Joss (eds.) (2017) Mass Intellectuality and Democratic Leadership in Higher Education. London and New York: Bloomsbury Academic.

Hall, Stuart, Critcher, Chas, Jefferson, Tony, Clarke, John, and Roberts, Brian (2013) Policing the Crisis: Mugging, the State and Law and Order. London and New York: Palgrave Macmillan.

Hall, Stuart, Massey, Doreen and Rustin, Michael (2013) After Neoliberalism: Analysing the Present. Soundings 53 - http://www.ingentaconnect.com/content/lwish/sou/2013/0 0000053/00000053/art00002, accessed 17 April 2018.

Hallwood, Peter (2011) A New Strategy is Needed for a Brutal New Era. Clare Solomon and Tania Palmieri (eds.) Springtime: the New Student Rebellions. London and New York: Verso, 36-9.

Hammer, Dean (2015) Authoring Within History: the Legacy of the Roman Politics in Hannah Arendt. Classical Receptions Journal Vol 7 1, 129-39.

Hanson, Steve (2017) Language, Juridical Epistemologies and Power in the New UK University: Can Alternative Providers Escape? Journal for Critical Education Policy Studies 15 3 - http://www.jceps.com/archives/3630, accessed 28 December.

Harasim, Linda (1983) Literacy and National Reconstruction in Guinea-Bissau: A Critique of the Freirean Literacy Campaign. University of Toronto: https://search.library.utoronto.ca/details?2087140, accessed 28 December 2018.

Harney, Stefano and Moten, Fred (1998) Doing Academic Work. In Martin Randy (ed.) Chalk Lines: The Politics of Work in the Managed University. Duke University Press, 154-80.

Harris, John (2011) Global Protests: Is 2011 a Year that will Change the World? The Guardian https://www.theguardian.com/world/2011/nov/15/global-protests-2011-change-the-world, accessed 17 April 2018.

Harrison, Andrew and Hutton, Les (2014) Design for the Changing Educational Landscape: Space, Place and the Future of Learning. Abingdon and New York: Routledge.

Holloway, John and Picciotto, Sol (1977) Capital, Crisis and the

State. Capital and Class. Volume 1 2, 76-101.

Harvey, David (2007) A Brief History of Neoliberalism. Oxford: Oxford University Press.

Holloway, John (2002) How to Change the World Without Taking Power. London: Pluto Press.

Holloway, John (2019) We Are the Crisis: a John Holloway Reader. Oakland CA: PM Books.

Holmwood, John (2011) A Manifesto for the Public University. London: Bloomsbury Academic.

Humboldt, W. von (1810), *Über die innere und äußere Organisation der höheren wissenschaftlichen Anstalten in Berlin*. Weinstock, H. (Ed.) (1957), *Wilhelm von Humboldt*, (Frankfurt: Fischer Bücherei), 126-34.

Hudis, Peter (2013) Marx's Concept of the Alternative to Capitalism. Chicago: Haymarket Books.

Humboldt, Wilhelm von (1993) The Limits of State Action. Cambridge: Cambridge University Press.

Invisible Committee (2009) The Coming Insurrection. Los Angeles: Semiotexte.

Jappe, Anselm (2013) Sohn-Rethel and the Origins of Real Abstraction: A Critique of Production or a Critique of Circulation. Historical Materialism 21 1, 3-14.

Jappe, Anselm (2017) The Writing on the Wall: On the Decomposition of Capitalism and its Critics. Winchester and Washington: Zero Books.

Jessop, Bob (1990) State Theory: Putting the Capitalist State Back in its Place. Cambridge: Polity.

Kay, Geoff and Mott, James (1982) Political Order and the Law of Labour. London and Basingstoke: Macmillan.

Kirkendall, Andrew (2104) Freire, Paulo and the Cold War Politics of Literacy. University of North Carolina Press.

Kishik, David (2015) The Manhattan Project: a Theory of the City. Stanford: Stanford University Press.

Klein, Melanie (2008) The Shock Doctrine: the Rise of Disaster

Capitalism. London: Penguin.

Knoll, Joachim and Siebert, Horst (1967) Wilhelm Von Humboldt. Inter Nationes.

Kojeve, Alexandre (2014) The Notion of Authority. London and New York: Verso.

Kumar, Ashok (2011) 'Did Anything Change?' Evaluating the Effectiveness of the 2010 Student Protests - https://www.academia.edu/3722137/_Did_We_Change_Anything_Evaluating_the_Effectiveness_of_the_2010_UK_Student_Protests, accessed 29 December 2018.

Kurz, Robert (2007) Grey is the Golden Tree of Life, Green is Theory https://libcom.org/library/grey-golden-tree-life-green-theory-robert-kurz, accessed 27 December 2018.

Kurz, Robert (2013) World Power and World Money: the Economic Function of the US Military Machine with Global Capitalism and the Background of the New Financial Crisis. Mediations: Journal of the Marxist Literary Group 27 1-2 - http://www.mediationsjournal.org/articles/world-power-world-money, accessed 27 December 2018.

Kurz, Robert (2014) On the Current Global Economic Crisis; Questions and Answers. Larsen, Neil, Nilges, Matias, Robinson, Josh, Brown, Nicholas (eds.) (2014) Marxism and the Critique of Value. Chicago and Alberta: MCM, 331-57.

Indymedia (2010) Personal Accounts of Time Inside the Student Protest Kettles -https://www.indymedia.org.uk/en/2010/12/470581.html?c=on, accessed 18 February 2019.

Irwin, Jones (2012) Paulo Freire's Philosophy of Education: Origins, Developments, Impacts and Legacies. London and New York: Continuum.

Labour Party (2016) Alternative Models of Ownership - https://labour.org.uk/wp-content/uploads/2017/10/Alternative-Models-of-Ownership.pdf, accessed 27 December 2018.

Labour Party Manifesto (2017) https://labour.org.uk/wp-content/uploads/2017/10/labour-manifesto-2017.pdf, accessed 4 June

2018.

Lambert, Cath (2011) Psycho Classrooms: Teaching as a Work of Art. Social and Cultural Geographer 12 1, 27-45.

Larson, Michael (2013) Book Review. Proletarian Nights: the Workers Dream in Nineteenth Century France Interstitial Journal - https://interstitialjournal.files.wordpress.com/2013 /03/larson-proletarian-nights.pdf, accessed 18 February.

Larsen, Neil, Nilges, Matias, Robinson, Josh, Brown, Nicholas (eds.) (2014) Marxism and the Critique of Value. Chicago and Alberta: MCM.

Lefebvre, Henri (1969) The Explosion: Marxism and the French Upheaval. New York and London: Monthly Review Press.

Leslie, Esther (2000) Overpowering Conformism. London and Stirling, VA: Pluto Press.

Leslie, Esther (2009) Revolutionary Potential and Walter Benjamin: A Post War Reception History. Jacques Bidet and Stathis Kouvelakis (eds.) Critical Companion to Contemporary Marxism. Chicago: Haymarket Books, 549-66.

Linebaugh, Peter (2006) The London Hanged: Crime and Civil Society in the 18th Century. London and New York: Verso.

Lockwood, Dean and Winn, Joss (2013) Student as Producer is Hacking the University. Helen Beetham (ed.) Rethinking Pedagogy for a Digital Age. London and New York: Routledge.

Lowy, Michael (2005) Fire Alarm: Reading Walter Benjamin's On the Concept of History. London and New York: Verso.

Lukacs, Gyorgy (1971) History and Class Consciousness: Studies in Marxist Dialectics. Massacusetts: MIT Press.

Lunghi, Alessio and Wheeler, Seth (2012) Occupy Everything! Reflections on Why It's Kicking Off Everywhere. Minor Compositions. http://www.minorcompositions.info/?p=372, accessed 29 December 2018.

Lunn, Eugene (1984) Marxism and Modernism: an Historical Study of Lukacs, Brecht, Benjamin and Adorno. Orlando: University of California Press.

Lyotard, Jean-Francois (1984) The Postmodern Condition: A Report on Knowledge. Manchester: Manchester University Press.

Luxemburg, Rosa (2006) Reform or Revolution and Other Writings. New York: Dover Publications.

Magna Carta Universitatum Observatory (2018) http://www.magna-charta.org/magna-charta-universitatum, accessed 29 December 2018.

Maisuria, Alpesh and Cole, Mike (2017) The Neoliberalisation of Higher Education in England: There is An Alternative. Policy Futures in Education - http://journals.sagepub.com/doi/abs/10.1177/1478210317719792, accessed 29 December 2018.

Mallot, Curry, Elmore, John and Cole, Mike (2013) Teaching Marx: the Socialist Challenge. USA: Information Age Publishing Inc.

Marx, Karl (2003) The 18th Brumaire of Louis Bonaparte. International Publishers Co., US.

Marx, Karl (2018) Critique of the Gotha Programme. International Publishers Co., US.

Marx, Karl (1990) Capital Volume 1: A Critique of Political Economy. London: Penguin Classics.

Marx, Karl (1993) The Grundrisse. London: Penguin Classics.

Mason, Paul (2008) Live Working or Die Fighting: How the Working Class Went Global. London: Vintage.

Mason Paul (2012) Why It's Kicking Off Everywhere: the New Global Revolutions. London and New York: Verso Books.

Mason, Paul (2012) The Graduate Without a Future https://www.theguardian.com/commentisfree/2012/jul/06/graduate-without-future-q-and-a, accessed 4 June 2018.

Mason, Paul (2013) Why It's Still Kicking Off Everywhere. London and New York: Verso.

Mason, Paul (2015) Postcapitalism: A Guide to Our Future. London: Allen Lane.

Mason-Deese, Liz (2018) From #MeToo to #WeStrike: A Politics in

Feminine. Viewpoint Magazine - https://www.viewpointmag. com/2018/03/07/metoo-westrike-politics-feminine/, accessed 20 February 2019.

McCulloch, Alistair (2009) The Student as Co-Producer: Learning from Public Administration about the Student University Relationship. Studies in Higher Education 34 2, 171-83.

McGettigan, Andrew (2013) The Great University Gamble: Money, Markets and the Future of Higher Education. London: Pluto Press.

McCulloch, Andrew (2014) Charisma and Patronage: Reasoning with Max Weber. London and New York: Routledge.

McLaren, Peter (2015) Pedagogy of Insurrection: From Resurrection to Revolution. Bern: Peter Lang Publishing.

McNally (2014) The Global Slump: The Economics and Politics of Crisis and Resistance. Oakland: PM Press.

Meadway, James (2011) The Rebellion in Context. Clare Solomon and Tania Palmieri (eds.) Springtime: the New Student Rebellions. London and New York: Verso Books, 7-20.

Mieville, China (2005) Between Equal Rights: A Marxist Theory of International Law. Chicago: Haymarket Books.

Milovanovic, Dragan (2003) Introduction. Evgeny Pashukanis. The General Theory of Law and Marxism. New Brunswick and London: Transaction Books, vii-xxvi.

Miliband, Ralph and Liebman, Marcel (1985) Beyond Social Democracy https://www.marxists.org/archive/ miliband/1985/xx/beyondsd.htm, 29 December 2018.

Miliband, Ralph (1973) The State in Capitalist Society. London: Quartet Books.

Milne, Seamus (2012) The Revenge of History: the Battle for the 21st Century. London and New York: Verso Books.

Morrish, Liz (2018) Can Critical University Studies Survive the Toxic University? -http://criticallegalthinking. com/2018/06/11/can-critical-university-studies-survive-the-toxic-university/, accessed 18 February 2019.

Morsy, Hannan (2012) Scarred Generation. SSRN - https://papers. ssrn.com/sol3/papers.cfm?abstract_id=3093019, accessed 29 December 2018.

Moten, Fred and Harney, Stefano (1999) The Academic Speed Up. Workplace: A Journal for Academic Labour, 4, 23-8 - https:// ices.library.ubc.ca/index.php/workplace/article/view/184003, accessed 29 December 2018.

Mute (2010) Statement on the Goldsmiths' Occupation: http:// www.metamute.org/community/your-posts/statement-goldsmiths-occupation, accessed 29 December 2018.

Myers, Matt (2017) Student Revolt: Voices of the Austerity Generation. London: Pluto Press.

Naidoo, Rajani (2018) The Competition Fetish in Higher Education: Shamans, Mind Snares and Consequences. European Educational Research Journal, 17(5), 605-20.

National Union of Students (2010) NUS Condemns Violent Actions of Rogue Protestors for Undermining the Message of 50000 https://www.nus.org.uk/en/news/nus-condemns-violent-actions-of-rogue-protestors-for-undermining-the-message-of-50000/, accessed 29 December.

Nesbitt, Nick (2017) Value as Symptom. Nick Nesbitt (ed.) The Concept in Crisis: Reading Capital Today. Durham NC: Duke University Press, 229-80.

Neary, Michael (2002) Labour Moves: a Critique of the Concept of Social Movement Unionism. Ana Dinerstein and Mike Neary (eds.) The Labour Debate: An Investigation into the Theory and Reality of Capitalist Work. Aldershot: Ashgate, 149-78.

Neary, Mike (2010) Student as Producer: a Pedagogy for the Avant-Garde? Learning Exchange 1 1 - http://eprints.lincoln. ac.uk/4186/1/15-72-1-pb-1.pdf, accessed 29 December 2018.

Neary, Michael (2012a) Student as Producer: an Institution of the Common? [or how to recover communist/revolutionary science]. Enhancing Learning in the Social Sciences - www.

tandfonline.com/doi/abs/10.11120/elss.2012.04030003, accessed 29 December 2018.

Neary, Michael (2012b) Teaching Politically: Policy, Pedagogy and the New European University. Journal for Critical Education Policy Studies 10 2, 233-57 - http://www.jceps.com/archives/715, accessed 29 December 2018.

Neary, Mike (2012c) Beyond Teaching in Public: the University as a Form of Social Knowing. Mike Neary, Howard Stevenson and Les Bell (eds.) Towards Teaching in Public; Reshaping the Modern University. Continuum, 148-64.

Neary, Mike (2013) Student as Producer: Radicalising the Mainstream in Higher Education. The Student Engagement Handbook: Practice in Higher Education. Bingley: Emerald Group Publishing Limited, 587-602.

Neary, Mike (2014) The University and the City: Social Science Centre, Lincoln – Forming the Urban Revolution. Paul Temple (ed.) The Physical University: Contours of Space and Place in Higher Education. London: Routledge, 203-16.

Neary, Mike (2015) Educative Power: the Myth of Dronic Violence in a Period of Civil War. Culture Machine, 16,1-28 - http://svr91.edns1.com/~culturem/index.php/cm/article/viewFile/586/591, accessed 29 December 2018.

Neary, Mike (2016) Value: Critical Pedagogy, Participatory Art and Higher Education - a new Measure and Meaning of the Common(s). Sam Ladkin, Robert McKay and Emile Bojesen (eds.) Against Value in the Arts and Education. Disruptions. London: Rowman and Littlefield, 355-74.

Neary, Mike (2016) Student as Producer: the Struggle for the Idea of the University. Other Education - https://www.othereducation.org/index.php/OE/article/view/163, accessed 29 December 2018.

Neary, Mike (2017a) Critical Theory and the Critique of Labour. Keynote presentation to Marx and Philosophy Conference. University College London June 24. University of Lincoln

Repository - http://eprints.lincoln.ac.uk/35049/, accessed 22 February 2019).

Neary, Mike (2017b) Pedagogy of Hate. Policy Futures in Education 15 5, 555-63 - https://journals.sagepub.com/toc/pfea/15/5, accessed 29 December 2018.

Neary, Mike (2017c) Academic Voices: from Public Intellectuals to the General Intellect. Richard Hall and Joss Winn (eds.) Mass Intellectuality and Democratic Leadership. Perspectives on Leadership in Higher Education. London and New York: Bloomsbury, 41-54.

Neary, Mike (2019) Reading Ranciére Symptomatically. Stephen Cowden and David Ridley (eds.) The Practice of Equality: Jacques Ranciére and Critical Pedagogy. Oxford and Berlin: Peter Lang International, 167-86.

Neary, Mike and Amsler, Sarah (2012) Occupy: a New Pedagogy of Space and Time? Journal for Critical Education Policy Studies 10 2 - http://www.jceps.com/archives/726, accessed 29 December 2018.

Neary, Mike and Hagyard, Andy (2010) Pedagogy of Excess: an Alternative Political Economy of Student Life. Mike Molesworth, Richard Scullion and Elizabeth Nixon (eds.) The Marketisation of Higher Education and the Student as Consumer. Abingdon: Routledge, 209-24.

Neary, Mike and Saunders, Gary (2011) Leadership and Learning Landscapes: the Struggle for the Idea of the University. Higher Education Quarterly 65 4, 333-52.

Neary, Mike and Saunders, Gary (2016) Student as Producer and the Politics of Abolition: Making a New Form of Dissident Institution? Critical Education 7 5 - https://ices.library.ubc.ca/index.php/criticaled/article/view/186127, accessed 29 December 2018.

Neary, Mike, Saunders, Gary, Cretlin, Giles, Parekh, Nayan, Harrison, Andrew, Duggan, Fiona, Williams, Sam and Austin, Simon (2010) Learning Landscapes in Higher

Education. Higher Education Funding Council for England, Wales and Scotland: http://learninglandscapes.blogs. lincoln.ac.uk/files/2012/05/Learning-Landscapes-in-Higher-Education-2010.pdf, accessed 29 December 2018.

Neary, Mike, Saunders, Gary, Hagyard, Andy and Derricott, Dan (2015) Student as Producer: Research Engaged Teaching, An Institutional Strategy. Higher Education Academy: York - lincoln_ntfs_2010_project_final_report_fv, accessed 29 December 2018.

Neary, Mike, Valenzuela-Fuentes, Katia and Winn, Joss (2018) Co-operative Leadership in Higher Education: Four Case Studies. Leadership Foundation for Higher Education - https://www.lfhe.ac.uk/en/research-resources/publications-hub/index.cfm/SDP2016Lincoln, accessed 29 December 2018.

Neary, Mike and Winn, Joss (2009) The Student as Producer: Reinventing the Student Experience in Higher Education. Les Bell, Howard Stevenson and Mike Neary (eds.) The Future of Higher Education: Policy, Pedagogy and the Student Experience. London and New York: Continuum, 192-210.

Neary, Mike and Winn, Joss (2012) Open education: Common(s), Commonism and the New Common Wealth. Ephemera: Theory & Politics in Organization 12 4, 406-22 - http://www.ephemerajournal.org/contribution/open-education-commons-commonism-and-new-common-wealth, accessed 29 December 2018.

Neary, Mike and Winn, Joss (2015) Beyond Public and Private: a Model for Co-operative Higher Education. Krisis: Journal for Contemporary Philosophy - http://krisis.eu/beyond-public-and-private/, accessed 29 December 2018.

Neary, Mike and Winn, Joss (2017) Beyond Public and Private: a Framework for Co-operative Higher Education. The Abolition of the University. Open Library of Humanities - https://olh. openlibhums.org/articles/10.16995/olh.195/, accessed 29 December 2018.

Neary, Mike and Winn, Joss (2019) Co-operative University Now. Tom Woodin (ed.) Learning for a Co-operative World: Education, Social Change and the Co-operative College. London: Trentham Books. (in production).

Neocleous, Marx (2000) The Fabrication of Social Order: A Critical Theory of Police Power. London and Sterling VA: Pluto Press.

Neocleous, Mark (2014) War Power, Police Power. Edinburgh: Edinburgh University Press.

Newfield, Chris (2016) The Great Mistake: How We Wrecked Public Universities and How We Can Fix Them. Baltimore: Johns Hopkins University Press.

Newman, Fred and Holzman, Lois (1993) Leo Vygotsky: Revolutionary Scientist. London and New York: Routledge.

Newstadt, Eric (2013) The Value of Quality: Capital, Class and Quality Assessment in the Re-Making of Higher Education in the United States, The United Kingdom and Ontario. PhD thesis. University of York, Canada http://citeseerx.ist.psu.edu/viewdoc/download?doi=10.1.1.879.7019&rep=rep1&type=pdf, accessed 29 December 2018.

Noble, Malcolm and Ross, Cilla (ed.) (2019) Reclaiming The University for the Public Good: Experiments and Futures in Co-operative Higher Education. Critical University Studies series London and New York.

National Union of Students (2010) NUS Condemns Violent Actions of 'Rogue Protestors for Undermining the Message of 50,000' - https://www.nus.org.uk/en/news/nus-condemns-violent-actions-of-rogue-protestors-for-undermining-the-message-of-50000/, accessed 23 February 2019.

O'Cadiz, Maria del Pilar, Wong, Pia Lindquist and Torres, Carlos Alberto (1998) Education and Democracy: Paulo Freire, Social Movements and Educational Reform in Sao Paulo. Colorado and Oxford: Westview.

O'Kane, Chris (n.d.) The Theory of the Form and the Development of Forms, Fetishism, Methodology and Social Theory in New Readings of Marx - http://www.academia.edu/14832529/_The_Theory_of_the_Form_and_the_Development_of_Forms_Fetishism_Methodology_and_Social_Theory_in_New_Readings_of_Marx, accessed 9 April, 2018.

Pashukanis, Evgeny (1989) Law and Marxism: A General Theory. London: London: Pluto.

Palmier, Jean Michel (2017) Weimar in Exile: the Anti-Fascist Emigration in Europe and America. London and New York: Verso.

Pearson, Harry (1983) Hooligans: A History of Respectable Fears. Basingstoke: Palgrave Macmillan.

Perlman, Fredy (1968) On Commodity Fetishism: an Introduction to I I Rubin's Essay on Marx's Theory of Value - https://theanarchistlibrary.org/library/fredy-perlman-commodity-fetishism-an-introduction-to-i-i-rubin-s-essay-on-marx-s-theory-of-valu, accessed 22 February 2019.

Pitts, Harry and Dinerstein, Ana (2017a) Corbynism's Conveyor Belt of Ideas: Postcapitalism and the Politics of Social Reproduction. Capital and Class 41 3 http://journals.sagepub.com/doi/abs/10.1177/0309816817734487, accessed 30 December 2018.

Pitts, Harry and Dinerstein, Ana (2017b) Postcapitalism, Basic Income and the End of Work. Working Paper in International Development and Well Being, University of Bath. No 55 - http://www.bath.ac.uk/cds/publications/bdp55.pdf, accessed 30 December 2018.

Pitts, Harry (2017) Beyond the Fragment: Postoperaismo, Postcapitalism and Marx's Notes on machines, 45 years on. Economy and Society 46, 324-45.

Postone, Moishe (1980) Anti-Semitism and National Socialism: Notes on the German Reaciton to 'Holocaust'. New German Critique 19 1, 97-115.

Postone, Moishe (1993) Time, Labour and Social Domination

- a Reinterpretation of Marx's Social Theory. Cambridge: Cambridge University Press.

Postone, Moishe (2003) Lukacs and the Dialectical Critique. https://platypus1917.org/wp-content/uploads/readings/postone_lukacsdialecticalcritique2003.pdf, accessed 30 December 2018.

Poulantzas, Nicos (2013) State, Power, Socialism. London and New York: Verso.

Power, Nina (2012) Dangerous Subjects: UK Students and the Criminalisation of Protest. South Atlantic Quarterly 11 2, 412-20 - https://libcom.org/files/dangeroussubjects.pdf, accessed 30 December 2018.

Power, Nina (2010) Interview with Jacques Ranciére. Ephemera 10 1, 77-81 http://www.ephemerajournal.org/contribution/inteview-jacques-ranci%C3%A8re, accessed 9 April 2018.

Pritchard, Rosalind (1990/1992) The End of Elitism?: Democratisation of the West German University System. Berg Publishers.

Pusey, Andre and Russell, Bertie (2012) Do the Entrepreneuriat Dream of Electric Sheep? Alessio Lunghi and Seth Wheeler (eds.) Occupy Everything: Reflections on Why It's Kicking Off Everywhere. Brooklyn: Minor Compositions - Autonomedia, 75-80.

Pusey, Andre (2014) The Really Open University, Creating Commons, New Cracks and Values In and Against Academic Capitalism. Phd University of Leeds, School of Geography.

Pusey, Andre and Sealey-Huggins, Leon (2013) Transforming the University: Beyond Students and Cuts. Acme – an International Journal for Critical Geographies 12 3 - https://www.acme-journal.org/index.php/acme/article/view/975, accessed 30 December 2018.

Pusey, Andre (2017) Towards a University of the Common: reimagining the University in Order to Abolish It With the Really Open University. Open Library of Humanities 3 1 13,

1 - 27 – https://olh.openlibhums.org/articles/10.16995/olh.90/, accessed 30 December 2018.

Rampell, Catherine (2009) Great Recessions: A Brief Etymology. New York Times, March 11 - https://economix.blogs.nytimes. com/2009/03/11/great-recession-a-brief-etymology/, accessed 30 December 2018.

Ranciére, Jacques (1991) The Ignorant Schoolmaster: Five Lessons in Intellectual Imagination. Stanford: Stanford University Press.

Ranciére, Jacques (1999) Disagreement: Politics and Philosophy. Minneapolis and London: Minnesota University Press.

Ranciére, Jacques (2004) The Philosopher and his Poor. Durham: Duke University Press.

Ranciére, Jacques (2010a) Communists without Communism. Slavoj Zizek and Costas Douzinas (eds.) The Idea of Communism, 167-77 http://abahlali.org/files/Ranciére. communism.pdf, accessed 9 April 2018.

Ranciére, Jacques (2010b) Ten Theses on Politics. Dissensus: On Politics and Aesthetics. London and New York: Continuum, 27-44.

Ranciére, Jacques (2011a) Althusser's Lesson. London and New York: Bloomsbury.

Ranciére, Jacques (2011b) Staging the People: The Proletariat and his Double. London and New York: Verso.

Ranciére, Jacques (2011c) The Thinking of Dissensus: Politics and Aesthetics. Paul Bowman and Richard Stamp (eds.) Reading Ranciére. London and New York: Continuum, 1-17.

Ranciére, Jacques (2012) Proletarian Nights: the Workers Dream in Nineteenth Century France. London and New York: Verso.

Rees, John (2011) Students Revolts: Then and Now in Michael Bailey and Des Freedman (eds.) The Assault of Universities: A Manifesto for Resistance. London: Pluto Press, 113-22.

Reid, Donald (2012) Introduction. Jacques Ranciére. Proletarian Nights: the Workers Dream in Nineteenth Century France.

London and New York: Verso, xiii-xxxv.

Reiner, Robert (2010) The Politics of Police. Oxford: Oxford University Press.

Roswitha, Scholz (2009) Patriarchy and Commodity Society: Gender without the Body. Mediations. Journal of the Literary Marxist Group. Vol 27 1-2 - http://www.mediationsjournal. org/articles/patriarchy-and-commodity-society, accessed 22 February 2019.

Reinvention Centre (2011) Student as Producer User Guide (2011-2012) - http://studentasproducer.lincoln.ac.uk/files/2010/11/ user-guide-2012.pdf, accessed 30 December 2018.

Reinvention Centre (2007) Interim Report - https://warwick. ac.uk/fac/cross_fac/iatl/cetl/about/evaluation/reinvention_ evaluation_july_2007.pdf, accessed 22 February 2019.

Reinvention Centre (2010) Final report -https://warwick.ac.uk/ fac/cross_fac/iatl/cetl/about/evaluation/reinvention_centre_ final_evaluation_report.pdf, accessed 30 December 2018.

Rifkin, Jeremy (1999) The End of Work: the Decline of the Global Labour Force and the Dawn of the Post Market Era. New York: Jeremy P Tarcher/Putman Book.

Rikowski, Glenn (2002) Fuel for the Living Fire: Labour Power! Ana Dinerstein and Mike Neary (Eds.) The Labour Debate: the Theory and Practice of Capitalist Work. Basingstoke: Palgrave Macmillan, 179-202.

Roberts, John and Penzin, Alexei (2017) (eds.) Art and Production: Boris Arvatov. London: Pluto Press.

Roggero, Gigi (2011) The Production of Living Knowledge: The Crisis of the University and the Transformation of Labour in Europe and North America. Philadelphia: Temple University Press.

Ross, Kristen (1991) Introduction. The Ignorant Schoolmaster: Five Lessons in Intellectual Emancipation. Stanford: Stanford University Press, vi-xxiii.

Ross, Kristen (2002) May 68 and its Afterlives. Chicago:

University of Chicago Press. Rubel, Maximillian (1962) Notes on Marx's Conception of Democracy, New Politics 1962: 78-90 https://www.unz.com/print/NewPolitics-1962q2-00078/, accessed 17 December 2018.

Saunders, Gary (2017) Somewhere Between Reform and Revolution: Alternative Higher Education and The 'Unfinished'. Richard Hall and Joss Winn (eds.) Mass Intellectuality and Democratic Leadership in Higher Education. Bloomsbury Academic Publishing: London and New York, 157-70.

Saunders, Gary (2019) Reimagining the Idea of the University for a Post-Capitalist Society. PhD thesis. University of Lincoln.

Seymour, Richard (2016) Corbyn: the Strange Rebirth of Radical Politics. London and New York: Verso

Shattock, Michael (2012) Making Policy in British Higher Education 1945-2011. Maidenhead: McGraw-Hill and Open University Press.

Simbuerger, Elisabeth and Neary, Mike (2015) Free education! A 'live' report from the Chilean student movement, 2011-2014 - reform or revolution? [A political sociology for action]. Journal for Critical Education Policy Studies, 13 (2), 150-96.

Simbuerger, Elisabeth and Neary, Mike (2016) Taxi Professors: academic labour in Chile - a critical practical response to the politics of worker identity. Workplace: a Journal for Academic Labour 28, 48-73.

Sinclair, Ian (2013) Reconsidering the Failure of the Anti-Iraq War March https://www.opendemocracy.net/ourkingdom/alex-doherty-ian-sinclair/reconsidering-failure-of-anti-iraq-war-march, accessed 30 December 2018.

Slaughter, Sheila and Rhoades, Gary (2009) Academic Capitalism and the New Economy: Market States and Higher Education. Baltimore: John Hopkins University Press.

Social Science Centre Collective (2017) Making a Co-operative University. Wonkhe, http://wonkhe.com/blogs/making-a-co-operative-university/, accessed 30 December 2018.

Solomon, Clare and Palmieri, Tania (eds.) (2011) Springtime: the New Student Rebellions. London and New York: Verso.

Shukaitis, Stevphen (2010) Sisyphus and the Labour of Imagination: Autonomy, Cultural Production, and the Antinomies of Worker Self-Management. Affinities 4(1), 57-82.

Shukaitis, Stevphen (2013) Can the Object be a Comrade: the Politics of Consumption. Ephemera. 18 1 237-244.

Swain, Hilary (2017) Coming Soon, a University Where Students Set their own Tuition Fees. The Guardian https://www.theguardian.com/education/2017/sep/12/university-students-set-own-fees-co-operative-college, accessed 30 December 2018.

Taylor, Marcus (2006) From Pinochet to the Third Way: Neoliberalism and Social Transformation in Chile. London: Pluto Press.

The Guardian/LSE (2012) Reading the Riots: Investigating England's Summer of Disorder - http://eprints.lse.ac.uk/46297/1/Reading%20the%20riots%28published%29.pdf, accessed 31 December 2018.

Taylor, Paul (1993) The Texts of Paulo Freire. Buckingham: Open University Press.

Taylor, Diane (2017) Mark Duggan Family Lose Appeal Against Lawful Killing Verdict. The Guardian, 29 March: https://www.theguardian.com/uk-news/2017/mar/29/mark-duggan-family-lose-appeal-against-lawful-killing-verdict, accessed 31 December 2018.

Thompson, Edward (1971) The Moral Economy of the English Crowd in the Eighteenth Century Past and Present 50, 76-136.

User Guide (2012) Student as Producer https://cpb-eu-w2.wpmucdn.com/blogs.lincoln.ac.uk/dist/e/185/files/2010/11/user-guide-2012.pdf, accessed 3 February.

University of Utopia (n.d.) http://www.universityofutopia.org, accessed 14 May 2018

Victoria and Albert Museum (2014) Disobedient Objects. Exhibition, 26 July 2014-1 February 2015. London.

Vieta, Marcelo (2014) The New Co-operativism. Special Issue Affinities 4 1 - https://ojs.library.queensu.ca/index.php/affinities/issue/view/574, accessed 31 December 2018.

Vradis, Antonis (2012) A Funny Thing Happened on the Way to the Square, Alessio Lunghi and Seth Wheeler (eds) Occupy Everything: Reflections on Why it's Kicking Off Everywhere. Brooklyn: Minor Compositions - Autonomedia 62-7.

Vygotsky, Lev (1986) Thought and Language. Cambridge: Massachusetts Institute of Technology.

Warwick Institute for Employment Research (2016) Graduates in Non-Graduate Occupations. Published by HEFCE. http://www.hefce.ac.uk/pubs/rereports/year/2016/gradoccup/, accessed 31 December 2018.

Weber, Max (1978) Economy and Society. Oakland: University of California Press

Weeks, Kathi (2011) The Problem with Work: Feminism, Marxism Antiwork Politics and Postcapitalist Imaginaries. Durham NC: Duke University Press.

Weil, Simone (2003) The Need for Roots. London and New York: Routledge Classic.

Weil, Simone (2013) Oppression and Liberty. London and New York: Routledge.

Weir, Robert (1996) Beyond Labor's Veil: The Culture of the Knights of Labor. University Park PA: Pennsylvania State University Press.

Wellmon, Chad (2015) Organising Enlightenment: Information Overload and the Invention of the Modern Research University. Baltimore: Johns Hopkins Press.

Wiggershaus, Rolf (2007) The Frankfurt School: Its History, Theories and Political Significance. Cambridge: Polity Press.

Williams, Zoe (2018) Politicised Students are a Nightmare for the Government. The Guardian, 28 February: https://www. theguardian.com/commentisfree/2018/feb/28/toby-youngs-appointment-was-scandalous-so-was-the-blacklisting-of-former-nus-members, accessed 31 December 2018.

Winn, Joss (2013) Hacking in the University: Contesting the Valorisation of Academic Labour. Triple C : Communication, Capitalism and Critique, 11 2, 486-503 - https://www.triple-c. at/index.php/tripleC/article/view/494, accessed 31 December 2018.

Winn, Joss (2015a) The Co-operative University: Labour, Property and Pedagogy. Power and Education 7 1 39-55 – http://eprints.lincoln.ac.uk/14593/, accessed 31 December 2018.

Winn Joss (2015b) Writing About Academic Labour. Workplace: a Journal for Academic Labour 25 1-15 – http://ices.library. ubc.ca/index.php/workplace/article/view/185095, accessed 31 December 2018.

Wilding, Adrian (2009) Pied Pipers and Polymaths: Adorno's Critique of Praxisism. John Holloway, Fernando Matamoros, Sergio Tischler (eds) Negativity and Revolution: Adorno and Political Activism. London: Pluto Press, 18-40.

Williams, Jeffery (2006) The Pedagogy of Debt. College Literature 33 (4), 155-69.

Withers, Deborah (2013) An Interview with Joyce Canaan. Alec Wardrop and Deborah Withers (eds) The Para Academic Handbook: a Toolkit for Making-Creating-Learning-Acting. Bristol: Hammeron Press, 39-60 - http://hammeronpress.net/ wp-content/uploads/2015/04/PHA_Final.pdf, accessed 31 December 2018.

Wright, Chris (2014) Worker Co-operatives and Revolution: History and Possibility in the United States. Booklocker.com.

Woodin, Tom (2017) Co-operation, leadership and learning: Fred Hall and the Co-operative College before 1939. Richard Hall and Joss Winn (eds.) Mass Intellectuality and Democratic

Leadership in Higher Education. London: Bloomsbury.

Yeo, Stephen (2015) The Co-operative University: Transforming Higher Education. Tom Woodin (ed). Co-operation, Learning and Co-operative Values. London and New York: Routledge, 131-46.

Yeo, Stephen (ed) (1988) New Views of Co-operation. London and New York: Routledge.

Zizek, Slavoj (2008) Violence: Six Sideways Reflections. Profile Books.

Zizek, Slavoj (2011) Shoplifters of the World Unite. https://www.lrb.co.uk/2011/08/19/slavoj-zizek/shoplifters-of-the-world-unite, 31 December 2018.

Zizek, Slavoj and Douzinas, Costas (2010) The Idea of Communism. London and New York: Verso.

CULTURE, SOCIETY & POLITICS

The modern world is at an impasse. Disasters scroll across our smartphone screens and we're invited to like, follow or upvote, but critical thinking is harder and harder to find. Rather than connecting us in common struggle and debate, the internet has sped up and deepened a long-standing process of alienation and atomization. Zer0 Books wants to work against this trend.
With critical theory as our jumping off point, we aim to publish books that make our readers uncomfortable. We want to move beyond received opinions.
Zer0 Books is on the left and wants to reinvent the left. We are sick of the injustice, the suffering, and the stupidity that defines both our political and cultural world, and we aim to find a new foundation for a new struggle.

If this book has helped you to clarify an idea, solve a problem or extend your knowledge, you may want to check out our online content as well. Look for Zer0 Books: Advancing Conversations in the iTunes directory and for our Zer0 Books YouTube channel.

Popular videos include:

Žižek and the Double Blackmain

The Intellectual Dark Web is a Bad Sign

Can there be an Anti-SJW Left?

Answering Jordan Peterson on Marxism

Follow us on Facebook
at https://www.facebook.com/ZeroBooks and Twitter at https://
twitter.com/Zer0Books

Bestsellers from Zer0 Books include:

Give Them An Argument
Logic for the Left
Ben Burgis
Many serious leftists have learned to distrust talk of logic. This is
a serious mistake.
Paperback: 978-1-78904-210-8 ebook: 978-1-78904-211-5

Poor but Sexy
Culture Clashes in Europe East and West
Agata Pyzik
How the East stayed East and the West stayed West.
Paperback: 978-1-78099-394-2 ebook: 978-1-78099-395-9

An Anthropology of Nothing in Particular
Martin Demant Frederiksen
A journey into the social lives of meaninglessness.
Paperback: 978-1-78535-699-5 ebook: 978-1-78535-700-8

In the Dust of This Planet
Horror of Philosophy vol. 1
Eugene Thacker
In the first of a series of three books on the Horror of Philosophy,
In the Dust of This Planet offers the genre of horror as a way of
thinking about the unthinkable.
Paperback: 978-1-84694-676-9 ebook: 978-1-78099-010-1

The End of Oulipo?
An Attempt to Exhaust a Movement
Lauren Elkin, Veronica Esposito
Paperback: 978-1-78099-655-4 ebook: 978-1-78099-656-1

Capitalist Realism
Is There no Alternative?
Mark Fisher
An analysis of the ways in which capitalism has presented itself
as the only realistic political-economic system.
Paperback: 978-1-84694-317-1 ebook: 978-1-78099-734-6

Rebel Rebel
Chris O'Leary
David Bowie: every single song. Everything you want to know,
everything you didn't know.
Paperback: 978-1-78099-244-0 ebook: 978-1-78099-713-1

Kill All Normies
Angela Nagle
Online culture wars from 4chan and Tumblr to Trump.
Paperback: 978-1- 78535-543-1 ebook: 978-1-78535-544-8

Cartographies of the Absolute
Alberto Toscano, Jeff Kinkle
An aesthetics of the economy for the twenty-first century.
Paperback: 978-1-78099-275-4 ebook: 978-1-78279-973-3

Malign Velocities
Accelerationism and Capitalism
Benjamin Noys
Long listed for the Bread and Roses Prize 2015, *Malign Velocities*
argues against the need for speed, tracking acceleration
as the symptom of the ongoing crises of capitalism.
Paperback: 978-1-78279-300-7 ebook: 978-1-78279-299-4

Meat Market
Female Flesh under Capitalism
Laurie Penny
A feminist dissection of women's bodies as the fleshy fulcrum of
capitalist cannibalism, whereby women are both consumers and
consumed.
Paperback: 978-1-84694-521-2 ebook: 978-1-84694-782-7

Babbling Corpse
Vaporwave and the Commodification of Ghosts
Grafton Tanner
Paperback: 978-1-78279-759-3 ebook: 978-1-78279-760-9

New Work New Culture
Work we want and a culture that strengthens us
Frithjoff Bergmann
A serious alternative for mankind and the planet.
Paperback: 978-1-78904-064-7 ebook: 978-1-78904-065-4

Romeo and Juliet in Palestine
Teaching Under Occupation
Tom Sperlinger
Life in the West Bank, the nature of pedagogy and the role of a university under occupation.
Paperback: 978-1-78279-637-4 ebook: 978-1-78279-636-7

Ghosts of My Life
Writings on Depression, Hauntology and Lost Futures
Mark Fisher
Paperback: 978-1-78099-226-6 ebook: 978-1-78279-624-4

Sweetening the Pill
or How We Got Hooked on Hormonal Birth Control
Holly Grigg-Spall
Has contraception liberated or oppressed women?
Sweetening the Pill breaks the silence on the dark side of hormonal contraception.
Paperback: 978-1-78099-607-3 ebook: 978-1-78099-608-0

Why Are We The Good Guys?
Reclaiming your Mind from the Delusions of Propaganda
David Cromwell
A provocative challenge to the standard ideology that Western power is a benevolent force in the world.
Paperback: 978-1-78099-365-2 ebook: 978-1-78099-366-9

The Writing on the Wall
On the Decomposition of Capitalism and its Critics
Anselm Jappe, Alastair Hemmens
A new approach to the meaning of social emancipation.
Paperback: 978-1-78535-581-3 ebook: 978-1-78535-582-0

Enjoying It
Candy Crush and Capitalism
Alfie Bown
A study of enjoyment and of the enjoyment of studying. Bown
asks what enjoyment says about us and what we say about
enjoyment, and why.
Paperback: 978-1-78535-155-6 ebook: 978-1-78535-156-3

Color, Facture, Art and Design
Iona Singh
This materialist definition of fine-art develops guidelines for
architecture, design, cultural-studies and ultimately social
change.
Paperback: 978-1-78099-629-5 ebook: 978-1-78099-630-1

Neglected or Misunderstood
The Radical Feminism of Shulamith Firestone
Victoria Margree
An interrogation of issues surrounding gender, biology,
sexuality, work and technology, and the ways in which our
imaginations continue to be in thrall to ideologies of maternity
and the nuclear family.
Paperback: 978-1-78535-539-4 ebook: 978-1-78535-540-0

How to Dismantle the NHS in 10 Easy Steps (Second Edition)
Youssef El-Gingihy
The story of how your NHS was sold off and why you will have
to buy private health insurance soon. A new expanded second
edition with chapters on junior doctors' strikes and government
blueprints for US-style healthcare.
Paperback: 978-1-78904-178-1 ebook: 978-1-78904-179-8

Digesting Recipes
The Art of Culinary Notation
Susannah Worth
A recipe is an instruction, the imperative tone of the expert, but
this constraint can offer its own kind of potential. A recipe need
not be a domestic trap but might instead offer escape – something
to fantasise about or aspire to.
Paperback: 978-1-78279-860-6 ebook: 978-1-78279-859-0

Most titles are published in paperback and as an ebook.
Paperbacks are available in traditional bookshops. Both print and
ebook formats are available online.
Follow us on Facebook
at https://www.facebook.com/ZeroBooks
and Twitter at https://twitter.com/Zer0Books